Praise for *Information Science*

'In *Information Science,* Seadle takes a hitherto unforeseen, and yet a novel and multifaceted approach to discuss the evolution, implications and applications of information as a concept, and information science as a discipline. The discussions, observations and commentaries appearing in the chapters throughout this book are a product of Seadle's rich knowledge, research and scholarship, and senior management experience in the field of information science at national and global levels. This is a must-read for anyone who wants to know and understand the role of information in the evolution of our society from the stone age to the modern era of Artificial Intelligence.'
Gobinda Chowdhury, Professor of Information Science, University of Strathclyde and co-author of *AI and Information Access*

'Michael Seadle draws on his extensive background in information science to present an account of how information and its institutions have evolved over time, and why and how information matters now. Drawing together themes of language, culture, technology, and integrity, this work offers readers a framework for understanding the field's development and its ongoing relevance, situating contemporary debates within a broader historical context.'
Heather Moulaison-Sandy, Associate Professor, School of Information Science and Learning Technologies, University of Missouri, USA

'This book navigates the universe of information science, brilliantly illuminating all the galaxies (theories) and stars (concepts), and masterfully explains them in a plain and easily understandable way. This book is essential for anyone with an interest in the field of information science. I am rebuilding my Information Management 101 class using this book. I am sure students will love it!'
Lihong Zhou, Professor (Full) and Associate Dean, Wuhan University, China

Information Science

Information Science

History, Ideas, Applications

Michael Seadle

facet publishing

Published by Facet Publishing
www.facetpublishing.co.uk

Facet Publishing is wholly owned by CILIP: the Library and Information Association.

British Library Cataloguing in Publication Data
A catalogue record for this book is available from the British Library.

ISBN 978-1-78330-694-7 (paperback)
ISBN 978-1-78330-695-4 (hardback)
ISBN 978-1-78330-696-1 (PDF)
ISBN 978-1-78330-697-8 (EPUB)

First published 2026

MIX
Paper | Supporting responsible forestry
FSC® C013604

The manufacturer's authorised representative in the EU for product safety is Logos Europe, 9 rue Nicolas Poussin, 17000 La Rochelle, France (contact@logoseurope.eu, www.logoseurope.eu).

Typeset from author's files by Flagholme Publishing Services in 10/13 pt Palatino Linotype and Open Sans.
Printed and made in Great Britain by CPI Group (UK) Ltd, Croydon, CR0 4YY.

This book is dedicated to my wife, Joan Luft, for all of her help and advice, and to my colleagues Elke Greifeneder and Melanie Sterzer for their ongoing support.

Contents

About the Author

Michael Seadle, PhD, is a full professor at Humboldt-Universität zu Berlin, where he has served since 2006 in various roles as director of the School of Library and Information Science (2006–18) , as Dean of Humanities (2010–16), University Council Chair (2015–17), member and chair of the Commission Wissenschaftliches Fehlverhalten (Commission on Research Malpractice) (2014–18). Before coming to Berlin, he served in a variety of library capacities at Michigan State University Libraries including Assistant Director for Information Technology and Head of the Digital and Multimedia Center (1998–2006). He chaired the iSchools 'iCaucus' (2012–13) and was one of the signatories of the iSchools incorporation in 2014. He served as Executive Director of the iSchools until May 2024. He was editor of the peer-reviewed academic journal *Library Hi Tech* from 1997 to 2016. He continues to serve on the editorial board of *Bibliothek Forschung und Praxis* (2007–) and as editor of *World Digital Libraries*. He has published a number of books, including *The Measurement of Research Integrity* (Routledge, 2021), *Quantifying Research Integrity* (Morgan Claypool, 2017) and *Educating the Profession: 40 years of the IFLA Section on Education and Training* (DeGruyter, IFLA Series, 2016). Earlier works include *Automating Mainframe Management: Using expert systems with examples from VM and MVS* (McGraw Hill, 1991) and his dissertation, *Quakers in Nazi Germany* (Progressive Publisher, 1978). Over the decades, he has received millions in grant money from the US National Science Foundation, the German Forschungsgemeinschaft and corporations like Elsevier.

Preface

The idea for this book came from the need to explain to a broader academic audience what 'information science' means in the modern world, because the term fits imperfectly within the narrower boundaries of modern academic disciplines. Andrew Abbott explains that disciplinary boundaries provide 'a general conception of intellectual existence, a conception of the proper units of knowledge' (Abbott, 2001, 130). Information science has the problem that it cuts across many 'proper units of knowledge' and may fit best with history, philosophy and the humanities, where ideas often matter more than jobs or applications.

Acknowledgements

No one really writes a book of any substance on their own. Dinner-table conversations with my wife, a scholar and professor, played a role. I also want to acknowledge the real intellectual contributions of my friend and former doctoral student Elke Greifeneder, as well as discussions with Melanie Sterzer, Stefanie Havelka and my friend Gobinda Chowdhury.

Introduction

Identity

Information is ubiquitous, and that ubiquity is part of the problem when defining information science as a discipline. It lacks natural boundaries. In the *Chaos of Disciplines* (2001), Andrew Abbott explains why disciplinary boundaries are important: 'The first of these is the Geertzian function of providing academics with a general conception of intellectual existence, a conception of the proper units of knowledge.' In other words, disciplinary boundaries provide a basis for identity. This is particularly important when that identity determines where the discipline belongs within an organisation such as a university. One goal of this book is to describe information science in a way that makes its identity clear. Examples can help.

When a person comes to the reference desk of a library and asks for information about Berlin, Germany, in order to plan a trip, the librarian behind the desk will typically conduct a classic reference interview to learn about the person's information needs. This might include whether the person wants sightseeing options, a list of museums, background about the city's history, or perhaps an explanation of the city's social and political structure. Public transit information could be relevant. Hotels and restaurants could be relevant. The purpose of a reference interview is to understand the person's goals and to match them with available resources. Information in context is what matters, and each new detail can make the search more precise and more effective. Information scientists do a reference interview for every task they undertake.

Another everyday example comes from the decisions that a serious chef makes when preparing a meal. It is not merely a matter of recipes, but of finding the right ingredients in the store, knowing their nutritional value, what they cost and perhaps the ecological impact of the choices. Information about the cooking tools matters, such as knives, bowls, pots and pans, range tops and ovens. Understanding the essential hand skills also matters for tasks like bread baking. Tactile information helps to decide how much liquid a dough really needs (recipes are not always accurate). Olfactory information plays a role in choosing spices and in determining whether an ingredient is fresh. The behavioural preferences and information about diners' allergies matter for choosing and excluding ingredients. This wide range of information cannot always be reduced to predefined lists or to mechanical processes. A good cook must think like an information scientist. Again, context matters.

A more technical example involves the installation of new software. While software generally comes with installation instructions, those instructions rarely satisfy more than a portion of the information needs. Knowing the capabilities of the computer hardware and the current version of its operating system matters. Possible interactions with other installed software should be considered. Details about the software vendor and the computing environment may determine long-term viability and how much support is likely available. The person doing the installation also needs training and expertise to solve unexpected problems. Knowing how to decipher error messages matters. Theoretically, all of this kind of information should be available in the documentation, but often is not. Knowing which information is relevant depends on the context.

A professional information scientist is always context aware, because context matters for almost every information choice. The core role of the information scientist is to integrate different streams of information into a whole that makes sense for a particular problem and can answer particular questions. Every scholarly field, and every practical one, needs people who can carry out such integrative tasks. They may not call themselves information scientists, but they are carrying out information science tasks by drawing together the necessary sources and resources.

Background

Information science is not just a product of the 'information age', which is a concept that grew in part from the work of Claude Shannon at the start of the computing era (University of Michigan, 2019). The role of information stretches back before the computer age, because information itself is at least as old as the earliest writing systems, and is arguably as old as or older than human speech. Everything humans do involves some form of information, and the range of types and ways of understanding that information are endless. An integrative 'science' of information is needed precisely because information as a concept is unbounded.

The word 'science' in modern English often implies a connection to the natural sciences, especially when used without a qualifier as in the 'social sciences', but the original English word had a meaning more like '*science*' in French or '*Wissenschaft*' in German, and described systematic knowledge. This original meaning is relevant when discussing modern information science. There was a time when the social sciences hoped to discover natural laws along the lines of the natural scientists. Claude Lévi-Strauss is just one example. Information science today does not and should not claim to be developing natural laws. It is pragmatic rather than theory driven. The role of language itself in information science will be discussed more completely in Chapter 4. This book focuses on how contemporary information science fits into modern scholarship. No academic field exists without its information components.

Vivien Petras offers a definition that builds on that of Michael Buckland. As she writes: 'Information science, as implied by the name, could be defined as the discipline that studies information in all its forms and theoretical conceptions.... Information science is concerned with how information is manifested across space and time' (Petras, 2023, 579–96).

This is consistent with the importance of being context aware, but with a slightly less historical emphasis, since Petras is not a historian.

Analogy with history

Information science is not unique in its breadth. History is equally broad because it covers the past in all of its aspects, just as information science is about information in all of its forms. A few notable historians, like Arnold Toynbee (1934–61), have tried to imitate the natural sciences by formulating theories about historical change, but without long-term success. History is too diverse to be reduced to algorithms.

Historical methodology is also not easily reduced to a unified set of approaches. One reason is that historians borrow tools and methods from all fields. Doctoral students in history must first learn what it means to think historically, which is a matter of consciousness rather than of technique. Understanding the past goes beyond discovering the right texts. As the French historian Marc Bloch (1953, 34) wrote, 'to the great despair of historians, men fail to change their vocabulary every time they change their customs'. In other words, even clear labels can be misleading and the professional historian must look beyond them, much as an information scientist must look beyond simple labels or particular needs to understand the context of an information problem as a whole.

Like historians, information scientists are eclectic in their use of tools. The craftsman's principle applies here, because of the importance of selecting the right tool for the job, which may mean the right combination of types of information. Just as a fully trained carpenter knows which tool to use to cut a specific type of wood for a particular purpose, the well-trained information scientist needs to know how to select the right information out of all of the possible forms and types. As Bloch suggested for historians, labels can be misleading over time. The defining characteristic of an information scientist is the ability to see the whole context of an information problem.

Structure of the book

This book builds on a range of topics that show how information science fits in the scholarly and real world. The intellectual context is important precisely because information science is new as a discipline, although information itself is ancient. One important aspect of information science as a discipline is that it cuts across almost all contemporary academic subjects and integrates them in ways that expand their meanings.

Chapter 1: A History of Information

Information itself is older than any human awareness that information even exists. Modern concepts of information evolved as people began to understand the natural world and their own psychological world better. Reliable sources are an integral part of information science, as they have been for historians since the time of Herodotus in the fifth century BCE. From an information science viewpoint, the history of information is a search for authoritative sources.

Chapter 2: A History of the Discipline

Information science is a 20th-century concept that evolved from library science, since libraries manage the largest sources of scholarly information. When Daniel Atkins became dean at the University of Michigan and established its School of Information, he invited faculty from a broad range of disciplines to join the new iSchool. He wrote in 2003: 'Using advanced cyberinfrastructure must be done in a systemic context that exploits mutual self-interest and synergy among computer and information, and social science research communities who see it as an *object of research* …'. This represents his vision of information science.

Chapter 3: Information Science Organisations

Most scholarly organisations are in fact information science organisations, because special kinds of information is part of their identity. Today, however, the leading organisations that explicitly claim an information science connection originated in the library community, including iSchools Inc., ASIS&T (Association for Information Science and Technology) and ALISE (Association for Library and Information Science Education).

Chapter 4: Language and Information Science

Language is one of the key sources of information, though not the only one. Words in different languages carry different meanings and connotations, which shape our understanding about information. One simple example is the word 'science', whose meaning varies with language, with context and across time.

Chapter 5: Culture and Information Science

Culture is the context in which people understand information. Even people conveying information in common terms may understand it differently because of different backgrounds. For example, in some cultures the institutional title 'professor' implies greater authority than 'doctor', which indicates only a level of education. The trust issues in analysing information sources often have cultural origins.

Chapter 6: Technology

Today, information and technology are so closely interrelated that much of the communication about information runs via technology tools. That is not new. Writing and, later, printing were once new forms of technology. Communication platforms can also influence the information itself.

Chapter 7: Internet Technology

In the minds of many people, the internet has become such a basic source of information that older forms of information access have lost their importance. Many people look online first to read news, to read e-mail and to chat with friends via social media. It has changed people's expectations.

Chapter 8: Information Integrity

Information integrity affects everyone inside and outside of the research community, and it is a matter of active debate. Recent examples of the importance of information integrity come from misinformation about the COVID-19 pandemic. Most universities have commissions to evaluate integrity breaches, but research into the causes of integrity violations is rare.

Chapter 9: Artificial Intelligence

Artificial intelligence (AI) usually refers to external systems that are capable of solving problems in ways that appear to resemble human thought. Information scientists should be aware that most systems with the means to make a variable response to external stimuli display some measure of intelligence. The idea of AI is old, even if the current name and the hype around it suggests something new.

Chapter 10: Information Behaviour

Information behaviour is a distinctive field with its own conference and an active leadership group. As a sub-discipline, it is relatively new. How people decide what information they want and what they do with it varies with social, cultural and historical situations. This includes the choices about what information people seek and how they use it.

Chapter 11: Data Science

Data science belongs to information science in part because it allows the quantification of many, if not quite all, forms of information. A few university programmes find the concept attractive because it implies a strong technical foundation. Some forms of information are best understood when quantified.

Chapter 12: Non-verbal Information

Non-verbal information includes all sources of information that do not primarily rely on the use of words as the means for communication. A facial expression such as a smile or a frown can indicate whether a person takes the information seriously or positively and whether or not the speaker trusts the information.

Chapter 13: Information Retrieval for Technology

Information retrieval is a historical carry-over from library science, but it has taken on much broader aspects as the complexity of information has grown to the point where searches succeed best when the searchers understand the context. This is an area where all the complexities of the information interactions play an important role.

Chapter 14: Information Curation

Research on information science topics requires long-term access to sources, which is one part of curation. The context of the sources also needs to be preserved, apart from the bits and bytes and books. Technology plays a role, as does metadata, in explaining what the information is. Open access for retrieval matters.

Chapter 15: Information for Education

Separating information from education is practically impossible. Many factors influence the information choices for educating students, some cultural, some political, some based on how best to make use of a student's abilities.

Chapter 16: Information and Politics

This conflict is particularly evident during times when democratic societies are making decisions about their futures, but it was never absent from political discourse in the past. Personal claims have often mattered more than reproducible facts.

CHAPTER 1

A History of Information

Every aspect of the world implicitly contains information, even at a time when humans had not yet discovered or named it. Dretske (2007, 274) writes that '[I]nformation is always information about something.' And that *something* can logically exist before information about it does. But what exactly is information in scholarly and philosophical terms? Things only formally have information content once thinking creatures assign meanings to them. Even the simplest living creatures interpret the world as they perceive it and make decisions based on their understanding. Bees are a good example, since they make judgements about what flowers to seek out for the nutrients they need. Once creatures endow the elements of their world with meaning, then context becomes an element of how they understand the information.

Context is an aspect of information that should never be ignored. The fact that a full-grown lion is roaring angrily takes on a different meaning if the context is a zoo where the lion is behind bars in a cage. The environment is always rich with contextual information that influences the meaning of the information around it. Purely abstract information, a mathematical theorem, for example, might seem potentially context free, but the background of the person who is contemplating the purely abstract information is itself a context that cannot be disregarded because it influences what meaning the theorem has for that person at that time. Context plays an especially important role when thinking about the history of information, where the circumstances change over time.

Origins

The discovery of information occurred before any enduring records were kept, but through archaeology it is possible to discover information objects for early humans, such as the Neanderthals. Perceptions of the Neanderthals have changed radically over time, and today they offer a good example of how information changes as the factual context grows. For a long time scholars have known that the Neanderthals had large brains, were physically strong and represented the dominant form of the genus *Homo* 'from roughly 400,000 years ago until 40,000 years ago' (Krishnan, 2023). There is now evidence that they had a good mastery of fire, since '[e]xcavation sites are full of pieces of flint that show evidence of fire-making' (Krishnan, 2023). Thanks to modern techniques that allow extracting DNA from ancient bones, scholars know that 'Eurasians today have between 1.5 and 2.1% of Neanderthal DNA' (Krishnan, 2023). Neanderthals were genetically so similar to modern humans that they could interbreed. Interbreeding is a part of the context that cannot be ignored.

DNA information was not available in 1856 when workers found Neanderthal bones near Düsseldorf in a valley ('*Thal*' in German) that had belonged to a family originally named Neumann (new man) who, like many at the time, renamed themselves using a pseudo-Greek term for new (*neander*), so that the valley became the 'Neander Thal'. For over a century after the discovery, the popular image of the Neanderthals implied brutish, ape-like creatures fundamentally different from modern humans and implicitly inarticulate. It is hard to know whether the Neanderthals communicated with each other in spoken language, but the objects found with their remains suggest a level of planning that implies intelligent communication. In other words, the context suggests that they used information in order to survive.

This does not mean that the history of information began with the Neanderthals. No one knows whether and how many other early forms of the genus *Homo* had the ability to give meaning to objects or to their own experiences, but it suggests that 400,000 years ago may not be too early to count as a starting point for the history of information. It also makes it clear that writing was not an essential starting point. Writing is just the first and most reliable way for information to reach into modern times.

It is plausible enough that pre-modern humans used some form of language-like communication, even if it diverged so radically from the complexities of modern language that it could seem like a series of grunts and gestures. Scholars can only estimate the origin of speech indirectly by guessing to what degree early humans needed some form of language to create the tools that archaeologists have found with their remains. By this method, the earliest speech may have been as much as two million years ago (Balter, 2015). Other methods look at the pathway between the auditory cortex and the frontal lobe in the brains of humans and their near relatives. Friederici and Anwander (2020) write: 'Although only humans have speech and language, the link via the auditory pathway in other primates suggests an evolutionary basis in auditory cognition and vocal communication. The discovery pushes back the evolutionary origin of the human language pathway by at least 20 million years.'

Language may not be essential to information, but it helps when assigning meaning and sharing that meaning with others.

Written language

Written language appeared much later. Again, the exact dates are unclear. Scholars today generally accept the idea that the first writing appeared on Sumerian clay tablets in the form of cuneiform markings at around 3400 BCE and that hieroglyphs appeared soon afterwards, in 3200 BCE. China had written language by at least 1300 BCE, and likely somewhat earlier. The Indus Valley civilisations may well also have had a form of writing that seems to have vanished over the centuries. Exactly how early writing was used is unknown, but the physical context of Sumerian tablets supports the argument that the records involved accounting and business contracts. In Egypt, writing was found in tombs, which suggests a religious role.

The Egyptian hieroglyphs and the Chinese characters are both pictographic, which means there was no clear association between pronunciation and the written language. The meaning of the Chinese characters has passed down through time. The Egyptian hieroglyphs appeared at one time to have a reliable Greek translation based on the Rosetta Stone, but more recent research by Susan Brind Morrow radically reinterprets the meaning of the hieroglyphs. She 'has dispensed with Egyptologist Kurt Heinrich Sethe's system of numbered "utterances" and treats the inscriptions as a poetic whole …' (Werner, 2015, 91–3).

> Morrow gives us a completely different translation of the texts, upending more than a century of scholarly analysis. Until now, Egyptologists have said the beginning of the texts deal with the private parts of a baboon. Morrow reveals it is actually a description of the constellation Orion!! Maybe the fact the ceilings of the pyramid are covered in stars should have given earlier researchers a clue as to what the texts are about.
>
> (Cunningham, 2016, 233)

The contextual role of the ceiling in this revision is not without significance.

Phonetic writing systems dominate today, except in China; but today Chinese who use computer keyboards must input text sequences in Pinyin to suggest the right character. Phonetic systems using letters change over time. Modern German spelling has gone through many reforms, most recently in 2006. English and US spelling also diverge moderately, thanks in part to Noah Webster's spelling reforms in the USA. Written words in modern French also diverge from how they were spoken in old French. In other words, the phonetic information in many written languages only approximates the spoken.

Languages change radically over time. Shakespeare's plays offer an example, since even native speakers do not necessarily understand the vocabulary unless they studied it in school. Some contemporary social media language needs explanation for older generations, and the language of the natural sciences has a specialised vocabulary that is opaque to outsiders. Each scientific speciality is also different. While language is an important way to store and communicate information, special circumstances can become a problem. Indigenous people, for example, sometimes have a range of words for smells or tastes or for objects that other languages lack. Words are frequently an imperfect means for communicating the information content of visual, olfactory or taste perceptions.

Ancient information

Information in the ancient world made different assumptions about information, because the context was very different. Religious explanations played both a causal and explanatory role, because religion provided meaning to events and objects that had seemed to have no other explanation. Empirical evidence in the modern sense was interpreted in different ways. A thunderbolt not only was a natural phenomenon but could also be an expression of anger by the gods. Chance events were sometimes assigned deterministic origins of a sort that gave people a sense of control. Managing their environment was one purpose of ancient information, and the reliability of information represented a key problem then, as now.

Weather is an example: reliable weather information was important because harvests depended on it. Weather predictions were fraught with risks. When people asked the gods about future weather, the gods maintained a discreet and obscure silence about details by speaking through interpreters, whose reliability troubled even true believers. The reliability problem for evidence has not gone away. There are people today who consider much of the epidemiological evidence about a disease like COVID-19 to be unconvincing. Reliability concerns have not vanished in the modern world.

The ancient world did not lack reliable information, but it had conceptual limits that hindered broader-scale extrapolation. Seasonal information was generally good because changes in the seasons were well established in local cultural expectations, and large-scale changes to weather patterns were relatively limited. The facts of seasonal changes were evident to everyone, and awareness was high because harvests depend on seasons. Unexpected weather events mattered because they affected food supplies. As a general rule, in the ancient world weather information influenced everything from planting to military campaigns, and inaccurate weather forecasts had life-and-death consequences. People sought weather information that fitted their expectations, which included a mix of accurate observation, folklore and magical speculation, because they lacked better tools. Even today's better tools do not always seem more convincing than magic. Doubt about their reliability is commonplace, and weather scepticism remains a cultural norm. The modern doubt about climate change has ancient roots.

Even if the ancient world lacked modern tools to process certain kinds of information, people did their best to manage the information available to them. Navigation was economically important, and ancient cultures developed widely used star charts in order to cross moderately large bodies of water such as the Mediterranean. These charts were mostly accurate and unchanging, and reliance on the stars fitted the cultural context because of their religious significance. The stability of the star charts for navigation served a variety of other purposes. Horoscopes, for example, used the stars and planets to tell people about themselves and about their personal preferences in ways that probably influenced their choices. Horoscopes have not vanished from the modern world, and popular newspapers still carry them, even if, among educated people, their acceptance as an information source has diminished.

Horoscopes came from Babylon roughly 500 BCE. The culture of the Babylonians 'developed various mathematical techniques and tools that enabled them to mathematically calculate and predict the orbits of the planets and stars' (Egger, 2022). Tool development to process information was important in the ancient world, and some mathematical aspects of ancient tools still work today. While educated people no longer accept the predictive value of horoscopes, the early mathematical predictions of the star charts had a lasting value because they showed how to apply mathematical reasoning to other phenomena.

The ancient world valued practical information. The Roman army learned how to construct roads of better quality and durability than anything that had gone before, and in some cases better than anything that came afterwards for a surprisingly long time. One problem was the loss of exact information about the construction process, as well as about how to make such high-quality concrete. This is another important fact about ancient information: the more specialised the information was, the more vulnerable it became to loss over time. Ancient information systems tended to be ephemeral because record keeping was poor, preservation techniques were almost non-existent and even the idea of long-term information preservation was missing.

Ancient libraries

Libraries existed in the ancient world and played a role in passing down written forms of information. Most libraries were the private collections of wealthy people, often the writers themselves. Most of these collections were small. The famous 'library at Alexandria, founded by the first king of the Ptolemy dynasty around the start of the 3rd century BCE, eventually grew to house (at least) tens of thousands of volumes' (Nicholas, 2018).

The Alexandrian library did not resemble a modern library with lending policies, collection plans and preservation strategies, but it was arguably the largest collection of written material in the ancient world and played a role in preventing the loss of parts of ancient culture. Nonetheless, much of the information in the ancient world was not written, but was passed along only in oral tradition. The ancient world is today more foreign because of that loss.

The Chinese did not lack books in the ancient world, but the role of libraries there was less well defined:

> Ancient Chinese libraries, synonymously called book-storage houses or book repositories because of the emphasis on the collections until the term 'library' was used in Shi Wu Daily on September 27, 1896, 'originated from the Xia and Shang dynasties, came into being in the two Han dynasties, developed in the Sui and Tang dynasties, and their best development stages were in the Song and Qing dynasties'. (Huang, 2011, 2)
>
> (Yi, 2013)

In this they appear to resemble classical Western collections. Literacy may have been more limited because of the complexity of the characters, but that is only speculation. Information about information in ancient China is sadly limited, and the same is true for Indian civilisation.

Medieval information

This period encompassed radical changes in the lives of people in almost all regions and classes, which meant that the context of information changed more than surviving written works reflect. The world of the western portion of the Roman empire after the fifth century CE was once described as the 'Dark Ages', on the theory that literacy almost vanished. Literacy is not, of course, the same as having information, and in the ancient and medieval world most information was transmitted orally, even if the quantity and quality of that information is only indirectly measurable. Scholars know today that the era was not an information dark age, but was one in which non-textual sources dominated.

In the early medieval world many of the institutions that normally fostered written information struggled because of external problems like barbarian invasions. Such disruptions did not eliminate information, but they affected formal means of recording and preserving it. The Church preserved a higher level of literacy for the clerical orders, whose task was to copy the Bible and stories about the lives of saints. These manuscripts also included legends that gave details about daily life. Outside of the Church, military information grew and evolved as circumstances changed. Obvious examples are the introduction of horses and armour and better metal weapons. That was practical information that mattered to the leaders of the society.

The situation in China regarding written information was different. The examination system for entering the bureaucracy began in the Sui dynasty in about 567 CE and lasted into the 20th century (Lietzow, 2020). This guaranteed the importance of writing and written sources, even if the content of the examinations tended to emphasise philosophical and historical knowledge more than information about practical subjects. China suffered from internal warfare and barbarian invasions during much of the pre-modern period, but this no more stopped the growth of information there than in Europe.

China also absorbed information about other parts of the world, much like Europe during this period. The information came partly from trade, which was extensive, especially after the voyages of the 15th-century Ming court eunuch Zheng He. Zheng He brought Chinese fleets to parts of India and, in subsequent voyages, to the eastern coast of Africa. This was around the time when the Italian explorer Marco Polo visited China. These visits mattered not only for their trade but for the degree to which they brought information about other countries to China and to Europe. The details were less important than the growing realisation that other cultures existed and had other ways of looking at the world.

Information flows

Information flows even more quickly than trade, and the realisation that sophisticated other areas existed opened people's imagination. For the Europeans, the age of exploration culminated in an era of colonisation and exploitation. In contrast, the Chinese and their Japanese neighbours reacted more strongly to preserve and maintain their own environment. The cultural priorities were different: 'While in Europe branches of the mathematical sciences developed that were concerned with resource saving technologies like simple machines, this was not the case in China, where the mathematical sciences were mostly concerned with astronomy, numerology and harmonics' (Sivin, 1973, xiii, quoted in Schemmel, 2012).

Information during this era took on new meanings as the economic and social context changed. In Europe, the Catholic Church had played a critical but never an entirely monolithic institutional role, because beliefs were overwhelmingly local. Travel certainly enabled the spread of ideas, but limitations of contemporary communication tools reduced their impact. When the Hussites appeared in the 15th century, they inspired a rethinking of religious beliefs that was later reflected in the Reformation of the 16th century. Even though the Hussite movement did not spread, information about its ideas was not easy to contain, even before Gutenberg's printing press. These religious reforms reflected a changed relationship to the literal meaning of written texts, which the Protestant reformers emphasised, in contrast to established Church practices that emphasised clerical symbolic interpretations

The impact of the printing press on spreading access to religious texts is well known. Pamphlets, broadsheets and book-length treatises remained expensive and out of the reach of most people, but, as literacy spread, people read written texts out loud to audiences that had no competing forms of entertainment. Printing changed the language of communication as well, as local languages slowly replaced Latin in Northern Europe, and printing forced a degree of linguistic and orthographic standardisation. Dialects survived and still thrive in spoken form, even though they have become exotic in print. Printing appeared much earlier in China, probably 'around the year 700, … during the Tang dynasty (618–907)', but for cost reasons and because of the wealth of characters, 'wood- or metal-block printing remained the dominant technology' (Hoh, 2021).

The Enlightenment in the 17th and 18th centuries sought to view the world in a rational way that used information sources other than religion, and interest in the evidence-based scientific practice grew, with an increasing reliance on experiments in areas like electricity, chemistry and physics. Theoretical models generally did not appear until a century later. Looking for empirical evidence represented a significant change in people's awareness of what constituted reliable information. Ancient concepts of causation no longer seemed to explain phenomena in the physical world, although the more magical elements of pre-modern causation survived in isolated and less literate communities, where beliefs in traditional explanations persisted even as the Reformation caused people to re-evaluate many of their ideas about how the world worked. The intellectual context had shifted decisively. The same radical shift did not occur in China, perhaps because nothing quite so seismic happened to established beliefs.

Information 1800–1950

In Europe the French Revolution changed people's perceptions of the world. The importance of noble heritage and family background did not vanish overnight, but the difference between the birth elite and mere bourgeoisie declined noticeably, because the assumptions about the meaning of noble status lost some of their past validity. Mobility between classes also increased markedly during the Revolution and afterwards, in part because land ownership no longer played a decisive role in status. In other words, information about family background became less important in the social and political perceptions of people as time moved forward. This was true not only for France, but for most of Western Europe. Even in England, where the Revolution had no direct influence, landed gentry began to accept the influence of newly rich manufacturing families.

The technological changes in manufacturing that are broadly called the Industrial Revolution reflected a change in the nature of information. England became 'a country of tinkerers' (Voth et al., 2022). Tinkerers were largely inventors. An ordinary person who tinkered was not necessarily equivalent to a middle-class engineer with formal training, and might be little more than a hand-worker who had clever ideas about building new tools. Tinkerers could not generally make a fortune without support from people with sufficient access to capital to exploit the idea and the hand-worker's skill. In other words, information about how to make a new tool acquired a value that had not been recognised or rewarded earlier. This changed the perceptions of power relationships. Especially in England, and later elsewhere in Europe, wealth depended less and less on owning land. Many wealthy landowners also became industrialists, but merely having landed wealth ceased to imply the same level of influence that it had in earlier times. The context changed and the meaning of wealth shifted with it.

These changes in the information landscape took place without anyone calling them a revolution, even though their influence was wide ranging. Universities took on new importance as institutions that worked with information. Universities were not new in Europe. Bologna is generally recognised as one of the oldest European universities because of its 12th-century foundation, and the universities at Paris, Oxford, Cambridge, Prague and Heidelberg all pre-date the 15th century. What changed were the subjects. Theology and law retained their importance and their focus, but philosophy took an interest in new ways of looking at the world that eventually led to 'natural' philosophy, later called natural science. In the course of the 19th century, subjects like mathematics grew in value, and new universities like Berlin came into being, with its emphasis on seminars and research-oriented doctoral programmes. The social value of university attendance remained in many countries, but the emphasis on new forms of learning altered the thinking of the graduates.

Teaching remained heavily oral, both via lectures and in seminars where (in theory) the students had to speak and to share what they learned, instead of focusing on written exams. Context played a role in how students presented their work, especially in the laboratory sciences, which required a specialised infrastructure that was radically different from lecture halls and classrooms. Funding was an important factor in the development of the natural sciences because of cost, which meant that wealthier universities in wealthier countries could develop natural science programmes that attracted people from elsewhere, as long as they had the mathematical and linguistic skills for admission, and enough money to live on.

Japan slowly developed Western-style universities. The Imperial University of Tokyo was founded in 1877 and other institutions of higher education followed relatively quickly. Germany provided key models such as the 'Japan Society for the Promotion of Science, [which] was established in 1932, after the pattern of the German Kaiser-Wilhelm Gesellschaft in Berlin' (Hashimoto, 1963, 14). What model to imitate was itself an information decision, and the logic of that decision often depended on indirect factors. Japan already had an international rivalry with the Anglo-American world, especially in naval matters. That rivalry may have made it more socially and politically acceptable to look to Germany. The natural sciences and engineering in Germany were also widely recognised as first rate, as the list of Nobel prize winners in the natural sciences indicates. Einstein in physics and Fritz Haber in chemistry were examples. Since Japan was never a colony, English-speaking countries were also not obvious models.

The radio came into being at the end of the 19th century, but did not become a widespread communication medium until the 1920s. Radios were relatively expensive and the choice of programming was very limited. Nonetheless, they offered music, news, radio plays and other forms of entertainment that many found easier than reading newspapers. Radio opened new dimensions in information, not merely because of the real-time immediacy of events but because listeners could pick up clues from the tone of the presenter that added nuances to the spoken words. Live reporting arrived more slowly because of the equipment needs, but it added contextual information to what might otherwise have been dry events. One of the most popular forms of radio coverage was sporting events, where radio could capture some of the excitement of the players and the crowd.

Information since 1950

Television became available in the USA in the 1930s, but it was too expensive for most people until the later 1940s. The early television receivers were large, prone to technical problems and depended on vacuum-tube technology that was far less stable than the transistors that followed a decade or so later. Television began primarily as a source of entertainment, but expanded quickly into news. The visual information it presented created a greater sense of immediacy because the images offered more contextual information than radio or newspapers could provide. The effect of television on the US public during the Vietnam War was likely a cause of the widespread protests and growing anti-war sentiment. Television was less ubiquitous in most Western European countries during the 1970s, but also brought a measure of immediacy to student protests of the later 1960s and to the 1972 attack in Munich during the summer Olympics.

Television especially had an effect on sports. Physical attendance at the stadium mattered less, except for those who sought the social presence of other fans. Often, a person watching a game on television could see more clearly what was happening on the field or in the court, and replays later offered information that those physically present could not easily get. Physical presence nonetheless still offered context that television and radio could not, in the form of physical contact with fellow fans, the distinctive taste of stadium food and even the smell of the excitement of the crowd. Television is sometimes spoken of as a cool medium, meaning that it creates a sense of distance from the event, and the small size of early screens added to that sense of not really being there.

The traditional date for the start of the internet was with the US ARPAnet in 1969, but work on packet-switching systems started significantly earlier. The design of the internet protocol deliberately emphasised routing redundancy as a means of maintaining communications during a nuclear attack, a problem that seemed real at the time. E-mail grew rapidly as a means of communication, especially among people at universities. Not all networks used the standard internet protocol. BITNET ('Because It's Time Network') transferred packets from host to host and had an international reach. Its weakness became obvious after a Cornell computer science student created the first self-propagating virus that used people's contact lists to send itself to everyone on the list.

France developed its own 'Minitel' system in the 1980s. It expanded rapidly, thanks to its connection with the French Postes, Télégraphes et Téléphones system, and was discontinued in 2012 after about 30 years of service. Germany was a late adopter of the internet, and substantial usage began only after 1990 and unification. China was also a late adopter, presumably for political reasons. In practical terms, internet protocol became ubiquitous in the 2000s. This enabled videoconferencing using the H.323 protocol after 1996. Interactive video and audio communication grew rapidly as tools like Skype added new features, and as new products like Zoom came on the market. WeChat in China grew to become almost ubiquitous in that country. While the ability to see and converse with people half-way around the world significantly increased information sharing, it did not directly increase the amount of information.

Videoconferencing changed where people worked, and effectively eliminated some of the contextual information available in face-to-face meetings. This is one reason for the ongoing preference for physical conferences, despite the travel expense for those who could afford it. The virtual conferences are more democratic because of the lower costs, but participants may also feel that the experience is less fulfilling. Physical conferences have become a class-based privilege. The density of interaction opportunities can open doors to better jobs and to broader co-operation, but the participants must find the resources to pay for it. Those at elite universities generally can.

The shift from handwritten letters to typed letters to e-mail markedly improved the speed and clarity of communication at the expense of context signals. For most people, handwriting signals something about mood and the intensity of feeling because of how the author formed the letters. Typing stripped away some of those emotional signals, due to its uniformity. A good writer could fill in the emotional context and a poor writer could not conceal it. E-mail in effect also increases the advantage of those skilled in selecting and using words, because word choice must substitute for other context-based signals. In that sense, the improvements from information technology gave advantages to an elite with good linguistic skills and internet access.

Conclusion

Some improvements in information technology have indeed increased the amount and quality of information available in the world. Information sharing and interactions with people in distant places changed the parochial views of people who grew up with the view that their immediate context was normal, right and proper, but cultural assumptions change slowly. People in the 21st century certainly have the opportunity to know more about the natural world, about people elsewhere and about the variety of social and economic environments. For any individual this means a change in the information available, but in the end information itself is fundamentally what it always was: a mix of perception, context and learning from others.

CHAPTER 2

A History of the Discipline

What defines a discipline?

The French historian Marc Bloch noted that '[t]o the great despair of historians, men fail to change their vocabulary every time they change their customs' (Bloch, 1953, 34). This statement is especially true for the meaning of the word 'discipline', since it evolves from generation to generation and has subtly different meanings in different cultures and countries, depending on the legal structure.

For fields like accounting or law, the job market provides a mechanism for defining the discipline, but job markets change over time and take on different characteristics that change the discipline. Methodology may work as a definition for some disciplines, because methodology can determine how members address problems, but today few academic disciplines employ a single methodology and many borrow liberally from related fields. This chapter looks at how the idea of information science developed out of a tangle of precursors into a 21st-century discipline.

The academic world lacks a simple and consistent definition of the intellectual contents of disciplines. Sociologist Andrew Abbott, a well-known scholar on the subject of disciplines, argues that 'disciplinary functions are cultural rather than social structures. The first of these is the Geertzian function of providing academics with a general conception of intellectual existence, a conception of the proper units of knowledge' (Abbott, 2001, 130).

The culture of a discipline typically reflects what it regards as the 'proper units' of knowledge. For example, historians look at change over time, economists at money, psychologists at the workings of the mind, and philosophers (insofar as philosophers limit themselves at all) look at thought itself. The context in which scholars define their discipline influences how they understand what it represents, and of course context is itself part of their culture. The context in which Abbott was writing was the US university system, where a scholar's disciplinary identity defined the person's immediate department or college. Abbott himself notes a few other models: 'the personalism of nineteenth century Germany, the French research cluster, the ancient British system with its emphasis on small communities of common culture' (Abbott, 2001, 128). Abbott's list is not exhaustive and is certainly time bound to the post-World War 2 era, but his core definition about the units of knowledge applies across time and cultures.

Information science as an intellectual discipline has only recently acquired an organisational identity, but has ancient roots, much like history and philosophy. Information is a topic as old as time and has long existed outside of any organisational unit, because information is an element in everything people write or say. The word 'science' in this context does not imply any resemblance to the natural sciences, but refers to the much older root concept. Until the 20th century the English word science had the same meaning as the original French word science, meaning knowledge. In that sense, information science resembles other academic fields that address core elements of human understanding before they ever acquired organisational trappings. Scholars naturally thought about how minds and societies function before any labels like 'psychology' or 'sociology' came into being. Today, information science is slowly defining its own 'proper units of knowledge', which includes an awareness of the factual and contextual information that all fields use to make discoveries. No scholarly field stands alone, and none exists today without information at its core. Fields like history and philosophy have survived changes over time, because their ways of looking at the world endure despite change. Information science as a field today may have a new name and new identity, but its core subject is fundamentally timeless.

Since concepts of information have changed over time, and the names used for people working with information have changed as well, information science may count today as a 'new' discipline in academic terms, but its intellectual roots reach well back in time.

From authority to academic status

The first information scientists may in fact have been theologians, since it took the Western world centuries to think about information as something distinct from the 'authority' of sacred texts. Texts like the Bible once defined official knowledge, and many other forms of sacred works have existed since the beginning of human communication. Their origin was generally oral, although people switched to written forms once writing systems became available, in order to preserve the sacred words in an unchanging form.

Such sacred texts could not represent every possible type of information, but provided a structure for understanding information. The meaning of the texts varied with each interpretation, but their nature as undeniable truth was accepted within Christian and later within Muslim society, since they share a common heritage. Sacred texts like the Bible or the Koran told their readers everything that was deemed significant about the world they lived in, even when day-to-day details remained for people to discover for themselves.

It is hard to say exactly when the Bible and the works of the Church Fathers lost their status as a complete information source. Ironically, the change may have coincided with the Reformation, which made biblical texts more important, while freeing them from traditional interpretations. In the 17th century, Blaise Pascal's famous wager about the existence of God did not rely on references to biblical authority. It depended only on logic, an information tool that had existed since the time of Plato and Aristotle, and had mainly applied to natural laws. The shift away from a strict belief in biblical literalism took centuries. Biblical teachings about creation seemed to be indisputable in some places as late as the 19th century, when challenges arose both to Darwin's *Origin of the Species* (1859) and Charles Lyell's *Principles of Geology* (1830). Empirical evidence (as a form of information) only slowly came to matter more than biblical authority. A few religious minorities even in the 21st century still favour biblical claims over other forms of evidence.

No field springs into existence from nothing, and information science had many precursors after religion ceased to dominate people's thinking. The emerging interest in empirical information represented one starting point, but an enduring change in what constituted information took centuries. In the 16th century, 'history and legal activity shared a concern with evidence' (Smith, 1997, 81), as shown in the earlier rejection of the so-called 'Donation of Constantine'. The important fact is that both history and law relied increasingly on solid evidence as a form of information, and that prepared the way for contemporary expectations about reproducible information.

Library science, which today generally counts as one of the disciplinary precursors of information science, first acquired its own distinct identity in the 19th century as a practical training for people handling book collections. The title of librarian has long existed to describe any person responsible for important text collections. Those who worked in libraries in the ancient and medieval world counted as library practitioners in both the Western world and in China. Over time, the focus of their jobs led intellectually oriented librarians to begin to reflect on and eventually to write about the nature of the information they collected and preserved.

In purely institutional terms, the first place to establish a programme designed to think theoretically and abstractly about the management of written works may have been the University at Göttingen, which invited Karl Dziatzko to found a library programme in Göttingen that included doctoral-level scholarship in 1886 (Rohde, n.d.). The programme profited from the subsequent Prussian law of 1893, which created a justification for professional training for people working in libraries – essentially, a job market. Dziatzko was himself a classical philologist (Deutsche Biographie, n.d.). His successor was Richard Pietschmann, an Egyptologist (Deutsche Digitale Bibliothek, n.d.). While the medieval relationship between philology, history, language and evidence-based information remains visible in the University's choice of these professors, the creation of a philosophically distinct programme shifted its focus.

A first doctoral programme

The importance of the first doctoral programmes in library studies is hard to overemphasise, because it introduced a new measure of abstract discourse that raised the study of books to a level that resembles information science today. Book history played an important role in early library studies, partly because of the rarity and monetary value of older texts, but also because of the strong academic emphasis placed on the importance of evidence by well-known scholars like the German historian Leopold Ranke, who famously argued for writing history as it actually was ('wie es eigentlich gewesen [sei]') (Deutsches Historisches Institut, 2019). Ranke was well known beyond Germany and beyond the field of history. People who studied book history certainly knew of Ranke both because of their own connections to history and because of his fame within the German academic world. What they gained from him was a sense that information in the form of reliable evidence mattered for all types of scholarly work. The idea was not new, but Ranke provided a level of scholarly legitimation that had previously been less explicit.

Concerns about reliability of information began in the Renaissance, well before Ranke. People who practised natural science research in the 18th and 19th centuries cared greatly about the accuracy of the information, and they had the advantage that their results could be tested. For example, Isaac Newton's laws of gravity and his three laws of motion were empirically testable. Volta's 'voltaic pile' quickly attracted attention and was tested in a series of public experiments, including one in Paris in 1801 before Napoleon I, and it mattered that the experiment worked (Britannica, 2025a). Charles Babbage worked on creating a calculating machine beginning in 1823, when he received a government grant (Freiberger and Swaine, 2023). The important fact about these inventions was that people could demonstrate visibly that in their theories worked and that the results were reproducible. Information science was not yet self-aware enough to embrace this, but as background it represented an essential step.

Denis Diderot and the *Encyclopedia* contributed substantially to the spread of reliable information in text format. In a sense, they could claim to be early information scientists, since their mission included assembling as much of the known information in the world as they could. Like the leaders of the first academic programmes in library studies, the encyclopedists were not natural scientists, and they found it more natural to think about information in terms of written works and references than experiments. The important fact is that the encyclopedists sought to collect information in all of its variety, even when they did not completely understand it.

Information access

The jump from creating an academic field called library science to a scholarly discipline like information science required a shift that broke with the widespread tendency of increasing academic specialisation. New academic fields like psychology or sociology or genetics wanted to distinguish themselves from the vague generalities of the past. Information at the time seemed like a mere tool, a useful subunit, not an abstract core concept as extensible as atoms or cells or energy or history. Information simply seemed too nebulous as a concept to play a practical role as a worthwhile tool. To some it still does, which has led a few academics to want to rename it as 'data science' in order to make it seem less abstract and more concrete.

What changed was a dramatic growth in the awareness of the sheer quantity and variety of information in the world. People at the beginning of the 20th century complained about the pace of change. Often they meant visible physical changes involving so many rapid technical developments that continuity with the past seemed to be lost. A key technical transformation began with the steam presses mid-19th century, which dramatically increased the production of information in printed form. It was not long before radio replaced print as a means for rapid information distribution, and by the mid-20th century television made information transfer visual for all who could afford it. A consequence was that information no longer had to limit itself to print media, and this had political repercussions, as well as consequences for information science as a discipline.

Goebbels' mastery of the political power of the radio played a role in the Nazi election victory of 1933. In the USA, Franklin Roosevelt also became an expert in using the same medium for his fireside chats, as had Benito Mussolini years earlier in Italy. The information that Goebbels and Mussolini conveyed was untrue by contemporary standards, but the dramatic quality of their presentation style convinced many listeners to believe their claims. The listeners cared less about an abstract standard of reliability than whether the statements reflected their personal beliefs. Expectations about information validity required attitudes towards evidence that much of the public neither shared nor understood. Evidence, for a broad portion of the public, often meant trust in the speaker rather than objectively questioning their claims. This attitude still exists in contemporary politics and harkens back to the traditional belief in authority as the true measure of information.

Reliable information

Expectations about the importance of reliable public information changed slowly, in part because the public had no established mechanism that helped people to challenge non-factual claims, or even an awareness of how to proceed. Within the natural sciences the measures of empirical truth were easier to establish, because replicating results had come to matter more than preconceived expectations. Nonetheless, replication was not always easy. When the German chemist Fritz Haber (a Nobel prize winner in chemistry) developed a process to extract gold from sea water, he based his approach on data from an 1878 article that claimed that 'there were 65 micrograms of gold per litre of sea water' (Buck, 2023). In fact, he 'found that the concentration of gold was more than 10,000 times lower than he expected', which meant that Haber's plan could not work (Buck, 2023). Awareness of the need for truly reliable information grew slowly, and even in the 21st century is imperfectly understood or accepted, as could be seen in the public reaction to COVID-19.

Several disciplines felt the need for reliable information. Journalism is one example, but it suffered from the pressures of economic factors favouring sometimes outlandish claims that increased sales. Newspaper sales and media market share mattered more than mere facts to the people paying salaries. Nonetheless, the best practitioners of journalism still cared about the reliability of what they wrote and said, when they sought to influence the public. Journalism first became an academic subject at the University of Missouri in the late 19th century, and by 1912 Columbia University in New York had a graduate programme in journalism. Broadcast journalism was a logical next step. Journalism quickly became an established profession because it had a clear job market.

Journalism could have renamed itself as information science, and today some universities group it in the same unit as library and information science, but journalism has remained largely separate, in part because of market forces. The best journalists have engaged broadly with all forms of information, even though they do not necessarily share the librarian's interest in making information a durable and lasting commodity.

As Andrew Abbott said, disciplinary definitions are cultural, and the cultural nuances of disciplinary identity vary widely from region to region. Journalists have not been free in all countries to pursue or to save documentable facts. In some places they are more rigidly controlled than librarians, whose work sometimes has the advantage of escaping political and public notice, though in recent times that has changed. The Nazis banned books they disliked politically, and today certain states in the USA have started interfering with library collections, Florida most notably. In general, though, journalists have faced more restrictions on their freedom because of their more public role.

The birth of a field

Historically, information science took its current name and form in the USA, and in the USA today the job market plays a core role in defining disciplines for university graduates. It is important not to confuse the job focus of a particular culture with the intellectual and philosophical basis of a discipline, which typically cuts across artificial commercial boundaries. One example of disciplinary cross-cutting comes from people who have won Nobel prizes in economics, even though they have held positions in other fields. Trans-disciplinary examples can also include psychology, which was variously part of philosophy or medicine before taking on an independent identity. Psychology continues to have complex connections to both the medical and social science worlds.

Research methodology has played a more important role in defining disciplines in the modern world than it did previously. Until the 20th century, the idea of a discipline was so vague that when James Angell (later president of the University of Michigan) wanted an academic position in the mid-19th century, the president of Brown University offered 'a choice of jobs as chairman of either the Civil Engineering or Modern Language Department' (Wikipedia, 2025a), two fields that are methodically so widely different that today it seems hard to imagine that one person could be appropriate for either job.

Information science as a discipline sometimes struggles precisely because of the breadth of its focus, since information is everywhere and the field lacks the respectability of ancient roots like history. Another criticism has been that information science lacks any claim to a unifying theory, but in a philosophic sense theory is itself only a viewpoint. The mechanisms of theories often evolve over time. Viewpoints in the broader cultural sense do so more rarely.

The idea that information science first became a discipline after the invention of computers comes largely from those who built the tools that became the contemporary means of information exchange. It is true that computing, networking and the processing and storage capabilities of computing changed society's relationship to information. People talk about the Gutenberg revolution in printing in the same way, and certainly the printing press was no less transformative than computing systems in making information broadly accessible. Many contemporary practices for communicating information, especially scholarly information, grew out of print-based models that information science has inherited and largely adopted. The scale and speed have changed, but, compared to content, the long-term role of technological change should play only a minimal role in defining a field of study.

The name 'information science' has virtually no history as a term, because it was a creation of the mid-20th century. The first references to information science appeared in the 1960s: 'After the Georgia Institute of Technology established the first formal information science programme in 1963, the discipline quickly developed at a number of other universities either as an independent field of study or as a specialty within such departments as library science, computer science, or engineering' (Britannica, 2025b). It does not matter whether this date as the original information science programme is universally accepted, or even that the programme's focus was strongly computing oriented. It provides a starting point, after which many university departments began thinking simultaneously about the potential for the study of information as an academic discipline.

The ability of computers to transform how people thought about information became a widespread topic of discussion, including exaggerations similar to those in contemporary discussions about artificial intelligence. Even the name 'computer science' was new in the mid-20th century, before which computers were mostly women performing calculations by hand. Early computer training began at many institutions in the mathematics departments, in part because understanding mathematical logic played a key role in understanding machine language in its alphanumeric form as assembly language, which itself merely represented the machine codes (e.g. LR for Load Register for Hex "18" in IBM 360 Assembly language). The ability to read hexadecimal commands played a non-trivial role in early programming training, since the compilers for higher-level languages like Fortran (1953) and COBOL (1959) were imperfectly reliable even decades after these so-called third-generation languages became widely established.

According to Shallit (1995) in his 'Brief History of Computer Science', the first department of computer science was at Purdue University in 1962, only slightly earlier than the Information Science Department at Georgia Tech. The long engineering tradition at Purdue makes this claim as plausible as the Georgia Tech date, since both universities had a strong technical orientation. The dates and places for the establishment of new disciplines matter less than the fact that the ideas they represented began to take more concrete form approximately around that time. A decade later the opportunity to study computer science formally became more widespread among those US universities which had the advantage of both the money and staff resources to buy expensive machines, often initially for administrative purposes and only later opened to teaching or research on a limited basis.

While discussing the rise of computer information processing as a model for other kinds of human information processing, Roger Smith wrote in his book about the human sciences: 'Information science, visible in material form in computing technology, became what has been called a defining technology, a technology which gives a culture its dominant models for investigation and understanding and structures the way we think about the world' (Smith, 1997, 837). The link between computing and information science seemed obvious at the end of the 20th century, and for many it still is, but Smith himself implies that information science is more than computing because it has to do with how people think about the world. The field was in the process of gaining more definition precisely when Smith's book was published.

Information science gains identity

Less important than establishing a name for the discipline was to establish an identity that fit the broader long-term philosophic concepts of what information science should and could represent. That required a wealthy university that already had a substantial research reputation and, perhaps more importantly, a dean that was ready to take a major risk. Daniel Atkinson, the new dean at the University of Michigan, was such a risk-taker dean. He did not merely rename a successful library studies programme, but built a new intellectual basis for information science by hiring people from an unusually broad set of disciplines. He himself came from engineering, and worked to attract notable faculty from diverse fields like psychology and economics to create a unit with an explicit and intentional focus on information itself. An important factor was the ability of those new faculty members to attract money, which matters above all in the US university world, and they succeeded. Not everyone was happy, especially those specialising in topics specifically related to library studies, because they felt sidelined, but in the American context financial success mattered above all else.

Many other US schools took an interest in Michigan's success and also claimed to be information science leaders, among them Syracuse University, the University of Illinois and the University of Washington. Some of them had earlier information science programmes and were moving in similar directions, though with fewer resources and less public attention. When Humboldt-Universität zu Berlin decided to transform its library studies into genuine information science, it turned to representatives from the University of Michigan for advice. Both of those whom they invited had, by chance, PhDs from the University of Chicago. The intellectual connection to the importance of serious doctoral studies mattered.

Berlin made a conscious choice to reinvent itself along new lines that included a much closer relationship to computing. One of the new professors at the Berlin School was the head of the computer centre and had a computing doctorate. A second new professor had a complex background that included a doctorate in history, a degree in information science and decades of hands-on computing experience. He was also bilingual in German and English. The two new professors were also good friends, and together they offered a transformative set of connections and backgrounds. Their influence on the university can be seen in the fact one became the dean and later chair of the University Council, the body that elected presidents and vice-presidents. Berlin made a deliberate choice that was, in its way, as unexpected and dramatic as Michigan's.

It helped that the University also began to win German Excellence Initiative awards. The new 'iSchool' played only a minor role in the awards, but benefited from the enhanced recognition. The first non-US-based chair of the iSchools governing body came from Berlin, and the first non-US iConference took place in Berlin, under the leadership of Elke Greifeneder, then a professor in Copenhagen. It was fundamentally important for the development of information science as a discipline that it became genuinely international. Wuhan University also became an active information science partner and brought with it strong connections to Sheffield University in the UK and close ongoing ties also to Berlin.

The intellectual leadership of information science in modern times has multiple roots where no individual played a leading role but, rather, sets of people with ties of friendship and a recognition that the field was undergoing a level of transformation that called for co-operation and support. There are too many names to list. They understood that information as a form of knowledge crossed established boundaries. The discipline took form not as a way for students to get jobs or as a way to exclude methodologies, but as something that truly defined itself around the abstract concept of information.

The idea was what mattered and has become the true definition of a field that has outgrown older and narrower descriptions.

It is typical of a field whose self-definition has a genuine philosophical basis that its boundaries are, as Andrew Abbot wrote, cultural rather than a matter of institutional structures. Information science is not an attempt to give a name to a field with a large number of practitioners trying to create distinctions that separate their ideas and interests from other scholars but, rather, an intellectually consistent approach to thinking about the modern world that transcends employment issues. Information science is about ideas. This does not mean that jobs do not matter to information scientists, only that information scientists should look beyond short-term interests to the core ideas that define the field.

Information science today

Perhaps it is a sign of a mature discipline that scholars with an interest in data science view information science as an established point of comparison. An example comes from the article by Mayernik (2023), who writes, 'This analysis highlights the historical parallels between the emergence of data science in the 21st century and the emergence and evolution of information science over the past 100 years to provide insight into interdisciplinary challenges facing data science as a professional and academic endeavour.' This article is also one of the few discussing information science as a discipline separate from library and information science. Mayernik (2023) argues against the 'formalization of a discipline and profession with agreed-upon curricula, skills, and professional responsibilities'. He notes that 'Similar issues have manifested in information science for a century or more and continue to be points of debate today.'

Data science has become a popular marketing term for university departments that want to evoke a connection to data processing as a way to promote the technical skills of their graduates in the same way that earlier units emphasised the connection between information science and information technology. As Seadle and Havelka (2023) wrote:

> Data are the eunuchs of the information world because data and data sets are functionally sterile and meaningless without reference to the intellectual, spatial, temporal, and social environment that represents their context. A serious researcher can prove nothing with data without knowing where they came from and what they mean. Information must always include context, and information science as practiced today represents the union of context and data.

The trouble with context as a defining element of a discipline is that it changes constantly, which is inconvenient when trying to set disciplinary boundaries even though it nonetheless reflects reality.

Information science has become a formal discipline, with departments and graduates and journals that use some form of information science in their name. Whether those characteristics will continue to define information science as an academic field over time remains to be seen. Disciplines that once seemed important, like philology (the study of the historical development of language and linguistic structures), shrank and faded because the context in which they had seemed important either changed or was absorbed into other disciplines. This does not mean that their contents are less important, only that other fields absorbed their characteristic elements as they grew to seem too specific and narrow for modern purposes. It seems less likely that information science will suffer a similar fate, because information covers such an intellectually broad spectrum. Its future depends on whether scholars who pursue information science maintain their intellectual breadth.

Conclusion

What happens to disciplines that no longer seem to represent the cutting edge of scholarly thought and lose their connection to the workday life of practitioners? What happens when some other new concept replaces them in the popular mind? There are plenty of historical examples, such as philosophy, which once covered a wide range of intellectual discourse that includes what is now called natural science. Another example is history, which once covered topics that seem now to belong to political science or sociology or even economics. Academic fashions change over time, in part because people want something new. Adopting a new academic fashion is a way of escaping stale conventions in order to discover and to say new things.

This is not necessarily bad or unprecedented. Scholars sometimes need to be able to start afresh, much as they did when the concept of information science came into being. That does not mean that information science will vanish as a way of thinking, but it could mean that organisational units that use the name of information science today may grasp at new terms that seem to reflect new goals. As Marc Bloch wrote, vocabularies change over time. Core ideas generally survive regardless of the short-term infrastructures that seem to embody them.

CHAPTER 3

Information Science Organisations

What criteria define an information science organisation?

While the criteria should ideally be as broad and inclusive as the idea of the field itself, institutions prefer more specific boundaries in order to define themselves. In practical terms, most organisations that explicitly associate themselves with information science include some implicit or explicit reference to 'information' in their name. Some organisations that collaborate with information science organisations may not use the appellation 'information science', but nonetheless fit into the broader conceptions, such as computing, statistics, sometimes even business.

The North American landscape has at least three groups that lay claim to being information science organisations. The youngest is iSchools, Inc., whose formal incorporation as a non-profit dates only from 2014. Its headquarters are in Germany. The Association for Information Science and Technology (ASIS&T) was founded in 1937 as the American Documentation Institute and changed its name to Association for Information Science and Technology in 2013, when it dropped the 'American' from its name. Older still is the Association of Library and Information Science Education (ALISE), founded in 1900 as the Association of American Library Schools. These three organisations collaborate under the umbrella term iFederation, which was first suggested at a 2015 wedding in Germany, where the chair of the iSchools and the president-elect of ASIS&T were both guests. Personal connections matter.

There are other organisations that could and sometimes do claim to be part of information science. Some of the more active examples can shed light on the nature of information science. The International Federation of Library Associations (IFLA) represents an example of an organisation that has information science interests but still resolutely defines itself in traditional library terms. Libraries are centres for information and many of the members of IFLA have at least indirect connections to information science in their home countries. Libraries in some member countries still put a heavy emphasis on printed books, but that is slowly fading as digital sources have come to dominate much of the academic discourse.

The American Library Association intentionally kept the word 'Library' in its name, but the British Chartered Institute of Library and Information Professionals (CILIP) chose to add the word 'Information' to its title. This does not mean that the Americans are less interested in information science, or that the British libraries wish to be closer to the concept. It was a marketing choice as much as anything. Both organisations offer accreditation to educational programmes that specialise in information science, which indicates how clearly they recognise the overlap. Likewise, the German library association (Bibliotheksverbund) has retained the word library in its title despite its close connections with information science programmes. In Germany, libraries play a role in society that is more established and perhaps more important than computing.

Names do not always reflect the amount of interest in information science. The India Library Association is an example of an organisation that routinely uses the acronym LIS (library and information science) when talking about education or programmes. The Chinese Libraries Association does not use the Western term 'information science', but many of the leading academic programmes are members of the iSchool organisation and recognise the importance of information science. Language and culture make a difference in understanding the nuances between a more traditional book-oriented organisation and a more inclusive approach to the nature of information. In the past, a number of organisations adopted the appellation 'information science' without having clear information science content. Today the situation is reversed, with more actual information science content than names suggest.

The next sections will describe the three explicit information science organisations that belong to the iFederation.

iSchools

In 2008 Ronald Larsen of the University of Pittsburgh wrote a history of the origin of the iSchools dating back to 1988, when Toni Carbo (University of Pittsburgh), Donald Marchand (Syracuse) and Richard Lytle (Drexel) 'formed the Gang of Three' that became the first explicit gathering of school leaders who had an interest in information science (Larsen, 2009). It was an exclusively US group of deans who had an interest in orienting their programmes more towards information technology. The group was informal and focused on practical topics like 'How do you explain information science (IS) to your provost?' (Larsen 2009). The group grew over the years to ten members, all US, and continued to grow so that by 2008 it included one Canadian university and one from Singapore, whose head was an American.

The group slowly began to think how best to define the content of information science. 'Marcia Bates defines "the domain of information science [as] the universe of recorded information that is selected and retained for later access", and posits that applied information science is "primarily concerned with the form and organization of information, its underlying structure, and only secondarily with its content …"' (Larsen, 2009). This description strongly reflects its library science roots with the emphasis on selection, access and structure, to the exclusion of content. Bates asked in particular 'What are the features and laws of the recorded-information universe?' (Larsen, 2009). The quest for 'laws' especially reflects a long-standing desire to emulate the natural sciences that was a leitmotif of the social sciences in earlier centuries. What is important here is that people were beginning to think in more abstract and philosophical terms about what information science might be.

Discussion about possible theories played a role, and academic ideas made an appearance in the form of 'broad context including understanding capabilities and practices, human behaviors, usage, and impacts' (Larsen, 2009). John King and Kalle Lyytinen offered a view of 'the core of the discipline as a "market of ideas" where the IS field is defined as "the study of the design and management of information and associated technologies in organized human enterprise"' (Larsen, 2009).

The human focus of information science slowly grew more explicit and more important. Some people adopted the term 'movement', despite (or perhaps because of) its quasi-religious connotations. The word suggested ideas that people wanted to believe in and implied the possibility of rapid mass growth without institutional structures that set limits on its development. The word 'movement' served largely as a marketing term. Information science represented too explicitly an academic approach to understanding the world, without the theological elements of authority that have long characterised 'movements'.

Hype played an especially large role in the early days of the iSchools. In addition to the term 'movement' people invented the term 'iField':

> The iField also empowers people in other fields to create, find, store, manipulate, and share information in useful forms. It may be unique in that, despite its elusive core, its subject, information, is at the heart of what individuals, organizations, and societies need in order to advance human endeavors, from acting to zoology. The iField's most visible and viable outcome is the delivery of the right information at the right time to the right people in the right form.
>
> (Larsen, 2009)

This was all fundamentally true as a set of shared goals, but not ones that defined the iSchools as fundamentally different from existing library organisations.

Historically, the iSchools came into being at a time when many existing library programmes faced two problems. One was a slow decline in the social and economic role of libraries as a primary source of information. In the mid-20th century most substantial companies had their own libraries to provide reference information to professional staff. These libraries were not large, but a medium-sized insurance company might, for example, have one or two trained librarians to make sure that key information remained available. Few training programmes for librarians emphasised corporate jobs, but the latter added to the jobs market and were sometimes paid better than other librarian positions. The advent of computer-based records eliminated many corporate libraries.

The second problem grew out of a change in publishing and marketing. Delivery costs fell, thanks to distributed printing, and companies like Amazon commercialised delivery so effectively that people ordered from them rather than going to a local bookstore or a library. Many bookstores fell victim to Amazon's success, and bookstores had also once been employers for trained librarians. Electronic editing and reviewing also changed how publishers worked. Gains in efficiency enabled publishers to offer more content, while reducing the jobs market for trained librarians.

Reducing the focus on library education seemed like a way for university programmes to escape the shrinking jobs market. As a result, many programmes began to emphasise computing skills. This was not purely a North American response. Both of the new professors at the Berlin School of Library and Information Science in 2006 had strong computing and digital backgrounds, which reshaped the focus of the courses even before the course titles changed to become more explicitly technical. This was not a sharp break with tradition any more than it was at the US schools, but represented a deliberate tilt towards a technological emphasis. The change at some US schools alienated some alumni donors, but the increase in the number of applicants more than balanced the donor loss. Some schools, notably the University of Washington, benefited from the support of Microsoft and similar technology companies. Library-oriented vendors never had much money to give to academic programmes, but technology companies recognised that information schools produced graduates with a useful mix of technological and social expertise, whose salary expectations were more modest than those of computer science graduates.

The number of iSchool members grew slowly as long as eligibility for joining was set at US$1 million in external grant funding, which only Berlin and two other European schools had. The annual dues were US$5,000, which many potential members could not afford. Both rules changed at the time of incorporation, thanks to a recognition that elitist old rules hindered both growth and internationalisation. The iSchools also adopted a regional structure that divided board seats between North American, European and Asia-Pacific members and required a regional rotation of the chair and the annual conferences. The iSchools effectively ceased to be American, despite its incorporation in Washington, DC. Its business offices shifted to the Berlin area, where they have remained.

As of 2024 the iSchools had over 130 members on all inhabited continents. The formula for distributing board of directors seats was a compromise that gave more votes to the schools that paid higher dues, with the result that initially three of the six directly elected board members came from North American schools. The rotation principle guaranteed a more global distribution of officers. The only officer with no specific regional affiliation is the treasurer, who is currently a well-known scholar from Asia. The long-standing pattern of mobility in the academic world has helped to make the iSchools more international. For iSchools, leaders from Australia, Korea and Germany played a leading role in enabling a greater level of internationalism than the founders had envisioned.

The iSchools organisation has a strong academic orientation, with international doctoral seminars during the teaching semesters, an active group for early-career academics and regular news features that focus on topics like research integrity. Since the COVID-19 pandemic, the annual iConference has included a virtual component, so that members from all regions can participate without significant travel costs. No one should imagine that the iSchools have no tensions among the regions, but the commitment to respect for other cultures and regions is strongly embedded in the organisational culture.

ASIS&T

ASIS&T has a significantly longer history than the iSchools. It began in 1937 as the 'American Documentation Institute (ADI), a service organization' (ASIS&T, n.d.) 'Its initial interest was in the development of microfilm as an aid to information dissemination.' It is worth remembering that microfilm at the time was a new and important technology. In the 1950s ASIS&T began to evolve: 'ADI became the national professional society for those concerned with all elements and problems of information science. With the 1950's came increasing awareness of the potential of automatic devices for literature searching and information storage and retrieval' (ASIS&T, n.d.). In 1968 the name of the organisation changed to 'the American Society for Information Science.' (ASIS&T, n.d.), making it the first organisation actually to use 'Information Science' in its name. It was the first 'national professional organization for those concerned with designing, managing, and using information systems and technology' (ASIS&T, n.d).

An important feature of ASIS&T was its interest in social involvement and publication, and ASIS&T

> made the Mid-Year Meeting an annual event focusing on a single topic of current interest, sponsored a bicentennial conference (1976) on the role of information in the country's development, was an active participant in the planning and implementation of the White House Conference on Library and Information Services, and the Bulletin of the American Society for Information Science appeared and became a mainstay membership publication of the Society.
> (ASIS&T, n.d.)

The organisation established 'groups on office information systems and personal computers as well as international information issues and rural information services' (ASIS&T, n.d.). In the 1980s it also established 'its first non-North American Chapters.... In 2013, the Society changed its name to the Association for Information Science and Technology (ASIS&T) to reflect its growing international membership' (ASIS&T, n.d.).

In 1952 ASIS&T began to admit individual as well as institutional membership (ASIS&T, n.d.). Individual membership has become its mainstay, with a complex set of membership rates to reflect personal status (student, early career, retired or community only) and the economic status of the home country, based on two tiers for developing countries with a 'full waiver of dues for two years from join date' for some developing countries and significant reductions in the annual costs for others (ASIS&T, n.d.). This was a practical attempt to make membership affordable internationally, which has been largely successful. According to Lydia Middleton, ASIS&T executive director (ASIS&T, 2025), total membership includes just over 2,100 members worldwide. About 47% of the membership is North American, 32% come from the Asia-Pacific area, especially from India, which alone represents over 15% of the membership; Africa has 6%, Europe just under 10% and South America not quite 1%. The important fact is that ASIS&T has gone from being primarily North American to more broadly international.

It is important to remember that the iSchools membership is largely institutional, while ASIS&T now primarily has individual members. This leads to different governance structures and statistics that are not directly comparable. People who are paying for membership directly may be more inclined to take an active role, while institutional membership means that everyone who belongs to the institution can claim membership. In practical terms the people who feel most involved with the iSchools are the 130 heads of the member schools. ASIS&T offers webinars on a range of information science topics including artificial intelligence, ethical issues and sustainable information management. ASIS&T also sponsors a doctoral colloquium, though only at its annual meetings, which have remained mainly face-to-face events. The ASIS&T digital library includes the highly regarded Journal of the Association of Information Science and Technology (JASIST), which Wiley publishes. Structurally, ASIS&T has elected officers, including a president and treasurer, who change annually. As with the iSchools, these officers are not responsible for operational decisions, but for policy discussions with the board.

In 2024 ASIS&T decided to partner with a commercial organisation: 'ASIS&T is excited to share that as of January 1, 2025, ASIS&T has partnered with Global Management Partners (GMP) to provide management support services for ASIS&T. While Lydia remains the Executive Director fully employed by ASIS&T, GMP is providing all other staffing for the association' (ASIS&T, 2025). This means that the management of the organisation has moved into the hands of a North American corporation, leaving the iSchools as the only information science organisation with its own staff, all of whom have advanced degrees in Library and Information Science.

ASIS&T typically holds its conferences in October, and historically they have generally been in North America. But in 2016 the conference was in Copenhagen, Denmark, in 2019 it was in Melbourne, Australia and the 2023 conference was in London. The iSchools board also took the opportunity to meet in London during the ASIS&T conference, since it was convenient for both the European and Asian members. That could have been seen as a sign of closer co-operation between the organisations. In fact, in 2023 ASIS&T proposed closer structural co-operation among the three information science organisations, but both ALISE and the iSchools board ultimately rejected the proposal.

ALISE

The Association for Library and Information Science Education focuses on education for information professionals, with an emphasis on training librarians. The organisation 'grew out of a series of informal meetings of library school faculty at the American Library Association conferences'. The group 'voted in 1915 to form a permanent organization and to be identified as the Association of American Library Schools', and in 1983 it changed its name 'to reflect more accurately the mission, goals, and membership of the Association' (ALISE, n.d.).

The ALISE Board of Directors has seven members, all from the USA. ALISE does not have its own staff, but uses the services of a management company called Barcami Lane with which the iSchools also have a service agreement to handle US banking. ALISE offers both individual and corporate membership and has a 'Council of Deans, Directors, and Chairs [that] consists of the chief executive officer of each individual ALISE Institutional member school.' In structural terms, it may be somewhat more like the iSchools (ALISE, 2024a).

ALISE produces an annual statistical record that is widely used within the academic librarian community because of the depth of reliable detail that it provides about the North American employment market. The statistics include topics like faculty, salaries, faculty size, salary ranges and other relevant information, including travel expenditures. It is hard to compare salaries across countries and cultures, and the differences between elite and non-elite institutions can be significant. Nonetheless these statistics offer a useful benchmark. The faculty salary information is uniquely interesting precisely because the strong North American focus means that the faculty titles and salary ranges are directly comparable. The statistics include the percentage of tenured faculty, which is mostly just over 50%, and the mean number of full-time faculty at member schools, which hovers around 20. The concepts of tenure and full time reflect cultural norms that are not universal. The information in the tables makes sense only for those familiar with the culture from which the numbers come, which is often true in information science.

The ALISE tables focus explicitly on American Library Association accredited programmes, a fact that reflects their origin and strong library focus. ALISE provides information about doctoral programmes, including statistics about the gender distribution and ethnic background of doctoral students. These categories have a political significance mainly in the North American context. The doctoral student numbers differentiate between those with a focus on library science and those primarily doing information science, which are about twice as high. This probably reflects the job market and a widespread belief that library science is a field in decline because the number of new positions for librarians has declined. The North American academic market focuses intensively on job prospects for graduates. One reason is the high tuition fees for their education. Many programmes in Europe are essentially free for citizens.

ALISE has its own journal called the *Journal of Education for Library and Information Science* (*JELIS*). It 'is a fully refereed scholarly periodical that has been published quarterly by the Association for Library and Information Science Education (ALISE) since 1960' (ALISE, 2024b). The University of Toronto Press serves as publisher for *JELIS*, and it appears quarterly. ALISE also has a book series that 'addresses issues critical to Library and Information Science education and research through the publication of epistemologically grounded scholarly texts which are inclusive of regional and national contexts around the world' (ALISE, 2024c).

Like the iSchools and ASIS&T, ALISE would like to have an international scope.

IFLA

The International Federation of Library Organisations never included 'information' in its title, but as a worldwide organisation of libraries it has a relationship to information science. IFLA was founded 'on 30 September 1927 at the Annual Meeting of the UK Library Association in Edinburgh, Scotland, IFLA officially began in 1929 with 15 members from 15 countries' (IFLA, 2024).

IFLA has too many active sections to describe them in detail, but some are especially worth noting because of their connection to information science. One section with a formal history describes '40 Years of Technology in Libraries' (McCallum, 2003), but the phrase 'information science' does not actually appear in the history, which focuses on automation, bibliographic standards and data exchange. Networks and online catalogues and digital archives have also played a role. None of this was cutting edge, but it has remained core to most library operations since the 1960s.

The IFLA series book about 'Educating the Profession: 40 years of the IFLA Section on Education and Training' by Seadle, Chu, Stöckel and Crumpton does talk about 'developments at schools of library and information science', since two of the authors (Seadle and Stöckel) worked for the Berlin School of Library and Information Science, and another (Chu) for the School of Information Sciences at the University of Illinois. In the introduction the authors wrote:

> [I]t is clear that students with strong computing skills get jobs more quickly, and often with better pay, than those with traditional library skills. Among the iSchools there is a strong trend to offer courses on programming or in conjunction with computer science programmes. Graduates with these skills also tend to find jobs in industry or research projects. This means a substantial drain of what are often top students out of the library world.
>
> (Seadle et al., 2016, xx)

Another IFLA series book from 2017 by Ismail Abdullah discussed 'Global Library and Information Science', and seven other titles explicitly included 'Information Science' in their titles, starting in 1995. Seven other topics focused on buildings or design, and six discussed digital topics such as digital preservation and digital libraries generally. Four discussed knowledge management, seven had 'marketing' in their titles and three focused explicitly on developing countries. The goal of the series was to give readers an understanding of topics of special importance to the library world. IFLA has a journal that dates from 1993 and is available digitally.

IFLA has a regional structure that to a certain extent inspired the regional structure of the iSchools. For IFLA, the regions are: Asia-Oceania, Europe, Latin America and the Caribbean, Middle East and North Africa, North America, and Sub-Saharan Africa. One of the problems is that the regions are uneven in size and resources. In terms of population, the Asia-Oceania region (including China and India) is the largest, but the European and North American regions often send the most delegates to the IFLA conferences. The IFLA Congresses shift regularly from region to region, though more take place in Europe with 11 Congresses there since 2000 – three in Asia, four in North America, two in Africa and one in Latin America. Finding host venues is often a problem because of travel costs for members and because the hosts end up assuming many burdens, while the compensation comes chiefly in the form of the honour of being a host site.

Anglo-American library associations

Both the American Library Association (ALA) and the British Chartered Institute of Library and Information Professionals can reasonably count as active information science organisations whose origins grow out of the library community. The 'information' connection is explicit in the case of CILIP, which describes itself as 'the leading voice for the information, knowledge management and library profession. We're here for everyone who has a professional connection to information, knowledge, data and libraries, and shares our belief in their power to change lives' (CILIP, 2024).

The ALA says little explicitly about information science on its website, though it does list David Bawden and Lyn Robinson's excellent book, *Introduction to Information Science*, on its website under 'News' (ALA, 2024). ALA's 'stated mission' is 'To provide leadership for the development, promotion, and improvement of library and information services and the profession of librarianship in order to enhance learning and ensure access to information for all' (ALA, 2024).

The ALA claims 6 October 1876 as the date of its founding at the Centennial Exposition in Philadelphia. Its history says that 103 librarians attended, including 90 men and 13 women. (ALA, 2024, 'History'). ALA's focus is more exclusively on physical libraries in the US than on broader information needs. Under the heading of 'transforming libraries' there is no mention of information or information science. Under 'strategic directions' Information science gets a brief mention in a list of six strategies: 'Work with graduate programs in Library and Information Science (LIS) to increase focus on equity, diversity and inclusion within LIS programs and within the subject matter of the curricula.' (ALA, 2024, 'Strategic Directions').

It is clear that the strategic emphasis is not on information science but on the issues of equity, diversity and inclusion that are active North American political issues.

More than any other library associations in the Western world, the ALA suffers from political attacks by people, especially politicians, who want greater censorship in the selection of books and who feel that libraries and library organisations are politically too left leaning. An example from the *New York Times* has the title: 'As libraries become battlegrounds in the nation's culture wars, their allies are fighting to preserve access to their collections and keep themselves out of jail, or worse' (Williamson, E., 2024). Jo Yurcaba (2023) wrote: 'The Montana State Library Commission left the American Library Association, because the ALA's president described herself as a "Marxist lesbian" in a social media post last year.' Florida also decided 'to sever connections with the nation's oldest library organization after the non-profit became embroiled in the ongoing culture war over what books should be available to students' (Stephenson, 2024). Other states to withdraw include Wyoming and Texas (Stephenson, 2024).

Funding libraries appears to have become a problem, especially in well-to-do suburban communities where social change, particularly immigration and integration, seems threatening. Ultimately this means that ALA has little capacity left to think about the philosophical aspects of information science because their identity seems to be under attack.

The Canadian Federation of Library Associations (formerly Canadian Library Association), the Australian Library and Information Association and the Library and Information Association of New Zealand all make some reference to information science, though the Canadian association's only mention of information science is that a membership requirement is a 'master's level programme in library and information studies accredited or recognized by the appropriate national body' (Canadian Federation of Library Associations, 2016), perhaps because Canada has an active 'Canadian Association for Information Science' which hosts an 'internationally recognized journal, the Canadian Journal of Information and Library Science' (CAIS, 2023).

European and other library associations

Essentially every country in Europe has a library association. Germany is the largest Western European country and the wealthiest, which does not explain why the Deutsche Bibliotheksverband (German Library Association) lists eight relatively independent German library associations, each with its own specialised focus. In a sense this reflects the US model with specialised subunits for academic, public and other types of libraries. The word information appears regularly, but '*Informationswissenschaft*' (German for information science) appears only in the context of degree programmes. Germany has a strong book tradition, though the number of bookstores is smaller than it was 20 years ago. German libraries also sometimes refer to the four 'national' libraries, including the official Deutsche Nationalbibliothek, which has two branches, in Frankfurt am Main and in Leipzig, plus the Bavarian State Library (Bayerische Staatsbibliothek) and the Staatsbibliothek zu Berlin (which was the Prussian State Library before World War 2). The German term for information science appears on all of the websites.

The French library association is the Comité français international-bibliothèques et documentation. It is an umbrella association formed in 1996 that includes associations for practising librarians (Association des bibliothécaires de France – ABF), for library directors (Association des directeurs de bibliothèques universitaires – ADBU), information and documentation professionals (Association des professionnels de l'information et de la documentation – ADBS) and Enssib, the national school for information science (l'École nationale des sciences de l'information et des bibliothèques), which is itself a member of the iSchools organisation.

The size of the national libraries may serve as an indication of the status of the library and information professions in European countries, where the cultures and resources are roughly comparable. The French National Library (Bibliothèque nationale de France, 2023) has about 16 million books, which is roughly the same as the German National Library (Deutsche Nationalbibliothek, 2024, 'Bücher') (not including the Bavarian National Library or the Berlin State Library (Staatsbibliothek zu Berlin, 2025a), both of which have about 11 million volumes). In comparison, the British Library has about 14 million and the Library of Congress 39 million.

The Library Society of China (www.lsc.org.cn) should be included in any list of organisations dealing with information and information science, especially since many of the academic programmes that train librarians belong to the iSchools and play an active role in discussions about information science. The website is, however, entirely in Chinese, and even with translation software the nuances of language regarding information science are lost.

Conclusion

Information science plays a leading role in the iSchools and in ASIS&T, which see information as their main focus. It plays a clear role also in CILIP and ALISE in addition to their strong orientation towards librarianship. The German and French library organisations have a clear relationship to information science, especially through the academic institutions that train most librarians in those countries. The same situation is true for the Library Society of China. Only the ALA remains largely silent about information science, although, as in other countries, the training programmes for American librarians have strong ties to information science programmes. That could change when the American political landscape ceases to focus on censorship.

CHAPTER 4

Language and Information Science

What is the role of language in information science?

Language is not the only way that people share information, but information science does rely heavily on words to convey ideas. Numbers, diagrams, pictures and photographs all contribute in important ways to information, but the academic world primarily counts success in the form of words, even when a text contains supporting material like numbers and diagrams. There are examples where images or numerical data convey information more directly and clearly than a word-based explanation can, but the integration of these information forms is less widely used than it might be.

This chapter focuses on spoken and written language, since these are the core building blocks of most academic works. It is important to remember that written and spoken language may convey different information, due to the tone the speaker uses, even if the words are theoretically the same. This chapter will also discuss non-verbal means of communicating information, because information science needs to take a broad view in the modern world, where non-verbal information is increasingly available. Historically speaking, forms of communication change constantly. Information scientists ought not to discount even the grunts and gestures of early humans. Some researchers claim that 'the art of elegant hand-toolmaking is an evolutionary advance that boosted their brain power and potentially paved the way for language ...' (Sample, 2010). Language is not an innate human skill, as anyone knows who has watched children grow.

All forms of language rely heavily on context. The tolerance for imperfect grammar and inexact word choice is considerable as long as the context and speaker are reasonably clear. People do not necessarily hear every word that an interlocutor speaks in a noisy or acoustically imperfect space. People with a limited language familiarity may especially have trouble when the context is unclear, because understanding depends on expectations. People with hearing disabilities or a sensitivity to acoustic problems may nonetheless have the ability to guess what the speaker might have intended to say. The same is true for reading. People who claim to be speed readers do not necessarily see every word precisely, and their performance may sink when faced with subjects where they cannot anticipate the meaning. A recent study discussed 'a reading process that is at least partially *anticipatory*: Readers could make predictions about a future word and allocate time to process it based on their expectation' (Pimentel et al., 2023).

Not all languages use alphabetic symbols that represent pronunciation, Chinese most notably, and that frees the written language from dependence on how people in different regions pronounce the words. Mandarin Chinese, for example, is spoken with dramatically different tones and pronunciation than Cantonese far to the south. Radicals (subunits of the characters) can influence both the meaning and sometimes (but not always) the pronunciation. 'For example, the Chinese radical 女 (nǚ) means woman. If you spot that radical in another character, it generally means that the character is related to women in some way' (Berlitz, 2024). Many inflected languages also have indications of whether a noun is feminine, but that does not necessarily imply an association with women.

Common languages

Common languages are those that people use in ordinary conversation. According to the website Ethnologue (2024), English has over one billion speakers, including non-native speakers, which makes it the most-spoken language on the planet, with Chinese a close second. Even measuring the number of speakers of a language accurately is a problem, because of questions like whether to include second-language speakers (and second-language speakers at what proficiency), and which variants belong to the main language, which are dialects, and which one-time dialects count as a new language. Swiss German generally counts as German, but Dutch counts as a separate language, even though it is linguistically so closely related to German that many native German speakers, especially '*plattdeutsch*' speakers, understand it. English generally counts as a single language, but some dialects in the more remote parts of Britain and North America can challenge those who know only the standard version.

English is relatively easy to learn at a very basic level, because it has a simple, non-inflected structure. At the beginning of the 20th century a number of authors, including Charles Kay Ogden and Ivor Richards, worked on how to design the elements of basic English with a 'core 850 words, plus 200 international words, and 1000 words for the general fields of trade, economics, and science …' (Wikipedia, 2025b). This suffices for everyday necessities such as ordering food in a restaurant, but not for topics requiring abstract thinking and greater nuances. Languages constantly need new ways of expressing unfamiliar ideas, which they do in a variety of ways. In German, for example, it is easy to combine words to create a new word representing a new concept. English and French tend to use phrases. The simple German word '*Geschwindkeitsbegrenzung*' is speed limit in English, '*limitation de vitesse*' in French and requires four characters in Chinese. This means that the process of conveying even relatively simple non-traditional concepts can take different forms, and the meanings may vary from culture to culture. In Germany speed limits are often taken literally, while in modern US English many drivers regard them as suggestions.

One of the problems with language as a source of information is that meanings change constantly. The word 'gay' offers a simple example. In the 1950s in American English it meant nothing more than happy and carefree. At present in American English it means homosexual and has multiple layers of political meaning that can be positive or negative, depending on the political leanings of the listener. In German the word for someone who is homosexual is plainer, perhaps because homosexuality is more broadly accepted. German has also adopted the English word 'gay' to mean '*schwul*', which is the standard German word for homosexual, but without the same political connotations.

Metaphors are an established part of language, so much so that people sometimes forget that their literal meaning is different. Jennifer Szalai (2024) writes in the context of a book about artificial intelligence – a topic that itself is a metaphor – 'Our sense of possibility is shaped by the metaphors we choose.' One advantage of a metaphor is that it compacts information in ways that make it accessible. Szalai (2024) cites an example from Tenen's book *Literary Theory for Robots*: 'It's easier to say, "The phone completes my messages" instead of "The engineering team behind the autocompletion tool writing software based on the following dozen research papers completes my messages."' Metaphors represent a standard part of how people use language to share information in ways that evoke a visual response: for example, a person who is caught 'red handed' implies being caught with blood on their hands. Information science itself may be seen as a metaphorical description by those who associate the word 'science' with their image of the reliability of natural science.

Writing languages

Writing is newer than spoken language, and the letters and characters for expressing words have changed substantially over time. This does not necessarily mean that the meanings of words have changed with the orthography, but the letters can have a social meaning that is part of the reader's context. German in the 19th century used several different but related ways of forming letters, both in handwriting and in print. The printed version was '*Fraktur*' and imitated a form of medieval handwriting that was different from the Latin script used in France and England. To political conservatives at the beginning of the 20th century *Fraktur* seemed more genuinely German (until Hitler unexpectedly decided it was Jewish). Students had to learn '*Sütterlin*' handwriting for the same reason, until after World War 2. The archaic and nationalistic association of these letters is so strong today that the scripts have fallen out of use. Many students today can read books in *Fraktur* only with difficulty. Certain letters are especially hard to distinguish, because the *Fraktur* 's' and 'f' differ by only a minor mark. The use of the sharp-S (ß) has officially changed over the years.

Entering text and commands is relatively easy for Western-language speakers because the keyboards use the standard Latin alphabet. The extra diacritical marks in French and German are few enough that setting up special keys was possible even with mechanical typewriters. Writing in Arabic, itself an alphabetic language, on a standard computer keyboard is also possible with a special keyboard or with appropriate settings, though adding in vowel markings can be slow, since they are more frequent than diacritical marks. On a mobile phone, some Egyptian students type in English because it is easier and many commands and URLs require the Latin alphabet (El-Zalabany, 2024). The South Asian syllabaries for languages like Hindi or Bengali or Tamil are not strictly alphabetic, but it is also relatively straightforward to adapt computer keyboards to these scripts, though they have the same problem with e-mail addresses and URLs that require Latin characters. Chinese characters present a different need for adaptation, because there are hundreds more characters than keys. One method is to use a Western keyboard to type in Pinyin, which is the modern alphabetic representation of the Chinese characters. The Chinese characters then appear in a suggestion box. Using Pinyin essentially means that the speaker has enough knowledge of the spoken language to know what to type. Some touch screens also allow a person to draw a character that the software can recognise.

Written languages do not work for everyone equally. For people who suffer from dyslexia, the letters may move around or fail to convey the sound of the word. The Mayo Clinic defines dyslexia as 'a learning disorder that involves difficulty reading due to problems identifying speech sounds and learning how they relate to letters and words (decoding).... Dyslexia is not due to problems with intelligence, hearing or vision' (Mayo Clinic, 2024). IFLA has dyslexia guidelines, because it affects library users. The guidelines say: 'The definition of dyslexia is as complex as the condition itself' (IFLA, 2014). Children with dyslexia who do not receive help may find most written information inaccessible, but people with dyslexia can also adapt and become professors and scholars. Some languages are also easier for dyslexics to deal with because the words are pronounced exactly as spelled, so that mapping of the spoken word to the written representation is easier.

Written language uses different techniques than speech to convey information, and the differences depend heavily on context. Those devoted to Strunk and White's *Elements of Style* prefer the active voice and write with compact sentences: 'Vigorous writing is concise. A sentence should contain no unnecessary words, a paragraph no unnecessary sentences …' (Strunk and White, 1959, 12). This degree of compact communication is often hard in ordinary speech, partly because planning whole sentences ahead of time takes both practice and certainty about what one wants to say. This is one reason why some professors prefer to read their lectures rather than speak freely without notes. The information content of written language may be poorer than spoken language because it takes more skill to supply the right emotional tone. E-mail discussions on heated topics sometimes go wrong, because it is hard for writers to choose words that signal an appropriate tone. A written response to a message by an unknown person from an unfamiliar culture can be difficult, which may be why social media offers so many icons to imitate facial expressions.

Technical languages

Technical languages are meant to convey specific kinds of information that may be so specialised that a person without the right technical background will not understand. Information science is rife with examples of this kind of situation, because no one can claim expertise in all technical or scholarly fields. This section will look at examples from computing, physics and economics.

Computing languages

Computing has long been an aspect of most university information science programmes, which today offer and often require programming languages. The goal of computing languages is to inform the machine what a human wants it to do. Programming languages let humans 'talk' with the machines, with all the inherent communication flaws that human-based languages have. The problem is that computers tend to be literal minded and do exactly what the programming language tells them to do, even when it makes no sense. The exceptions will be discussed below, but readers should first understand how technology enables human–computer interaction.

Machine language

Computers ultimately understand only 'machine language', where the commands are in hexadecimal or binary format. In the very early days of computing, programmers needed the ability to read a printed hexadecimal rendering of computer memory (called a 'dump'). One problem was that human-friendly languages like Fortran and COBOL required two sets of programs to transform commands into language that the machine could understand. The programs that do the first-level translation into 'assembly language' are called 'compilers'. Reliability is hard to achieve, for some of the same reasons that ambiguity is a problem in human languages. Those who write compilers must guess what a human programmer wants, and how the machine will understand it. Something as seemingly simple as saving a file requires a negotiation between the human-written program, the operating system and the algorithms that the operating system uses to tell the storage hardware where to store the data, which may involve a table to indicate where the various segments of the file are on the storage device. The simple 'save' command in a programming language like COBOL may seem meaningful to the human author, but can lead to a sequence of different actions depending on the operating system.

The need for human programmers to know the binary form of machine language has declined since the 1970s and 1980s because the reliability of compilers has improved. Compilers are now good enough that most programmers can ignore the details of how machines use registers or do mathematical operations, or how they manipulate strings with Boolean logic. A goal of the newer programming languages is to seem like human languages. C is perhaps an exception, since it is the oldest higher-level programming language still in regular use. Operating systems like Unix use it because it can imitate some aspects of assembly language commands while retaining word-like commands such as 'printf' to send information to the screen. Python and other contemporary 'interpreted' languages use an English-language word base, which means that native speakers of English begin with a modest advantage.

Special-purpose computing languages

The variety of special-purpose computing languages is too large to discuss here, but some special-purpose languages deserve mentioning. Special-purpose languages have always existed. Some of the earliest languages were LISP and Prolog, which were early artificial intelligence (AI) languages designed to make sense of strings of letters. LISP was specifically for list processing, hence its name, and was so widely used in North America that several dialects developed. Prolog was meant to be a more general logic-based language and was especially popular in Europe, where its developers lived. It was and still is used for AI applications. Computer languages are sometimes like rare human languages that have a limited number of native speakers and start to slowly die out over time. That may be the fate of both LISP and Prolog.

LaTex is perhaps less a computing language than a formatting language that contained the commands needed for printing documents in early computing days. It remains moderately popular among computer science students, and some computer science conferences accept papers in LaTex, but the numbers are declining. The advantage of LaTex is the degree of control it gives over formats and layout. It is powerful, but non-programmers often find it unfriendly.

Statistical languages deserve their own linguistic niche because so much of modern scholarship depends on reliable statistical output. The most important of these languages are SAS, from SAS Institute in North Carolina in the USA, and R, which comes from New Zealand. SAS is a commercial product, while R is not. SPSS today is more of a package than a language, but knowing how to set up the tests requires an understanding of how the programming behind the package works.

Anyone using these languages needs to have at least a basic understanding of statistical proofs. There are helpful books, but their language is specialised and may not immediately make sense to someone whose vocabulary does not include statistical concepts. The problem is that a statistical analysis will not give valid results if the data distribution deviates too far from the requirements of the theorem. Julie Pallant writes in her *SPSS Survival Manual*:

> Parametric equations … make assumptions about the data that are more stringent. For example, they assume that the underlying distribution of scores in the population from which you have drawn your sample is normal. Each of the different parametric techniques, such as T-tests, ANOVA, Pearson correlation, has other additional assumptions. It is important that you check these before you conduct your analysis.
>
> (Pallant, 2007, 109)

In the end, the data needs to meet the required assumptions.

Modern statistical programs frequently check on whether the data distribution matches the requirements, and if the distribution does not, they give a warning message. Pallant explains further: 'Many of the attributes we want to measure are in fact not normally distributed. Some are strongly skewed, with most scores, following at the low end (e.g. depression); others are skewed so that most of the scores fall at the high end of the scale (e.g. self-esteem)' (Pallant, 2007, 5). The explanation consists of common words, but in the context of statistics, words like 'skewed' or phrases like 'normally distributed' take on specialised meanings that may make sense only in the context of a discussion about statistics.

Other technical languages

The natural sciences also have their own specialised language that uses a mixture of non-standard vocabulary and explanations involving words and phrases from everyday language. Here is an example from an introductory work: 'Let us start with the very basic facts.... The particles involved are characterized by their spin, their mass, and the quantum numbers (charges) determining their interactions. The fermion content (spin = 1/2) is organized in three families with identical quantum numbers and different masses' (Romanino, 2009). The words themselves make sense in normal conversation, but a particle is not a bit of dust on a shirt, 'spin' is different from the spinning of a top and different from political 'spin'. The word 'mass' is similar to weight, but implies a different scale and density. Technical languages often have meanings so context specific that only a person who knows that context and the math behind it has a clear idea of the meaning. This is how language works when conveying non-standard information.

Biology, geology, and economics are equally rich in words with specialised meanings in the context of the field. Even librarians use words like stacks or catalogue that have specific meanings within the building and profession. The fact that information science does not have a private closed vocabulary may be one of the reasons why it seems not to fit Andrew Abbott's description of a typical discipline, because vocabulary represents a visible barrier that separates insiders from outsiders. Information science could develop its own nuanced meanings for words, but that risks undermining the goal of understanding information in the broadest sense of the word.

Dialects within languages

Languages have a wealth of dialects, some of which linguists formally classify as variants, and some of which are so limited by time and place that they merely puzzle the uninitiated. Sports can offer examples of the latter, because each sport has its own special vocabulary, along with names that may be location dependent. Football has a cluster of words of its own. American 'football' is played with a ball that is a prolate spheroid. Rugby football uses a different spheroid shape. The German and British meaning of 'football' implies a round ball in a form of the game that Americans call soccer.

Sports communities not only have their own languages but also information that is important to them, even if no one outside their fan community cares. This becomes especially noticeable after the American Superbowl or after the European football World Cup, where for a time it seems as if everyone desperately wants more information about how the game went. Communities sometimes define themselves on the basis of the sports dialect they share, such as tennis or golf or ice hockey, and the passion for information may even reach down to the team level. Sports are not a traditional focus for academic information science, but sports offer an example of how information takes on a life of its own outside of any discipline.

Ordinary regional dialects may slowly be dying out, due to the effects of television and educational systems that require children to learn and speak the standard language. High German (*Hochdeutsch*) and standard northern Mandarin are the official versions of German and Chinese. Standard French has no special name, but standard French certainly exists and can be problematic for those from other areas. Even Belgium, where standard French is one of the national languages, has different words for numbers like 90, and Québécois French has a distinctly different pronunciation and some different words, many from English.

English gives outsiders the impression of being standardised, and broadly speaking a native speaker can understand English in most countries, even when having to struggle occasionally with the pronunciation. Indian English offers an example because it is spoken with an intonation similar to Hindustani (the common spoken language whose literary form may be Hindi or Urdu). Black English, especially ghetto English, can seem almost incomprehensible to non-locals, in part because the grammar and vocabulary vary from place to place. Britain notoriously has strong regional dialects, though some, like Cockney English, are dying out.

Dialects are not unique to spoken languages. Written versions of modern languages sometimes incorporate dialects. So many social media expressions have become second nature to the people who use them that outsiders need to search online to find out the meaning. This is equivalent to using a dictionary, except that the words are too modern for most standard dictionaries. Computing languages also have dialects. Fortran IV became the standard version of Fortran in the 1960s, but 12 versions of Fortran exist today and incorporate new features, such as Fortran 95, which allows for parallel computing. COBOL has changed somewhat less, but still has had ten versions. Likewise C has seven ISO versions; C++, the object-oriented version of C, has 6 ISO versions; and C#, another C variant, has four ISO variants. The list of computing languages with dialects is long. The point is that new dialects are common in all forms of language, sometimes mutually comprehensible, sometimes incompatible.

Change over time in languages

All languages change over time. Sometimes the changes become new dialects, sometimes the changes vanish and sometimes the original language evolves to absorb them. It is easiest to see this process by looking at changes in one language over time. Latin serves well as an illustration, because it was used broadly within Western Europe from roughly the beginning of the Christian era to the end of the 19th century. While the spoken language must also have changed, it is harder to know precisely when spoken Latin evolved into something resembling modern romance languages like Italian or Spanish or French, because no recordings exist. The evidence relies mainly on the written form. Scholars should not suppose that spoken classical Latin was as uniform as modern Italian or Spanish. Regional dialects and external influences from invaders or occupiers presumably played their usual role. The written language may not perfectly reflect the changes, but it is the best record available.

Classical Latin from the time of Cicero and Virgil represents an ideal standard that remained so long that schools in the 20th century continued to teach it to significant numbers of students in countries like Britain and Germany, and sometimes the USA and Canada. Word order mattered relatively little in classical Latin because the endings indicated clearly whether a noun was a subject or object or prepositional object, and verb endings indicated past, present or future tenses. This made the words themselves more complicated, as many learners note who grew up speaking an uninflected language like English and want to learn an inflected one like German. It is reasonable to assume that ordinary speakers of classical Latin made a lot of mistakes.

A change that may have mattered especially for educated readers in the ancient world was a marked change in the style of formal language. Cicero wrote complex sentences with significant embellishment. At the time of Augustine and Jerome the use of embellishments remained, as can be seen in formal writing like the *City of God*, but the language of Augustine's *Confessions* was markedly simpler, which makes the *Confessions* easier for the modern reader and translator. Jerome's most famous work was the Vulgate Bible, which has a remarkably plain style, probably because Jerome's goal was for the Holy Scriptures to reach as wide a public as possible. By the time of Gregory the Great in the sixth century CE, the linguistic ornaments had fallen away.

The time of Gregory the Great can reasonably count as marking the beginning of Medieval Latin, a language that remained in active scholarly use for hundreds of years and was a key vehicle for providing religious, legal and practical information. Venantius Fortunatus, a sixth-century Latin-language poet, was popular enough that some of his poems have survived (mostly in translation) as hymns. Alcuin of York became one of the chief literary figures at the court of Emperor Charlemagne. His Latin remained plain and he is known for Carolingian minuscule, a form of writing that included upper- and lower-case letters, which earlier forms of writing had not differentiated.

This was an era when vulgar (non-classical) Latin adopted linguistic characteristics from local languages, including a reliance on word order, even though highly educated authors like Thomas Aquinas in the 13th century resisted such changes. Erasmus of Rotterdam in the 16th century returned to writing a version of Latin that was more purely classical, which may have been a factor in the death of Latin as the universal European scholarly language. It was too different and too hard to learn. The Reformation was probably more decisive in reducing the dominance of Latin, because Protestant church services in Northern Europe stopped using Latin in their services. Latin remained for some educational and diplomatic purposes, but it lost significance as the standard means for information exchange.

In the 20th century written Chinese went through a significant transformation when the People's Republic of China adopted simplified characters to make it easier for ordinary people to learn to read and write. Arguments against this change talked about the loss of literary tradition for people who did not know all the complexities of the classical characters. In some sense this was comparable to abandoning classical Latin for vernacular languages. De-emphasising Latin and simplifying the Chinese characters both probably helped to make language a better information transfer vehicle.

The language of pictures

Scholarly languages are full of diagrams whose intent is to help readers understand complex concepts and to make the interrelationships between ideas clearer than is possible with mere words. Sometimes that works, and sometimes the diagrams are either so complex that it is hard to make sense of them, or so simple that they seem superfluous. A really good graphic is a powerful tool, but many academics outside the natural sciences lack the skills to produce more than word clusters with connecting lines. Ideally, a good graphic would say more than the words that accompany it, but often they convey less and just fulfil the purpose of breaking up a mass of text. Authors sometimes feel pressure to create diagrams because others do. In the information science world, a diagram ought to convey something that words cannot.

A good picture can provide significant information. Paintings of everyday life in 16th-century Flanders, such as those of Pieter Bruegel the Elder, can tell a historian a great deal about living conditions. Bruegel's *The Wedding Dance* (1566) is a visual explanation of social custom, clothing, food and sexual relationships that is effective beyond what most people can say in prose. Even the expressions on the faces of the dancers give insight into emotions that modern writers can see, but can only imperfectly describe.

The advantage of photographs and visually accurate art like *The Wedding Dance* is that they engage with aspects of the human brain in a way that even good writers find hard to accomplish with words. Scholarship tends to emphasise abstract ideas, while photographs and realistic paintings appeal to parts of the human brain that touch more directly on emotions. That matters for information science as well, because the whole information landscape is a complex of words, images, sounds and even smell and taste. Scholars may not typically talk about the quality of the cakes on the wedding feast table in the background, but to a certain extent their flatness can give a visual signal as to how they probably tasted. How the cakes tasted to the peasants in the painting probably differed from how modern people accustomed to sugar and refined flour might regard them. A good picture tells many stories that never find their way into words.

Conclusion

People typically share information using words, which means that understanding language matters for understanding how information science works. That does not mean that every information scientist needs to be a linguist, but an awareness of how language works and how meanings change over time and across locations affects how people understand information, and what they think the information means. Purely factual information ought to be unaffected, but the context in which the facts appear can affect their meaning. The locations of stars and planets have not changed since people began noticing them, but what they represent no longer has supernatural implications for most people, even though artefacts of their supernatural meaning live on in newspaper horoscopes. Scientists sometimes even invent new words and phrases like 'quantum mechanics' to describe phenomena in modern science that have taken root in educated public discourse, even though many readers are unfamiliar with the mathematical formulae that describe their real meaning. Information scientists cannot realistically understand every word or every formula, but knowing what one does not understand is also a form of information.

CHAPTER 5
Culture and Information Science

What is the role of culture in information science?

All human-generated information has a cultural component that information scientists need to recognise and understand. While culture and context are not identical, culture is so integral to human context that disregarding it can lead to false conclusions. An everyday example is whether a task is easy or difficult. Americans tend to answer optimistically, and Northern Europeans pessimistically, as María Ramírez (2024) noted in the *Guardian*: 'There was a stark contrast between the deeply rooted American cultural belief that things could only get better, and the routinely bleak view that prevailed in many European countries, even the wealthiest and most privileged ones.' This affects answers to surveys and interviews, and colours the meaning of the data from those research instruments.

Pure information exists apart from culture. The law of gravity applies to objects in all cultural contexts. The laws of nature exist outside of human culture, but the values that people assign to these facts vary. People living in northern climates often find temperatures above 30 Celsius (86 Fahrenheit) to be uncomfortably warm, but in Singapore temperatures above 30 C are normal throughout the year. Those accustomed to living in mountainous areas like the European Alps or the American Rockies may find the more constricted views of flat areas like Brandenburg in Germany or the American Midwest boring. Unsurprisingly, performers interpret theatre scripts in different ways. Hegel found that French actors played their roles with less bluster than was done in Berlin, and English actors, in contrast, played more passionately (Kaube, 2020, 478–9).

Culture serves as a lens that can distort the meaning of political statements. Politicians in Western countries often find statements by Islamic leaders inflammatory, sometimes to the surprise of the speakers. British understatement and German bluntness can lead to misunderstandings within the same academic unit. The information content of e-mail easily gets lost because signals like tone of voice and facial expression, which vary across cultures, are missing. This was a factor in the e-mail wars of the 1980s, when people were unaware of the aggressive tone of their messages, or simply lacked the verbal skill to control it.

This chapter will look at the influence of culture on information in a number of different settings. One setting is time, since culture changes significantly over time. Another setting is physical space: China and India are culturally significantly different than the West, and even among Western countries, the cultural assumptions are different among individuals in the USA than in Germany or the UK. Virtual space is perhaps a culture of its own that may feel different to people from different generations. Universities have cultural identities that differ significantly, depending on their status and ranking in the world. Workplace cultures have especially changed over time as old assumptions about working hours and conditions evolve to adapt to new circumstances. Even home domestic culture varies across regions and across time. Culture is not a simple, stable concept, but is so varied that human perceptions of cultural norms can differ radically. The challenge for information science is to adjust its perceptions of information to fit cultural circumstances as they change.

Culture over time

Changes in culture over time should surprise no one, and yet teachers long assumed that succeeding generations of students would understand the language of Shakespeare and the realities of life in the 17th century. It is not just the language that changes, but the way in which the language interacts with circumstances. Shakespeare is in fact a valuable source of information about relationships between men and women and the complexity of attitudes towards people from other countries in 17th-century England. What is true for Shakespeare in English is equally true for notable writers in other countries: Goethe, for example, whose religious themes can seem antiquated to contemporary readers, even though his language still sounds more modern to German ears than Shakespearean English does to the typical Englishman or American.

Looking further back in time, ancient Roman attitudes towards the natural environment depended on factors that are so completely discounted today that they have become almost invisible. The pantheon of gods was real then. Today people no longer accept that the gods play a role in weather or agriculture or battles, and in consequence the once-important information about which gods need appeasing no longer plays a role in military strategy or in agricultural decisions. Religious assumptions are only some of the cultural changes. Social relationships have changed so that the patrician–tenant–slave hierarchies of the ancient world no longer directly resemble contemporary workplace life, even though artefacts of the class distinctions persist in the form of appropriate dress, office space and who serves whom.

This means that the context in which people evaluate information has changed, often unevenly. American slavery offers an example. In the Roman world, slaves were still people who had some rights, even if they were not free. That attitude persisted through the medieval world, but the need for human labour in the newly colonised Americas led to the systematic enslavement of native Americans and imported Africans, who in the New World became property with such limited human rights that an owner could kill (or rape) at will, with no consequences other than the potential financial loss of a worker. The US civil rights movement of the 1960s was one sign that the attitudes of white Americans towards people of different racial origin had changed less than the law. Police violence shows that the information that the police use in making decisions about the use of force has a cultural overtone. Skin colour is not the only factor. Aggressive language, clothing and attitudes towards authority also play a role in exacerbating tensions on both sides.

Some elements within society may resist change. This is particularly true of highly disciplined groups such as the military or religious societies. Examples can be found in the history of military coups in many South American and African countries, where the stated intention is often to preserve order, albeit a form of order that is comfortable to those with arms. While religious groups may eschew overt violence, it can nonetheless be forceful in compelling members to adhere to certain boundaries. In the 19th century and early 20th century the Society of Friends (Quakers) sometimes expelled members who married outside of the Society. It was a way to maintain a clear identity that nonetheless broke down over time, not because the distinctions grew weaker but because internal and external pressures to conform grew so strong that the Society chose to adapt rather than fade into obscurity.

Culture across physical space

Geography offers a physical separation that enables distinct cultural identities to develop. People talk about Great Britain as one country, and the British Isles are objectively small compared to Europe, but inside of that closely bounded space the range of identities includes people who consider themselves to be Scottish, Welsh, English and Irish, while simultaneously being British. They share language and history and sometimes a mutual distrust of outsiders. Even just within the boundaries of England, people identify themselves as coming from Yorkshire or Cornwall or Norfolk. The exact differences are not always evident to the outsider, but the self-consciousness exists nonetheless. Great Britain is not unique in having cultural distinctions based on geography. Germans are well aware of the differences between Bavaria and Berlin. US citizens know that Michigan (which is culturally international, with a substantial Muslim community) differs from Alabama or Mississippi.

Not everyone agrees on when geographical differences indicate cultural differences. Vladimir Putin claims that Ukraine is historically and culturally part of Russia, a claim that at the time of this writing the people of Ukraine are resisting militarily. Stalin wanted Ukraine to have a seat at the United Nations and claimed it was an independent country that just happened to belong to the Union of Soviet Socialist Republics. The same was true for Byelorussia (modern Belarus). Historically, national identities have been fluid across the plains of Eastern Europe, perhaps precisely because the flatlands do not offer any clear mountain and river demarcations. Yet geography is not always a determining factor. Germany and the Netherlands share a graphically undistinguished border, but a separate cultural identity became established in the 'low countries' (literally, the Niederländer) before any clear German national identity emerged.

Any physically large country, even one with a single national language and literature, will have cultural nuances. Mandarin Chinese in the north of China, around Beijing, uses four tones, while Cantonese, in the south, has six tones. The written language of both Mandarin and Cantonese is the same, but sharing information via speech can become challenging for those who do not speak both variants. It is not just a matter of a north–south split. Each province of China has its own nuanced version of Chinese, and it may take many generations of standard Mandarin broadcasting before China speaks one language. The situation in India is even more complicated. Both northern India and Pakistan share a spoken language, Hindustani, that is mutually intelligible despite different literary traditions and different writing systems, one based on Sanskrit using the Devanagari, the other using Arabic script. The languages of southern India belong to the Dravidian language group, with different scripts. Nonetheless the degree of interaction between Indo-Aryan and Dravidian speakers was significant: 'It is now well established that the Indo-Aryan and Dravidian language families developed convergent structures in sound system (phonology) and grammar owing to contact going back to the 2nd millennium BCE' (Krishnamurti, 2024).

English is widely used in India because of the country's colonial heritage. Geography still matters, but communication tools and information technology may be blurring the physical boundaries.

Culture across virtual space

Virtual spaces have their own cultural boundaries. Many of the social media apps do not talk with each other, so that persons active on X (formerly Twitter) or Facebook, or YouTube or Threema (Swiss/German) or WeChat (Chinese) may live in culturally distinct spheres. Donald Trump's Truth Social is theoretically open to anyone, but in practical terms the estimated 6.3 million users as of July 2023 (Wikipedia, 2025c) probably come from a political subset of the 500 million users of X. Threema's end-to-end encryption puts an emphasis on privacy that is especially popular in Germany. WeChat is enormously popular in China, partly because it incorporates a payment system called WeChat Pay, which people outside of China can also use with some restrictions. It is particularly valuable when travelling in China.

The oldest form of virtual space in the internet is e-mail, which is almost universally available, except in countries that control the network traffic closely. Mailing lists in the 1980s, when access was mostly limited to people at North American universities, sometimes degenerated into 'flame wars' until a list manager stopped them. The culture of the mailing lists calmed down as people grew accustomed to the new tool, which often meant learning how to conduct written discussion that lacked any moderating tone of voice and facial signals. Messages in all capital letters were sometimes considered equivalent to shouting. The use or absence of personal titles is more important in many cultures than for Anglo-Americans. Even the form of address can cause awkwardness. Americans tend immediately to address people in e-mail by their first name, which is rare in Germany, and perhaps even rarer in many Asian countries. This can lead to the anomaly that colleagues writing to each other in English use first names, but when writing in German use a title (at least Herr or Frau) and last names.

The advantage and the problem with videoconferencing systems is the degree to which some people find conversations in virtual space uncomfortable. Age probably plays a role in the discomfort. A video conference enables all of the nuances of voice and lets participants see facial expressions, but other forms of body language may seem more muted. The quality of the connection can play a role too. A poor connection distorts voices and establishes a psychological barrier on top of cultural differences. Videoconferencing is essential for highly international organisations that do not want to fly team members across the globe, but the direct verbal and visual connection may only mask genuine cultural differences involving status and language. Information scientists need to take cognisance of these challenges. Technology may enable the transfer of certain kinds of information, but cannot erase all cultural barriers.

Culture in education

Universities and research organisations exist in their own cultural spaces with assumptions and hierarchies that have no clear equivalence in the outside world. In many parts of the world professors have permanent positions, but permanence itself has different meanings in different places. A German professor at a state-funded university (which most universities are) is normally a civil servant (*Beamter*) and has a job for life. The 'tenure' system in the US works differently in that a university can decide to abolish whole departments and fire its professors. That happens so rarely that few people outside of the academic world ever notice, and mainly occurs at minor schools when enrolments fall.

Tenure has become a political issue in the US, with conservative politicians wanting to weaken or abolish it in order to force faculty to adopt opinions that are sympathetic to their cause. This strikes at the assumption that professors have the freedom to teach what they want in the way they want. Historically, that level of freedom has existed mainly in disciplines too technical for politicians to understand. A physicist talking about quantum mechanics has a level of freedom that a historian may lack: 'Since January 2021, a total of 70 bills have been introduced across 28 states that seek to restrict teaching on college campuses, with the bulk focused on topics related to race, racism or gender …' (Seltzer, 2022). New College, Florida has been a prime example, where a conservative governor and legislature have abolished programmes like gender studies that they considered too liberal. High schools in the US have come under even more political pressure: 'Since January 2021, researcher Jeffrey Sachs says, 35 states have introduced 137 bills limiting what schools can teach with regard to race, American history, politics, sexual orientation and gender identity' (Gross, 2022). Information scientists know that this will have an effect on how freely students can learn.

University culture is highly hierarchical. The hierarchies vary from country to country, but in general a dean holds top position, just below a vice-president in the university administration, who, in some countries like the US, often has little to do with teaching and research. In America a dean is often primarily an administrator and fundraiser. This is true especially of business schools. Exceptions exist, of course. In Germany a dean continues to teach with a reduced teaching load, so that all deans remain active teachers and mostly continue to do research because the culture expects it. There are, however, different levels of universities in all countries. Below the top layer of highly rated and respected universities, lower grades of institutions exist that still call themselves universities.

University status is not really a function of external rankings, but of impact and performance. Reputation endures over long decades. A university that has an established reputation will not suddenly lose respect despite short-term vicissitudes. Harvard University remains respected, despite recent problems. The same is true for Oxford and Cambridge, whose reputations rest on centuries of notable performance. That level of stability is not universal. In Germany, Friedrich-Wilhelms-Universität was founded in 1809, and famous professors like Leopold von Ranke, Georg Wilhelm Hegel, Theodore Mommsen, Max Planck and Albert Einstein made it into one of the leading universities in the world. After the Nazis drove out many notable scholars, and the Soviet occupation imposed new restrictions, the University's reputation suffered. Since the Soviet occupation ended, recovery has progressed slowly. Humboldt Universität zu Berlin (as it is now known) has returned to the rankings of excellent German universities according to the German Research Foundation (DFG), but still has not achieved the international dominance that it enjoyed in the 19th century.

In Germany some aspects of the academic hierarchy are set in law. The '*Fachhochschulen*' (universities of applied sciences) cannot give doctoral degrees (though they want to). The number of hours of required teaching is also double that of a standard university, which makes it harder for the professors to do substantial research. At one time there were also '*technische Hochschule*', which offered applied courses like engineering. Most of those have become universities, except the Rheinisch-Westfälische Technische Hochschule Aachen (RWTH Aachen), which had such an excellent reputation that it kept its name, though it counts in Germany as a full university. A few private universities also exist and in some cases, like the WHU (Wissenschaftliche Hochschule für Unternehmensführung), a business school that is also called the Otto Beisheim School of Management. WHU is well respected internationally, but has a very limited focus. German universities give doctorates in economics, but a business focus is rarer. The rankings of the German Research Foundation have become an indicator of status. Universities apply for the status, which also comes with substantial funding. A few universities have a strong record of success. The Munich universities have almost always won, and the Berlin universities have a strong record. One of the big surprises was the poor success of Göttingen, which had long been regarded as one of the best German universities, especially in mathematics.

American prestige rankings are complex and nuanced and operate at many levels. Sport plays a significant role in the popular mind, but the connection between academic performance and sports success is accidental. The 'Ivy League' is a sports league, some of whose members happen to be academically significant. The 'Big 10' sports league has an academic arm called the Committee on Institutional Consultation (CIC), which formally includes the university provosts, but has broadened to include representatives from other parts of the universities including the libraries. In terms of research significance, the CIC is the equivalent of the Ivy League, since it includes the University of Chicago, the University of Illinois, the University of Michigan and others with distinguished research records. Chicago dropped out of the sports side in the 1930s, since it was smaller and cared little about sports. Chicago is notable not for football victories, but for its long list of Nobel prize winners.

American universities are a mix of private and public institutions. While most of the Ivy League schools are private and most of the CIC universities are public, many have such substantial private funding that the notion that they are primarily public institutions is dubious. Cornell University is an Ivy League school with a double character, half public half private, with a street running through the campus that separates the two halves. All notable private US universities receive substantial state money in the form of grants for research, which are themselves highly competitive and become a form of ranking. There is also competition for students, because their tuition money supports the institutional infrastructure. Private school tuition fees tend to be higher, and the justification is that graduates earn more, which is sometimes but not invariably true.

In the USA there are institutions that mainly give out bachelor's degrees. The word 'college' does not always mean an educational institution (Etymonline, 2021), but in American English today it generally means a degree-granting institution. A few elite colleges have the right to grant doctoral degrees – Bryn Mawr College in Pennsylvania, for example – and more colleges offer master's degrees, but most do not go beyond the bachelor's level. The value of the degree varies enormously in the jobs market. A degree from a community college generally has less value than one from a better-known private college. The situation is different in the UK, where 'college' can mean an institution to help students prepare for getting into a university, but it can also be part of a university – Oriel College Oxford, for example, or King's College London. A university such as Oxford University or the University of London generally has its name on the degrees, but the independence of the London colleges varies over time. Today King's College London can give out its own degrees.

Many countries have adopted the Anglo-American names and degrees, but there are exceptions. Germany has long had universities and does not use the term 'college'. Essentially, everything that can award some kind of degree is generically a 'Hochschule'. Before the Bologna agreements in 1999, German universities did not typically give bachelor's or master's degrees, but rather a 'Magister' or 'Diplom' plus a doctorate. 'Magister' is generally translated today as a master's degree, but it took significantly longer to complete than a master's degree does today. The 'Diplom' was often used in more technical fields and may be translated as a bachelor's degree, though it also took longer to complete. Both degrees had a thesis requirement only modestly less extensive than a doctoral thesis. In information science terms, this leads to misunderstanding on the part of outsiders.

Culture at work

Work cultures are diverse and vary both within and across countries, despite an illusion of uniformity. It was arguably the Industrial Revolution in the 19th century that made employers more conscious of the relationship between profit, production, the physical workplace and the working hours, which made everyone more conscious of working conditions. A primarily agricultural world regulates itself by the sun, the seasons and the animals. Tracking hours plays no role. Those who worked at home, weaving or spinning, had to count how many pieces they produced, but not the time involved. Factory work, with people working together to produce a uniform product, led to a stricter discipline. Frederick Winslow Taylor often gets credit for creating a system of 'scientific management' in which employers specified tasks for each worker, with clear expectations for starting times, ending times and quantity. Its origin was in America, but the idea spread within the industrial world. Workers hated this because it stripped them of the freedom to decide their own schedules, including for human needs such as eating or going to the bathroom. The rigidity led to protests, unions and often violent confrontations.

Information in the regimented factory world was a commodity that had proprietary value. The way to build a particular product may resemble the way to build other similar products, but even car assembly lines had their nuances because of the complexity of the end product. The information that mattered became reduced to how to assemble a particular part in an environment where the worker focused only on one part, one bolt, one wrench, one way to do it right. Time pressure never let up. There was no opportunity to rethink options, because the right to rethink belonged to managers. A medieval serf had more personal freedom. People chose an assembly workplace for two reasons: because they needed the job and had no other choice, or because the pay was reliable, if not always sufficient.

This regimented work culture did not belong only to factories. The life of clerical staff had long required specific working hours and tasks. Anyone working as sales staff or as a clerk in government or as a small business operator had to conform to external expectations that limited their freedom.

The child of a peasant farmer might help periodically with the harvest or with the animals, but often had long periods of freedom – until the introduction of compulsory schooling. Schooling changed the work culture in many ways. First, it trained children to conform to particular times and tasks, and to expect non-family members to evaluate their performance. Second, schooling gave children information that mattered increasingly in the workplace. Reading comes naturally to some people, but not to everyone, and yet reading became an essential workplace skill. People with disabilities like dyslexia ceased to fit into the accepted mode. Many people and societies view dyslexia as a shameful disability, even though it 'is not due to problems with intelligence, hearing or vision' (Mayo Clinic, 2024). It is only one example of social expectations that constrained the workplace.

Workplaces in wealthy parts of the world today are comparatively safe and well regulated, but information scientists should not ignore areas where people work under conditions that allow almost no personal freedom to think or act, and where the 12- or 14-hour workday robs workers of volition. For these people, information matters for several reasons. Some want to have enough information to be able to escape. Some want to learn how to improve themselves. Information about how to survive is critical, but the information science literature rarely discusses how to appease an insistent boss, or to enable a meagre wage to feed children and family. This kind of information matters to millions every day.

Culture at work depends on factors such as education, wealth and how well staff understand the technology and social structure of the workplace. Transparency (or a lack thereof) about what information goes into hiring and promotion decisions can affect the workplace culture as well. This is all part of the information context of the ordinary workplace. It is important to remember how radically the information environment of the workplace has changed over the last centuries. A mid-level manager today has vastly more information available than contemporaries did at any time in the past. Whether AI or human distrust or other factors will change the situation is hard to say. The only real constant for the information needs of the workplace is the constant flux as new ideas and new tools become available. The job of information scientists is not to predict the future, but to understand the evolving context.

Culture at home

No two households make the same assumptions or react to personal or external issues in the same way. It is easy to stereotype how middle-class Americans or working-class British or German academics react to new situations, but information scientists need to recognise the full range of behaviours within these generalisations. Families with small children have different priorities than those with teenagers or those with nearby elderly parents. People in countries with comprehensive, affordable- high quality healthcare will still worry when a family member becomes ill, but their concern may focus on more personal issues than whether they can afford a physician or a particular medicine or an operation. Openness about health issues varies within and across cultures. Discussions about contraception and abortion are especially sensitive, and attitudes have changed significantly since the 1970s. Where people live, what religion they practise and what their friends think are factors that will influence their choices and sometimes their relationships within society.

Judgements about medical information may be especially variable. One of the challenges scientists had during the COVID-19 pandemic was to communicate scientific findings to a public that urgently needed to understand the risks. The tendency to ignore information that would force people to change their habits meant that some people, especially in the political world, discounted life-saving warnings because it was information many did not want to hear. Information science needs to recognise that discomforting information is often unwelcome. The problem becomes one of persuading listeners about the validity of warnings. Sometimes external circumstances help, such as the number of people dying without other clear causes. Florida offers an example: mortality statistics suggest that Florida had a disproportionately high death rate (Tampa Bay Times, 2022). The governor's unwillingness to trust the data may have been a factor (Columbia Law School, 2024). The problem of scepticism towards medical science may be repeating itself in Florida: 'The state is in the grip of a measles outbreak, yet Joseph Ladapo, the surgeon general, continues to ignore medical science to stop it' (Luscombe, 2024).

There was a time when both Europe and China had arranged marriages, and to some extent India still does. An arranged marriage sounds odd today, but it was a practical arrangement to guarantee that individuals had spouses with sufficient income and social status. Anyone who has read Jane Austen's novels knows that marriage solely for love was a luxury that many families could not afford. An arranged marriage did not mean that the partners disliked each other, only that their economic suitability played a significant role in matching them, and economics can still play a significant role in any marriage, regardless of culture.

Conclusion

Culture defines what individual information scientists regard as relevant for a particular question. The selection of facts is itself a cultural choice, and all forms of science require a reasoned justification, but even a good selection may not convince everyone. Some fields are especially sensitive to doubt. In a political discourse the number of legal indictments against a candidate may seem like a key fact for members of one party, while age and energy may seem more important to others. Even when both sides agree on the basic facts, the weight and implications of those facts may differ to the point that agreement becomes unlikely.

In technical fields and in the natural sciences the choices of facts may seem as if they should be clearer, and at some basic level they are. The processing chips in most computers function by making binary choices, even though the results of millions of binary choices may look very different in different systems because of complex choices programmed into the system. Windows operating systems use different algorithms to manage memory than do Unix-based systems. Most users have never encountered memory-management algorithms, but anyone who has hands-on experience with operating systems will recognise the philosophical differences involved in deciding which task gets what resources to run next. In the early 1970s it was sometimes a matter of deciding which tasks would go dormant while the system retrieved data from disk or tape storage, and which would complete so fast that they could run while others waited. The advent of time-sharing options made this less urgent. At some level the technical choices reflected preferences so long forgotten that the culture they came from has vanished from the consciousness of most programmers, but that context exists, even if the memory of it has vanished.

CHAPTER 6

Technology

What role does technology play in information science?

Technology in all forms is integral to information processing, and thus to information science. As is so often the case, the context matters. Technology has existed in many variations since people first began exchanging information. Well before computing technology existed, other forms of technology handled the exchange.

The Freie Universität zu Berlin (2011) describes the core issue, which is 'knowing how to use current information and communication technology, being able to structure your own learning process and gather information independently, as well as critically assessing information sources'. This describes the present and past relationship between information science and information technology, because the goals of assessing and gathering information have remained steady over time. Information technology has historical roots that contemporary discussions about computing and engineering too often ignore. The Cambridge Dictionary (2024) defines technology as 'the use of scientific knowledge or processes in business, industry, manufacturing, etc.'. Gregersen (2024) writes that technology is 'the application of scientific knowledge to the practical aims of human life or, as it is sometimes phrased, to the change and manipulation of the human environment.' Together, these definitions provide a good picture of what people mean by technology.

Writing and printing were at one time important new forms of technology, but even they were latecomers, because technology is about concepts as well as machines. Number systems offer a good example. What many call 'Arabic' numbers were actually a technological step forward from using Roman numerals for expressing quantity. The Arabic numbers actually originated in India but came to Europe via Arabic writers. It mattered that they included '0' (zero) and a positional notation where the digits furthest to the left represented the highest value. China today also uses 'Arabic' numerals, but has retained the old character-based numbers, much as the West continues to use Roman numerals for formal purposes where little or no calculation is necessary.

The technology of numbers quickly becomes complex: today the hexadecimal (base-16) representation of numbers uses letters of the alphabet to represent values higher than 10: for example, the letter 'A' in hexadecimal stands for 10 in the decimal system, and the letter 'F' stands for 15 in the decimal system. Numbers above hex F are represented as hexadecimal 10, whose value is the decimal 16. Hexadecimal representations are technology in its most abstract form. Creating words and word-combinations to describe technology processes represents a key facet of information science. The word 'computer' originally meant the people (mainly women) who did complex mathematical calculations.

Writing as technology

Many prior developments contributed to the technology that people use today for working on computers. Letters were an invention as important as numbers, and early writing systems did not invariably use letters in the same sense that they are understood today. The Babylonians inscribed information in clay tablets using cuneiform, which originated in about 3200 BCE and continued in use for about 3,000 years. 'The script – not itself a language – was used by scribes of multiple cultures over that time to write a number of languages other than Sumerian, most notably Akkadian, a Semitic language that was the lingua franca of the Assyrian and Babylonian Empires' (Archaeology Magazine, 2024).

Chinese characters are comparatively modern, since the earliest known examples come from 1250 BCE. While the script has certainly evolved over time, the core concept of using the characters has persisted. A notable modern change came when the People's Republic of China adopted simplified characters, whose goal was to make it easier for people to achieve basic literacy. In a sense, the Chinese characters resemble numbers because they represent concepts rather than sounds. Foreign names can nonetheless be represented by character combinations that sound like the name in modern Mandarin. The name Michael, for example, is rendered as 迈克尔, but it can be rendered differently for the name in different languages. The French version, Michel, is 米歇尔, and the Chinese word for the Archangel Michael is 米迦勒 (Wang, 2024).

The tools for writing numbers, letters and characters depended on the materials available. The stylus used to inscribe cuneiform in clay tablets was a simple and effective tool that was commonly available. Even without special treatment, the clay could serve as a reliable means for information storage, and enough clay tablets have survived to give modern scholars a view into the culture. The ancient Egyptians used a plant called papyrus that had many purposes: 'The ancient Egyptians used the stem of the papyrus plant to make sails, cloth, mats, cords, and, above all, paper' (Augustyn, 2024). The Egyptians wrote with brushes dipped in an ink mixture based on soot. Environmental conditions allowed papyrus and its ink to survive well over time, and it was lightweight to transport. The ancient Egyptians wrote on other surfaces too, such as temple walls. The Chinese used brushes and wrote on a variety of available media including bamboo, some of which have survived. While the technological means for writing were simple and available, the knowledge and skills needed for writing required training, and still do.

Handwriting persisted as the standard means for written communication in the West until about 1450. Pen technology improved modestly through the use of metal nibs and more standardised ink. The writing surface also evolved from papyrus to vellum (made from animal skins) to something resembling modern paper made from old rags and linen. Paper of every sort was expensive in the early 19th century, which is why frugal authors would sometimes write lines that ran in two directions on the page, even though that made it harder to read, as described in Jane Austen's novels. Paper made from wood pulp appeared in the early 19th century. Libraries discovered a century later that the acid used in the production process caused gradual oxidation, which made the paper fragile. This sparked major concerns. The use of pen and ink persisted as a key means of private information exchange until the mid-19th-century invention of the typewriter. The trouble with handwriting as a technology for information exchange technology was that it could not scale for mass production.

Printing as technology

Typewriters appeared long after printing, but represent a practical intermediate stage between the technology of handwriting, that of printing and that of computers. More than one person has claimed to have invented the first typewriter, and the early models were inefficient as compared with pen and ink. Nonetheless, even the inefficient typewriters had the advantage of a uniformity that many who wrote by hand could not achieve. Some professional writers like Henry James took to dictating their works in old age, and that affected their style. The typewriter allowed a skilled secretary to take down his words faster and with greater clarity than handwriting, and even

James acknowledged that the typed version was easier to read than his own handwriting (Vericat, 2015). Typing became a female profession, perhaps because it represented a technology that allowed women to enter the workforce (Kellaway, 2013). 'In the 1910 US census over 80% of typists were women' (Ravado, 2022). Even in the mid-20th century, schools offered typing classes that few men attended.

Printing developed 'around the year 700, in China during the Tang dynasty (618–907) ... During the Song dynasty moveable type printing was invented by Bi Sheng (972–1051) between 1041 and 1048 using earthenware type. This was not widely used within China itself, except for very large jobs, given the high upfront cost associated with it' (Hoh, 2021). The complexity of the Chinese characters made efficient printing harder. Johannes Gutenberg's mechanism relied on movable type applied to an existing technology for pressing wine and olives. Movable type made Gutenberg's mechanism flexible, thanks to the relatively small number of letters. An obvious early candidate for printing was the Christian Bible, which combined nicely with the demand created by the Protestant Reformation. Printing this way was not fast compared to handwriting for a single copy, but could produce quantities of consistently readable text at a scale not previously known, and the technology required only modest capital investment. This changed a key parameter in the availability of information. It was not until the 18th century that printing technology evolved to where steam-driven cylinder printing made large-scale printing of newspapers like *The Times* of London realistic (Lechêne, 2025).

Printed works are so established today that their weaknesses are easily forgotten. One of the chief weaknesses is language itself, since not everyone could read the Latin of the Vulgate Bible, either because they were not literate or because Latin had changed so much that it seemed increasingly unfamiliar. The Church long preserved the use of Latin in the liturgy, but increasingly the words needed translation. Martin Luther and colleagues such as Philip Melanchthon created a German-language version of the Bible in the early to mid-16th century. Every translation involves shifts in meaning, and the Luther Bible famously included elements from the Greek that were not in the Vulgate. In a world where the Bible represented an authoritative source of information, these subtle and sometimes not so subtle differences changed the nature of 'truth' in ways that natural science experiments can today.

Engineering technology

The term 'engineering' covers a broad range of historical developments that have influenced how people receive and use information today. Every component of every computer is engineered, from current laptops to early room-sized devices that used vacuum tubes and were programmed by re-plugging cables and physical switches. 'In the early 1940s, IBM's president, Thomas J. Watson, reputedly said: "I think there is a world market for about five computers"' (Carr, 2008). Watson was probably right in terms of the kind of computers that existed at the time. Engineering standards for computers changed thanks to the invention of the transistor, which replaced the cumbersome and notoriously unreliable vacuum tubes. This changed the computer's size requirements as well as the internal wiring, and increased its speed and value. The next generation of computers relied on control systems that replaced wires-based programming with binary commands, which meant that engineers had to find a way to transmit the correct binary commands to the chips.

Punch cards or paper tape with commands became the standard way to program computers in the 1960s. This required the machines to understand encoded commands that were stored on cards or tape and then read into the computer. The technology already existed to allow people (mostly women) to type in the instructions. In the 1880s Herman Hollerith created punch cards to tabulate complex sets of data for the population census in several countries, and the machines to read numbers from those cards. Without punch cards as precursors, entering programming commands into computers would have required a new technology. Punch cards lasted well into the early 1980s, even after IBM introduced TSO (Time Sharing Option) in the early 1970s. TSO was resource intensive and required hardware (monitors with keyboards) that many companies found too expensive. Many firms had also invested in typing pools where skilled typists could enter handwritten computer code. These sorts of human investments were a part of the context that influenced information processing.

Other technical developments came quickly, including changes in how operating systems managed computer memory. Memory in a computer is an expensive resource. In early machines, memory often sat idle, waiting for data to load from card or tape or disk, which from a processing viewpoint was slow and wasteful. One of the key developments was to write algorithms to decide which tasks could wait while other faster tasks completed. This involved managing queues and setting priority standards. Different operating systems used different algorithms but sometimes borrowed ideas from each other. At one time such information was often shared among operating system developers. Newer computing chips made a difference. One of the reasons why Unix-like systems (including Linux) grew in popularity was their relative efficiency in managing memory. For an information scientist perhaps the key fact was how efficiently the ideas behind memory-management algorithms spread within the computing community, perhaps because people within this very specialised world talked openly with each other.

Radio technology

The date of the first radio is controversial. '[Nikola] Tesla was the first to make a wireless radio, and he had a public demonstration in March of 1893' (study.com, 2024). Other sources emphasise the development of radio technology half a century earlier: 'Hans Christian Oersted was the first to proclaim, in 1820, that a magnetic field is created around a wire that has a current running through it. In 1830, English physicist Michael Faraday confirmed Oersted's theory, and established the principle of electromagnetic induction' (Public Broadcasting Service, 2025). Candice West (2022) writes that 'Italian inventor Guglielmo Marconi is credited as the father of radio, having developed the idea in the 1890s.... By 1914, Canadian inventor Reginald Fessenden managed to develop a machine that could sustain a wave powerful enough to transmit voices and music over thousands of miles.' This uncertainty about the start date of a new technology is typical because it is rarely the creation of one person working in isolation, but represents a community of thought in which ideas and applications develop within a common context. What really mattered was the purposes for which radio came to be used.

The UK Science Museum (2024) claims the first British radio broadcast took place on 15 June 1920, but that regular programming did not start immediately. By the 1920s the radio was used widely in the USA for news, entertainment and music. Wikipedia (2025d) claims that the first news broadcast was on 31 August 1920 in Detroit. Detroit had a strong technology orientation, due to the engineering needs of the automobile industry. It was also relatively wealthy, which meant that many could afford to buy radios. The start date for radio broadcasts varies from country to country. In Germany the first broadcast appears to have taken place on 22 December 1920 in Königs Wusterhausen near Berlin. (Förderverein SenderKW, 2024). France was significantly slower to adopt the radio. What matters for information science is that this new medium offered a wider range of information than was possible for traditional print media, including music and real-time news.

Radio did not immediately undercut newspapers or magazines, which continue to flourish. Cost was one of the reasons, because the early radios used vacuum tubes that were liable to failure. Portable radios did not appear for another 40 years. Most homes had one radio in a central room, which meant that everyone in a household had to listen to the same programme.

Newspapers and magazines, by contrast, were portable, reliable and more than one person in a household could read them at their convenience. However, literacy was a barrier. Literacy in Germany and the USA was relatively widespread, and also in the UK among the middle classes, who were the ones who could afford to get information via radio. One of the advantages of radio was that it neither required literacy nor the free time to read, which many lacked in the working classes. Dialects were potentially a problem for radio listeners, because the broadcasts were almost uniformly in the language of the educated upper class. While radio helped to standardise the spoken language, this effect took generations.

Politicians quickly recognised radio's ability to reach mass audiences, but it took a dramatic speaking style to maximise the emotional content of a message. Careful nuances and dry facts did not carry the same impact, when spoken as did emotional appeals that relied more on feeling than facts or analysis. Demagogues especially profited from radio's ability to convey the feelings behind their messages, which in print could seem repetitious and/or fatuous to a critical mind. In effect, the radio enabled political rants to enter the home of every radio listener. In the 1930s politicians like Hitler and Mussolini took advantage of the new medium to reach many thousands more people than ever attended a physical rally. Franklin Roosevelt also did so in the USA.

It is easy to forget that the early days of radio's success were largely a Western phenomenon. According to Duits (2022), the first radio broadcast in Japan took place in 1925. Japan was a relatively rich Asian country, but radios were expensive and 'there was only one set for every five to six households'. In 1925 only 2% of households subscribed to radio. By 1935 the percentage had grown to 18% and by 1945 it had jumped to 45%. These figures are fairly accurate because Japan required people to register their radios. Nonetheless, Duits (2022) warns that '[t]hese figures can be slightly misleading, though, because the home was not the only place to listen to the radio. People would gather at radio shops and other locations where broadcasts could be heard.'

Radio technology was also slower to penetrate China. Alekna (2020) wrote that 'Radio first arrived in China in the winter of 1922–23, bursting into a world where communication was slow and disjointed, where less than ten percent of the population ever read newspapers –and these often took days or weeks to reach even relatively proximate locations.' This was before simplified characters made literacy more widespread, and radio also had the problem that a significant portion of the Chinese population did not understand Mandarin, especially not those in the southern provinces. This was offset by a level of social organisation that began in the 1930s, when '[t]rained radio monitors, posted in rural districts from the early 1930s onward, transcribed, reproduced, and redistributed news, information, and educational content broadcast from government stations'.

The news may well have had a government bias, but the hunger for news of any sort guaranteed an eager and substantial audience. It is hard to say what role radio broadcasts played in subsequent events after World War 2, but examples from other countries suggest that the impact was likely significant.

Visual technology

Finding a date for the invention of television is more complicated than for radio because television systems are technically more complex. Fischer and Fink (2024) suggest 1880 as a starting date, when 'a French engineer, Maurice LeBlanc, published an article in the journal *La Lumière électrique* that formed the basis of all subsequent television.... [T]he first demonstration of a primitive electronic system had been made in San Francisco in 1927 by Philo Farnsworth, a young man with only a high-school education.'

The key was a working cathode ray tube. 'At the 1939 World's Fair in New York City, Sarnoff inaugurated America's first regular electronic broadcasting, and 10 days later, at the official opening ceremonies, Franklin D. Roosevelt became the first U.S. president to be televised' (Fischer and Fink, 2024). The standards varied in the USA and Europe at this time, but this did not matter because systematic international broadcasting did not begin until the end of the 1930s. 'By 1941 the Columbia Broadcasting System (CBS), RCA's main competition in radio, was broadcasting two 15-minute newscasts a day to a tiny audience on its New York television station' (Stephens, 1999).

Serious television broadcasting did not begin until after World War 2, and was mostly an American phenomenon because few people in other countries could afford the expensive devices. The early shows were mainly taken from popular radio broadcasts. 'The number of television sets in use rose from 6,000 in 1946 to some 12 million by 1951. No new invention entered American homes faster than black and white television sets; by 1955 half of all U.S. homes had one' (Stephens, 1999).

Entertainment was not the only staple of television broadcasts. News played a significant role in its growth. 'In 1947 the House Committee on Un-American Activities began an investigation of the film industry, and Sen. Joseph R. McCarthy soon began to inveigh against what he claimed was Communist infiltration of the government' (Stephens, 1999). Television may have played a role in ending 'McCarthy's reign of fear. In 1954 the U.S. Senate censured McCarthy …' (Stephens, 1999).

Television began relatively early in Germany. Wikipedia claims the first broadcasts in Berlin took place in 1935 and grew again in the post-World War 2 era in both West and East Germany. Great Britain also had television broadcasts in the immediate post-war era. The number of television sets in France at this time remained small. In 1950 France had only 3,794 televisions and reception was available only in Paris (Lévy, 1998). The beginnings of television in China came later still. Wikipedia (2025e) claims the first broadcast took place in 1958, but does not cite any sources. The Great Leap Forward (大跃进) disrupted the growth of television, which resumed in 1960. Xiaoping (2001) claims that 'there are only two national television networks – CCTV and China Educational Television – in China. In addition, there are more than 368 provincial and local television stations around the country.' Today many Western networks are also available.

For information scientists television is important not only because a large number of people around the world now use it as a primary source of information but also because of the visual information it makes available. News programmes in the 1950s often showed only the news presenters. A viewer could tell something from their faces as well as from their voices, but the political impact grew when news cameras recorded live events such as protests and wars. Thousands took part in the civil rights marches in the USA in the later 1950s and 1960s, and television vastly increased the numbers who could see what was happening. The protests at German universities in the late 1960s and early 1970s were likewise broadcast. More significant was the television coverage of the Vietnam War, which brought a visual record of the violence into homes around the world. No longer was war and violence something people could only read about. The visual immediacy of events became harder to escape, and that influenced how people felt and voted. Humans react more strongly to visual than to verbal information. This is one reason why photography became an important element in newspapers once the costs of printing became manageable.

Telegraph and telephone

The first form of electronic communication technology was arguably the telegraph, which had precursors in naval flags and semaphore systems. The weakness of these systems was the need to know a precise set of codes. Samuel Morse developed a code system in 1832 that became standard in the early 19th century. Although telegraph usage lasted until well into the 20th century, its weakness lay in the specialised knowledge needed to understand the messages (McGillem, 2024).

The telephone, for which Alexander Graham Bell usually gets the credit thanks to his 1876 patent, had the advantage that it used spoken words. The early telephones were crude devices with such imperfect sound that people had to yell to make themselves heard. Operators at mechanical switchboards played a key role in making connections. Electronic switching did not appear in some regions until 1965 (Borth, 2024). Finding the correct phone number depended on printed telephone books with a special section (the Yellow Pages in the USA and UK) for commercial listings. In some countries the phone books were available at public centres such as post offices. International or long distance calls often had to be booked ahead of time even in the 1960s and 1970s, and the sound quality could be uneven.

Telephones that created an electromechanical pulse signal brought the word 'dialling' into use, since the devices used a rotary dial that turned at a sufficiently consistent speed to send electronic pulses to indicate the desired connection. Push-button telephones did not appear until the mid-1960s. International calling faced standardisation problems. The International Telegraph and Telephone Consultative Committee (CCITT) set standards that not all countries adopted, which eventually led to seven versions by 1991 (Borth, 2024). The infrastructure needed for telephone communication depended on a labour-intensive process of putting up wires and connecting the lines to places wanting telephones. Rural areas generally received telephone service after urban areas, and in many areas rural subscribers had no choice but to share a 'party' line, which meant that multiple households used a single line and could listen in on conversations, which made confidential conversations impossible. In many places there was a long wait, sometimes months, before a new telephone could be installed.

Mobile phone technology appeared in the USA in 1946, but at too primitive a level to be used by the public. Public service did not start for decades. Japan had a system as early as 1979, and the Scandinavian countries, the USA and the UK had mobile systems by the early 1980s. Mobile phones first became important for emergency services, but evolved beyond that to enable wealthy people to have a mobile phone to reach friends and colleagues at any time from any place. With mobile phones, the need to find a phone booth and insert an appropriate coin to place a local call became obsolete. This changed the physical landscape, though phone booths still mattered until the early 2000s. Phone booths were in fact problematic, since their soundproofing was generally poor, and the need for the correct coins remained an annoyance.

The European GSM (Global System for Mobile Communications) standard was established in 1988. The technologies continued to develop along with computer miniaturisation, with the eventual result that hand-held telephones that were capable of many basic computing functions became available at the beginning of the new millennium. For the information scientist, this was an important development because it meant that one could share verbal information with anyone, essentially worldwide, just by reaching for the miniature computer in one's pocket. The information being shared on these devices was often trivial. It was not the speech capability that mattered as much as having a computer in one's pocket.

Information exchange via telephone was nonetheless important. Although it generally did not involve high-value research, the private information exchange via telephony rapidly replaced handwritten letters. It is easy to assume that voice communication has advantages over handwritten letters, but that depends on the person and the circumstances. Not everyone finds voice preferable, and the ability to choose words carefully matters in some circumstances more than others. The immediacy of voice communication can be either a benefit or a curse.

Images

The popularity of images has ancient roots. Archaeologists have uncovered wall paintings from ancient Pompeii depicting everyday life and including both religious and salacious scenes. Medieval texts routinely contained initial letter elaborations or illustrations of the message in the text itself. This not only mattered for people whose understanding of written words was limited but helped readers to imagine the biblical scenes in greater detail. The illustrations were of course not accurate in historical terms, but included accurate depictions of the medieval world that gave biblical figures a level of immediacy beyond what the words conveyed.

Images remained costly to reproduce until well after the advent of printing. Chinese and Japanese woodblocks enabled the reproduction and distribution of images, and many of these works are still considered important works of art. The ban on images of persons in Islamic art (Department of Islamic Art, 2001) did not prevent elaborate plant or animal images that are still recognised as important art. Frescos, oil painting and all forms of line drawings had a level of popularity in the Western world that brought their creators lasting reputations and sometimes substantial incomes. The materials used to create images were not always easy to obtain. Canvas was more expensive than paper, and oils and other paints were not something the poor could afford unless someone recognised their talent. Nonetheless, the value of artistic talent meant that some patrons did provide the necessary financial resources. In some places, the Netherlands in the 16th century for example, relatively ordinary middle-class citizens saw enough value in artworks to spend money on paintings to decorate their homes.

Early 19th-century photography represented a revolution in the availability of images. The first black and white photographs were relatively crude compared to the drawings and prints of the era, but an exact and perfect image made an impression on viewers and buyers. The technology behind photography also improved quickly. 'In 1839, with an exposure time of just a few seconds, the daguerreotype became a means of using photography commercially for portraits' (Lumas Photo Art, 2024). This ensured that photography could become a serious competitor to the long and sometimes uncomfortable sittings necessary for a painter to make a convincing portrait. It also reduced the cost of making likenesses. 'In 1889, George Eastman created the roll of film, which made it possible to shoot multiple pictures one after the other' (Lumas Photo Art, 2024). Further developments came quickly: 'Introduced in 1925, the Leica prototype used a small-format, 35mm film. In comparison with the bulky box cameras previously in use, the compact Leica camera was a highly modern improvement' (Lumas Photo Art, 2024).

This meant that within less than a century, photography changed from a tool for professionals to one that many could use privately. Developing film remained an activity that required some technical knowledge and the right chemicals and equipment, but middle-class people could produce accurate images in their own homes. The advent of the Polaroid camera with film that developed photos instantly did not change how professionals worked, but it had an effect on a consumer market that liked instant results.

Photographs communicated information in ways that were fundamentally different to what words could achieve. Words could give a nuanced explanation of what a particularly good author understood, but most people lacked the descriptive skill to rival a photographic image. Quick and inexpensive photography brought about a fundamental change in how people received and processed information, even before the digital age made photographs so ubiquitous that everyone had a high-quality camera in their pocket as part of their mobile phone.

Conclusion

Technology is an integral element of information science, because technology has the ability to change how and where people find the information they need. The various technological revolutions were simultaneously revolutions in the production and availability of information. The increased availability of the written word, the spoken word and visual images fed directly into the core mechanisms by which humans could share information. The only senses that were left out of the technological revolutions were smell and taste, which matter to those who cook and eat, but seem never to have reached a level of importance that inventors have created ways to make that information widely available, except indirectly through verbal descriptions and images of food.

Technology enhances human understanding of information and greatly enhances its availability, but information scientists understand that the effectiveness matters only insofar as the medium communicates something that people understand, which varies enormously by context and person.

CHAPTER 7

Internet Technology

What is the role of internet technology in information science?

In the minds of many people, the internet has become so basic a source of information that older forms of information access have lost their importance. Many look online first to read news or e-mail and to chat with friends via social media. It has changed people's expectations about the speed and availability of both personal and public information. It has also created dependencies and anxieties, partly because the internet technology is so pervasive. For the information scientist, the speed of this transformation represents a change in how people relate to information, but it does not change information itself. Information scientists have played a role in creating this new environment.

Not everyone is happy about the capabilities of the internet. The Pew Foundation did a survey in 2004, which it published in January 2005. The internet was already over 30 years old at that point and had become so widely available that everyone had opinions and concerns. Among the survey results 66% of 'experts' who responded believed that 'At least one devastating attack will occur in the next 10 years on the networked information infrastructure or the country's power grid' (Pew Research Center, 2005). A few other predictions were equally dystopian: '59% of these experts agreed with a prediction that more government and business surveillance will occur as computing devices proliferate and become embedded in appliances, cars, phones, and even clothes' (Pew Research Center, 2005). And: '56% of them agreed that as telecommuting and home-schooling expand, the boundary between work and leisure will diminish and family dynamics will change because of that.' These predictions were not too far off. Some hopeful guesses were more imperfect: '50% of them believe that anonymous, free, music file-sharing on peer-to-peer networks will still be easy to perform a decade from now' (Pew Research Center, 2005). Nonetheless, a certain amount of free music is available today.

Stewart Brand supposedly first said that information wants to be free. Information scientists understand that this happy state probably cannot be achieved because of the cost of making information available. False information is just as expensive as true information, but is often subsidised. As a general rule someone or some institution subsidises both the access and the information itself. These costs go deeper than the internet itself. No one can access information on the internet without a computer, which may be as simple as a mobile phone, but costs rise steeply depending on the capabilities of the device. There are some free internet networks in public areas which institutions or governments subsidise, in part because it is cheaper to provide free internet access for certain services than to hire staff to answer patrons' questions. Advertising pays some of the costs of internet services, such as for Google search. The price comes in the form of unwanted advertisements. Information science cares about how information reaches people and what it means.

Origins of the internet

The internet is too complicated for any one person to have invented it, and it evolved over many years from its beginning as a military project. The chief initial funder was the US Advanced Research Projects Agency (ARPA) in 1958. The goal was to create a distributed network that would not be vulnerable in a nuclear war if one or more central nodes no longer existed. The key technology involved digital data in a process called packet switching. The first real test took place in 1965 between a computer at University of California, Los Angeles and one at Stanford University. More tests followed. 'By 1973, 30 academic, military and research institutions had joined the network, connecting locations including Hawaii, Norway and the UK' (National Science and Media Museum, 2020). This bore only a modest resemblance to today's internet, because it had no commercial services and was exclusively a research network. The set of protocols that managed the internet was TCP/IP, or Transmission Control Protocol/Internet Protocol. Essentially, the IP part made the connection and TCP handled 'many of the problems that arise from packet-based messaging, such as lost packets, out of order packets, duplicate packets, and corrupted packets' (Khan Academy, 2024). Even today, lost or corrupted packets are a problem, so check-sums and resend algorithms remain an important part of network operations today.

Numeric addresses worked for the first phase of internet development, but as the complexity grew, a simpler and more mnemonic system became desirable. The Domain Name System (DNS) came into being in 1983 (National Science and Media Museum, 2020), providing alphabetic names for computers connected to the internet. The initial distribution of DNS addresses did not envision the future international reach of the internet, and the early domain names reflected the dominance of US companies and universities. Today the domain name statistics show that almost 62% of domain names are not clearly associated with any country, which reflects the growth of companies wanting domain names whose meaning either fit their business or are location neutral. Excluding the 62% non-country names, US endings (including .com, .edu and .gov) dominate with 18.79%. The next largest are for China (2.86%), Iceland (2.65%) and Canada (2.36%). France, Germany, Japan and the Netherlands range from 1.06 to 0.63% (Domain Name Stat, 2024).

Population size plays no role in the distribution of domain names. The initial domain name distribution depended on who the early players were. A few US universities received larger domain name spaces than some countries did. This did not reflect prejudice so much as uncertainty, because it was unclear how fast the internet would grow, or how widely it would be distributed. Early attempts to limit the names failed for many reasons, partly because a country-name association implied limitations that not all companies wanted. Today 10.57% of the domains are 'xyz'. The name '.info' is 0.62%, and 'loan' is 1.94% (Domain Name, 2024).

The original US-based internet had close government ties, not only to the military but with the US National Science Foundation (NSF), which supported internet development as a means of fostering research. The NSFNET provided backbone services managed in co-operation with a number of US universities that had NSF computing centres. These included Cornell, Princeton, Pittsburgh (together with Carnegie Mellon University), Illinois and San Diego. When the NSFNET formally ended in 1995, the MERIT network took a lead role in managing the network through a complex set of partnerships. MERIT is itself a consortium of research universities in the US state of Michigan that began in 1966. It includes the University of Michigan, Michigan State University and Wayne State University. The end of the NSFNET in 1995 also marks the starting date for the commercialisation of the internet.

E-mail and browsers

As the name suggests, e-mail is the equivalent of a standard letter in digital form, and the purpose is similar. E-mail has the advantage that it costs the sender and receiver nothing, though discussions have taken place over the years that e-mail should have a minimal charge to discourage spam. The corporate world has an interest in keeping e-mail free because it profits from the free advertising.

A browser relies on a similar level of free internet usage. Many people think of browsers as generalised information sources, which to some extent is true, but not everything that looks like a browser gets information in a source-neutral way. Commercial apps, for example, typically rely on very specific information sources, which may not be available in browsers. Some internet apps are in fact older than browsers, as noted below.

E-mail is arguably the oldest of the internet applications. Early messages depended on a protocol for transferring files called FTP (File Transfer Protocol) – which made sense because the messages were essentially files. Soon it became clear that e-mail required better specifications, and SMTP (Simple Mail Transfer Protocol) came into being and standardised the ports and sub-protocols. As the use of e-mail grew, so too did its complexity. Companies developed applications to make reading and writing easier, including features that are now standard, like address books and formatting tools, none of which were available originally. From an information science perspective, the address books were especially important because their information defined a set of social relationships that was both more private and more immediately available than the telephone book.

Rules for how to use e-mail developed slowly as people gained experience with what was in fact a new medium, even though letter writing was old. A key difference from handwritten messages was privacy: e-mails could go to a larger audience, and system administrators could always read the messages. Individuals could forward 'private' messages to others, and mailing lists broadcast e-mails to a public that was sometimes broader than the author intended. In the early days of mailing lists, even among serious academics, 'flame' wars resembled people screaming at each other. Messages in all capital letters, or bold typeface or even just repeating phrases over and over again created a level of acrimony that impelled list owners to establish moderators to tone down the discussion. By the end of the 1980s, enough controls were in place to restrict outbursts, but such outbursts appeared again in later forms of internet communication, such as social media.

From an information science viewpoint e-mail is primarily a means to share comments. At its best, e-mail has been a venue for serious discourse about research, and still is today, but the gap between people's ability to express their ideas clearly and unemotionally in writing and their ability to do so orally remains a source of misunderstanding. Over the years e-mail has acquired symbols called emojis that help people to communicate emotions and personal intentions, such as whether the writer is making a joke and is not entirely serious. Such indicators help, and are today a common feature of social media.

Internet browsers appeared well after the advent of e-mail, and have played a significant role in making information available. Credit for the first browser depends on the context. Steve Worona wrote Cornell's CUINFO in 1982 (Seadle, 2021). This was not a browser in the current sense, but it was a precursor of later browsers. It used assembly language programs to capture internet packets to display on screens around the campus. It also included items like the advice column 'Ask Uncle Ezra'. One plausible claim for the first general-purpose browser is that Tim Berners-Lee wrote one on the NeXT computer. He explained: 'I could do in a couple of months what would take more like a year on other platforms, because on the NeXT, a lot of it was done for me already' (Berners-Lee, 2024).

In 1993 'Mosaic was created at the National Center for Supercomputing Applications (NCSA) at the University of Illinois Urbana-Champaign by computer scientist Marc Andreessen' (Mozilla, n.d.). 'The next year (1994), Andreessen founded Netscape and released Netscape Navigator to the public. It was wildly successful' (Mozilla, n.d.). There were also text-only browsers, such as Lynx, from the University of Kansas, which is still being used, according to Wikipedia (2025f). Browsers represent one of the most common ways that people search for information in the 21st century.

Libraries were eager to make their catalogues available online before browsers became common. 'NOTIS (Northwestern On-line Total Integrated System) was developed at Northwestern University Library beginning in 1967, installed at other sites starting in 1979, spun-off as a separate, for-profit company in 1987, sold to Ameritech in 1991 and last used by any library in 2012' (Specht, 2017). In other words, NOTIS provided access to library information before the first browsers became available. CUINFO displayed the NOTIS catalogues in the early 1980s on terminals at Cornell University.

From an information science perspective, browsers were not creators of information but became very successful tools for making digital information available. It was also important that that information was not merely words. Mosaic's importance lay in part in that it enabled visual images as part of the display. Images include not just photographs but diagrams and graphics of all sorts. This also changed the layout of web pages, so that they looked less dense and more attractive. Voice recordings and moving images followed quickly, so that contemporary browsers are multimedia tools.

Alternative networks

The internet was not the only network that used computing technologies to share information. BITNET ('Because It's Time Network') began in 1981, after the core internet infrastructure was in place but before the internet became commercial. It 'was originally based on IBM's VNET e-mail system and used the Remote Spooling Communications Subsystem (RSCS) and NJE/NJI protocols on the IBM Virtual Machine (VM) mainframe operating system' (Fuchs and Freeman, 2024). The VM operating system was widely used at top US universities at the time because it allowed the system programmers to run and test multiple other operating systems simultaneously. The VM systems programmers constituted a small group that met periodically and knew each other relatively well, which in social terms made it a logical platform to set up networks.

BITNET established connections to universities and research organisations in the UK, France and other countries including a large number in South America (Wikipedia, 2025g). The weakness of BITNET was its vulnerability. In 1988 a Cornell computer science student decided to play a prank on friends. He wrote a program that copied the addresses in e-mail directories and then sent messages to all the names in the directory along with the program, which began executing in every new environment. This is now known as the 'Morris worm' (Lennon, 2023). Part of the damage the worm did was to undermine reliance on BITNET. Many universities switched to using the Internet Protocol services exclusively.

Another network was Minitel, a service from the French PTT (Postes, Télégraphes et Téléphones) service. It went into operation in 1982, according to Wikipedia, and offered a wide range of services that resemble those of browsers today, including the ability to 'make online purchases, make train reservations, information services for business, search the telephone directory, have a mailbox, and chat in a similar way to what is now made possible by the World Wide Web' (Wikipedia, 2025h).

In the 1980s the World Wide Web did not yet exist and there was reason to believe that Minitel could expand beyond France. 'In 1991, France Telecom tried to reproduce their domestic Minitel success in the U.S. through a San Francisco-based venture called 101 Online' (Mailland, 2017). The weakness of the US venture was its desire to keep control:

> Instead of letting content providers manage their own services, as France Telecom had done, it replicated the dominant model for U.S. online networks of the era: curating all the content itself. Individuals and companies couldn't plug into the network and sell their content, goods, and services like their French counterparts had done, and as dotcom startups would soon do on the web.
>
> (Mailland, 2017)

An irony was that the French government, which has a known preference for control, ran a far more open version in France.

The argument that an urge for control caused Minitel to fail in the USA needs context. Internet users at the time were primarily people at universities, not a broader commercial public, and it was not until the end of NSFNET and the commercialisation of the internet that the demand for other services grew. Minitel in the USA never successfully expanded beyond its initial market area to other areas where keyboards and monitors were less common. The association with France may not have helped US marketing either, but the marketing efforts appear to have been modest at best. It was a time when many networking experiments were underway, and the internet had the advantage of an established international academic base that had grown accustomed to using it on a daily basis. After the Cold War ended, Germany quickly adopted the internet for its universities on a large scale. Despite the close political relationship between Germany and France, Minitel never became a serious competitor there.

Social media

In information science terms, social media are just another communication channel. The information on social media is frequently neither scholarly nor research oriented, nor even always true. Social media information matters because of how ubiquitous it is, and because the range of discussion provides context information, even when the ideas are unformed and imperfect. This section will look historically at a few social media examples out of the hundreds available.

The internet had social media aspects well before the name 'social media' was invented. E-mail was in a very real sense the first of the network-based social media systems, and was one that every internet user had access to, well before most people were aware of what the internet was. Jones (2015) offers the following definition: 'Social media is understood as the different forms of online communication used by people to create networks, communities, and collectives to share information, ideas, messages, and other content, such as videos.' He claims that under this definition sites like Six Degrees (1997) and Friendster (2002) were the first social media platforms. This ignores the fact that Listserv software provided a functionality similar to later specialised social media sites. According to Theresa Sintetos (2015), in 1986 'Eric Thomas created LISTSERV as a weekend project while a college student in Paris. This original idea formed the basis for social media as we know it today.'

At its most basic level, a LISTSERV is just a system that resends messages to a predefined set of e-mail addresses. A number of universities have hosted LISTSERVs on academic topics such as history. Regional LISTSERVs developed actively as well.

Social media sites collectively represent another way for people to communicate informally within groups of (mostly) like-minded people. Most social media sites do not have strict membership requirements, and literally anyone can join most sites without applying and without cost, which is both a strength of social media and one of its weaknesses, since managing the conversations often becomes difficult, even in cases when the host sets explicit rules. What distinguishes one social media system from another is not so much the technical platform as the kinds of conversations they encourage and enable.

Facebook is one of the older social media platforms. 'It began at Harvard University in 2003 as Facemash, an online service for students to judge the attractiveness of their fellow students. Because the primary developer, Zuckerberg, violated university policy in acquiring resources for the service, it was shut down after two days' (Hall, 2024). Facebook became a company the next year. Membership was initially limited to certain US universities, and it was in a sense a dating service for Ivy League students plus a few others from elite schools. Advertising played an early role in its history and provided the financial resources for further development. In 2012 Facebook became a publicly traded company. By then, its user base had expanded far beyond elite American universities. Privacy has long been an issue, as it is with many social media platforms: 'a survey of consumers in 2010 put Facebook in the bottom 5 percent of companies in customer satisfaction largely because of privacy concerns, and the company continues to be criticized for the complexity of its user privacy controls and for the frequent changes it makes to them' (Hall, 2024).

Politics also fuelled an interest in Facebook, whose 'groups' became active in elections in many countries, but not in all. China has long banned Facebook, as has Russia and other countries. China has its own social media. Completely uncontrolled political discourse is not always viewed positively, not even in the US, where some modest attempts have been made to curb excesses. Facebook took the unusual step of suspending Donald Trump in 2021:

> Last month, the Oversight Board upheld Facebook's suspension of former US President Donald Trump's Facebook and Instagram accounts following his praise for people engaged in violence at the Capitol on January 6.... Given the gravity of the circumstances that led to Mr. Trump's suspension, we believe his actions constituted a severe violation of our rules which merit the highest penalty available under the new enforcement protocols.
>
> (Clegg, 2021)

This was a strong step when applied to a former US president. The ban was rescinded in 2023. In response to the ban, Trump started his own social media network, called Truth Social, in 2021. A special-purpose investment company bought Truth Social in October 2023. The value of the company, as with other social media firms, depends on the size and activity of its user base, but the base has been slipping: 'According to a report from Similarweb, the monthly active users at Truth Social were down 23% in April when compared to the month prior. The firm also notes that mobile users on the website had decreased by 13%' (White, 2024). The strong political focus on Truth Social makes it unusual among the social media.

Twitter is another well-established social media company. It 'was created on March 21, 2006 by Jack Dorsey, Noah Glass, Biz Stone, and Evan Williams. It distinguished itself by limiting users to only 140 characters, a policy it held onto until 2017, when it doubled the character limits in all languages except Chinese, Japanese, and Korean' (Jones, 2015). The brevity of the posts resembled news headlines, and conversations had to be brief. When Elon Musk acquired the company, he renamed it to X and replaced its familiar bird logo with the letter X. Otherwise little visibly changed, other than that Musk opposed any free speech restrictions, except against himself (Timm, 2024). According to David Ingram (2024) of NBC news: 'The U.S. user base has been flat or down every month since November 2022, the first full month of Musk's owning the app, and in total it's down 23% since then …'.

'In 2009 China launched a social media platform called Weibo … that has grown to be one of the largest social media sites with over 400 million active users' (Jones, 2015). WeChat is another popular Chinese social media platform that was released in 2011 as Weixin and has 'well over one billion monthly users, the majority of whom are based in China' (Matthias, 2024). The Chinese social media are unlike the American systems in having little or no advertising. Instead WeChat earns 'the majority of its revenue from gaming, paid app upgrades, and digital payment fees' (Matthias, 2024). Privacy on WeChat is not guaranteed, but privacy seems not to be a major concern for its user base, which increasingly includes people from outside of China.

Other online tools could be called social media, depending on how strict the definition is. These include almost anything that allows people to post personal texts, pictures or voice recordings. Skype is an example. Niklas Zennström (Sweden) and Janus Friis (Denmark) founded Skype in 2003 in Luxembourg. Microsoft bought the company in 2011 (Britannica, 2025c), and eventually retired it on 5 May 2025. Skype had group features, but tended to be used more for business discussions than as an open platform, and perhaps for that reason had fewer problems with abuse. Security on Skype was also generally considered good, perhaps thanks to Microsoft policies. Apple has similar tools called FaceTime (for video) and Messages for text. Zoom was never meant as a public social media tool, but it serves a social function within organisations since it lets people interact visually in ways that more resemble normal human interaction than tools that rely more on text or photos.

Security concerns

Security concerns on the internet have long been an issue, in part because the openness of the architecture makes it vulnerable. The security problems break down into several types, of which financial fraud and personal harassment are notable examples. The internet has instituted a few technical measures to address security concerns, including HTTPS, which Netscape created in 1994. Google's Chrome browser began to label sites that did not use HTTPS as a potential security risk after 2018 (Wikipedia, 2025i). The security mechanisms are relatively weak: both HTTP and HTTPS depend on using the right port and a certificate from a trusted authority, and those certificates can be revoked, which has led to a need to check whether a certificate remains valid. The so-called 'dark web' (based on the Tor browser) offers a space for illegal activity because it is not traced.

Banks and other financial institutions are often targets, despite security improvements. Financial institutions and their customers have coped by requiring more passwords and two-factor authentication. In the days before internet banking, people went to a local bank to identify themselves in order to get cash. That was reasonably secure. For someone who wanted to pay bills by cheque, a signature represented a standard form of security, even though signatures are easily forged. Nonetheless, signature-based identification was so widely established in some cultures that countries like the USA still use signed paper cheques, even though this is slowly dying out in favour of electronic transfers.

In the mid-20th century a European cheque card allowed individuals to write special cheques to withdraw money from banks anywhere in Europe. The cheque card was essentially an ID-card from a bank, and itself had increasing layers of security as time went on. Various forms of traveller's cheques served a similar purpose for people on trips. A 'counter' signature matching the original was necessary, plus often another form of identification such as a passport. The companies that issued the traveller's cheques took no risks. They received the money first, and only guaranteed that the money was available. This form of pre-internet money transfer was cumbersome, but at some level reasonably secure. The concern remains that electronic transfer enables money transfers on a larger and less controlled scale. A password or PIN (personal identification number) has largely replaced signatures, and the possession of a bank-issued card is essential.

A range of forms of financial fraud occur on the internet, including 'phishing' (attempts to fool people into revealing sensitive information or installing malware) and direct attacks on an organisation's software, either to steal directly or to hold their sites hostage until they pay the attackers. Governments and institutions do what they can to avoid these kinds of risks, but this can be hard in a context where the attackers have sufficient resources from hostile countries or organised crime. Denial-of-service attacks are one of the actions that hackers have used against all forms of businesses. These attacks come in the form of message 'blasts' so intense that normal customers cannot reach the site. Often these are short term, but nonetheless effective. Some countries avoid these problems by close supervision of who can be active on their networks. This is a strategy that appears to work, but is criticised as a form of censorship.

Political concerns

A relatively uncensored and unrestricted internet, as is typical in Western countries, easily becomes a platform for political demagoguery and all forms of misinformation. The same has historically been true for gossip and tabloid newspapers, with the important difference that gossip and tabloids had a limited local scope, while the internet can broadcast worldwide. Scientific misinformation represents a particularly challenging issue for information science because it undermines the public trust in science and scholarship. This will be discussed in greater detail in later chapters.

Political misinformation is rife on the internet, but its nature varies widely and never was restricted only to the internet. In Germany, the Nazis used radio broadcasts to attack the Weimar government, and World War 2 propagandists in the USA suggested that anyone with Japanese heritage might be a spy. Facts and a balanced view of the truth faced difficult challenges, probably because such arguments did not appeal to the emotions and fears of the wartime public. What the internet has enabled in recent years is for essentially any person with strong opinions to broadcast them beyond their circle of immediate friends. Professional politicians routinely take advantage of the internet's openness to make their messages available, as do their opponents.

For a political message on the internet to be effective today typically requires more than words. Political websites offer full multimedia coverage. Advertisements in social media make regular use of images and videos as well, though sound is typically optional, since it becomes an unwelcome interruption. Those who want to get the latest opinions from their preferred candidate or party can go to the candidate's website. Increasingly, news programmes on the internet also have distinct political viewpoints, as was previously the case with newspapers and magazines. From an information science viewpoint, nothing fundamental has changed except the ubiquity of access and the intensity of the multimedia associated with the viewpoints. Nonetheless, intensity matters for hotly contested issues. In many Western countries a push for 'balance' has replaced the more abstract goal of 'fairness', perhaps because what seems fair to one side seems unfair to another. Balance tries to present all sides equally. In practice this means that the editorial judgement that used to set standards for requiring and presenting facts increasingly allows all sides to choose their own version of the truth.

Conclusion

Internet technology serves as a communication tool whose primary purpose, like that of printing or broadcasting, is to share new information. The internet has changed how to seek and distribute information, and it has radically changed the speed with which that happens. In a real sense the internet has democratised the capacity to communicate with large numbers of people. It has opened access to, for example, all members of organisations like the iSchools or ASIS&T, or to anyone searching for information in publicly available blogs or posts on widely read social media. The transformative element of internet access is that it has reshaped the context in which people seek and use information. In pre-modern times the typical context was hardly more than a few hundred people, often near neighbours whom they had known all their lives. It is only a modest exaggeration to say that the internet has changed the information context to become nearly planetwide, at least for those privileged enough to have the tools necessary for internet access.

CHAPTER 8

Information Integrity

What is information integrity?

Information scientists need to care about the integrity of information, which is not always easy. Integrity standards measure how truthful and reliable information is according to contemporary understanding. Since the standards change over time, the perception of integrity can vary, and often has over the centuries. That does not mean that information integrity lacks enduring value, only that the context so greatly affects the understanding of integrity that it may seem to change over time. There are plenty of examples even in relatively modern times. For example, it was not until well into the twentieth century that most people in the Western world accepted the factual evidence that humans evolved over time and were not created in exactly their current form.

The challenge in establishing information integrity goes back to the old problem of sources of authority, which shift over time. An even greater problem has been how to interpret the relevance of a particular authority for a particular kind of information. People commonly claim that they believe what they see, but sight can be deceptive. Size, for example, is hard to judge at a distance, and colours appear different in different forms of light. It is possible to set standards for information integrity within a context where most people can agree, but even agreeing depends on nuances of language and means of measurement. Precision is also not the same in all languages or places. A rough sea, for example, has a different meaning for a person who easily becomes seasick than for someone already accustomed to the waves. Information integrity has a political component too, when it involves making harmful accusations. The statement that someone cheated on their taxes could depend on how strictly the person understands the tax code, which is itself so complex that even experts may not always agree. The value of a claim that someone cheated may vary with the context. In a country where cheating on tax is common, it may not matter.

Problems with information integrity are generally complex because of the many possible variations of meanings and measurements and consequences. Information integrity is hard to enforce, even in the scholarly world, where the topic is often discussed. The sections below will address some specific issues.

Information integrity in the past

While humans have probably always disagreed, the disagreement only becomes an integrity issue when two sides disagree about the factual basis. The Reformation era in Western Europe provides a historical example. Topics like 'salvation' mattered intensely for scholars and ordinary people. A factual question arose from the sale of 'indulgences', which infuriated the early Protestants, who felt that the mechanism for forgiving sins by paying for prayers to be said and for absolution lacked the integrity of true biblical authority. It was as if a physicist today suddenly doubted basics like the law of entropy, or a 21st-century chemist claimed it was possible to change base metals into gold. Doubting the information integrity of one established 'fact' can also call others into question.

Natural scientists have often pushed against the established rules of their time. In the 19th century both the biologist Charles Darwin and the geologist Charles Lyell used physical evidence to support their arguments for why the planet is older than everyone had believed on the basis of the biblical Creation story. This in a real sense was not simply heresy but seemed absurd to people who had grown up in a world in which biblical authority had primacy. In practical terms, their evidence seemed unbelievable. From an information scientist's perspective, integrity problems arise when the consensus about relevant ways of gathering and applying evidence breaks down. This is a matter not just of change, but of changing assumptions that are so deeply ingrained in the culture that rational discussion becomes impossible. The facts of one side do not count as facts for the other. That is when accusations begin.

The more complex theories about the physical world become, the less that non-scientists play a role in the discussions simply because most ordinary citizens find formulations like $E = MC^2$ too abstract to discuss, even though that is the simple form of Einstein's more general formula: $E = (MC^2) / V^2/c^2$. And, of course, special relativity is a simpler version than general relativity. Few people attend schools where they must learn formulas like this. Today few grow up learning complex arguments involving biblical literacy. Education matters for how people judge integrity issues, which is unsurprising, because most integrity issues are complex.

The public focus on academic integrity issues in recent decades has become especially concerned with issues about copyright and plagiarism. Copyright laws themselves have changed significantly over the last three centuries since the British Statute of Anne in 1710 first established a model of basic protections for authors. In the 19th century Charles Dickens famously complained about American publishers stealing his works (Hudon, 1964). Dickens lived on the money from the sales of his books, and the rights issues were financially important to him. His novels were popular in the USA, but he did not profit directly since the USA never joined the Berne Convention for the Protection of Literary and Artistic Works until as late as 1989. From an information science perspective, an excessive focus on plagiarism distracts from other more important issues, since plagiarism itself does not invalidate the truth of scholarly evidence, only its economic value. Plagiarism is mainly an ethical issue, not one of scientific accuracy. Plagiarism was rarely an issue in the paper-based world, because small amounts of plagiarism were difficult to detect until new digital tools became available that could check digital documents for plagiarism at the word level.

The best of these plagiarism checkers allow operators to specify how many consecutive words are counted as plagiarism. Some can also leave out 'function' words that carry no meaning and only make an English sentence more comprehensible. A weakness in some plagiarism software is a failure to recognise well known facts and scientific phrases, including those involving standard ways of describing statistical results. A problem is a lack of clarity in plagiarism standards. There are also cases where the plagiarism becomes so extreme as to devalue the scholarship. German Defence Minister Karl-Theodor zu Guttenberg's doctoral dissertation contained so much plagiarism that it cost him both his doctorate and his political office (Pidd, 2011).

Many serious information integrity cases today involve some form of data falsification, which invalidates the results. A case that received a lot of attention during the COVID-19 pandemic and led to retractions in two highly respected journals, *The Lancet* and *The New England Journal of Medicine*, came about because a company called Surgisphere provided data that looked increasingly suspicious, and because the company itself ultimately declined to provide the whole of the data to the authors (Davey, Kirchgaessner and Boseley, 2020).

Ivan Oransky's *Retraction Watch* blog and his database documents cases of data fraud going back at least to 2010. There are many reasons why research data can have problems, including ordinary human error, and the more complex a study becomes, and the more time pressure authors are under, the more information integrity problems grow. It is easy to blame the researchers, and certainly every scholarly researcher should try to avoid error, but governments and universities are also to blame for the pressure they put on scholars to publish. Hanson et al. (2023) wrote about 'The Strain on Scientific Publishing'. The article addresses a well established concern and provides convincing data about the problem. Their concern is that the total number of papers submitted to journals has increased to the point that peer-reviewing is struggling to keep up, which means that problematic papers inevitably slip through.

Discovering integrity problems

Discovering information integrity problems represents an important task for information scientists, since false information undermines the public credibility of scientific and scholarly work. The task is hard because the ability to recognise problems and to prove them depends, as always, on the context.

Integrity problems in an area like medicine often also involve economic issues. For example, developing new medicines is expensive, and there is always pressure inside a company to show the medicine's effectiveness. Since the pharmaceutical industry funds research at universities, their support also affects the willingness of funded scholars to look for unfavourable results. Professor Lisa Bero (2019) writes: 'Industry funders can go to great lengths to suppress the findings of academic research when it's not favourable to the company …'.

The amount of money needed to do serious research in medical fields inevitably plays a role, but it is not the only factor. The training of the people who do that kind of research is highly specialised and expensive. In practical terms, researchers often come from high-ranked universities that may have had corporate funding for their training facilities. As a result, the personal and institutional desire to represent funded research results as valid is hard to ignore. This can also mean that the desire to test the integrity of potentially questionable scientific results may be limited.

Integrity problems in medicine get more press coverage than those in other areas. Integrity problems in medicine may be easier to spot because of their effect on people, but historically this has not always been simple. At one time research on heart disease focused primarily on men, on the assumption that men were more vulnerable. 'Heart disease was considered a man's disease. … That attitude persisted throughout the 20th century, a time when questions about a woman's health were centered on the parts of her body under her bikini, said Dr Gina Lundberg, clinical director of the Emory Women's Heart Center and a professor at Emory University School of Medicine in Atlanta' (Williamson, L., 2024).

This attitude counts as an information integrity problem because it suppressed relevant information about half of the human population, and such gaps could count as falsification. It is not quite fair to say that scholars deliberately ignored women's health. In the context of the time, women's 'problems' often seemed embarrassing to both sexes. Even in the mid-20th century one form of typical medical advice for gynaecological problems was for a woman to get married and have children.

While women cannot count as a minority, many minorities faced the same gap in health research. It is now well known that sickle cell disease especially affects people of African or Mediterranean heritage. The disease is deadly, and discoverable with appropriate testing. 'Graham notes that the cause of sickle cell anemia has been known since the 1950s. But for many generations, he says, sickle cell anemia has not had the funding and research attention it deserves' (DeNoon, 2005).

Less well known are other genetic diseases that affect Black Americans, including diabetes (60% more common in Black than white Americans), asthma (3 times as likely), lung scarring (15 times more common), lung cancer (50% more likely), strokes (twice the risk) and cancer (Black men have a 40% higher death rate than white men) (DeNoon, 2005). The point is that information integrity is not just about the mistakes that researchers make, but about information that no one had or had tried to discover.

Information integrity problems of every sort are hard to identify without being so directly involved in the topic that the errors stand out; and in a world where the research topics are highly complex, even those looking for problems may be concerned whether their own doubts could be errors. A cautious researcher might reasonably hesitate before accusing colleagues of integrity violations, even when those errors do not result from any fraudulent intention. A further problem is that the people who are responsible for quality in large labs frequently have the all-too-human problem of too little time to check everything.

Deliberate fraud is probably less frequent than ordinary human error, but it happens. Diederik Stapel was a successful psychology researcher in the Netherlands who was caught and ultimately admitted to making up the data in his papers (see also below). Stapel was not the only notable person who committed deliberate fraud: 'The once-celebrated South Korean stem-cell researcher Hwang Woo Suk stunned scientists in his field a few years ago after it was discovered that almost all of the work for which he was known was fraudulent' (Bhattacharjee, 2013).

Whose job?

The people officially responsible for finding research integrity problems are often journal editors, journal reviewers and dissertation supervisors, but that is generally secondary to evaluating the overall quality of a work. Integrity problems certainly affect overall quality, but actually finding and recognising such problems goes beyond what most can do. A particularly obvious error may stand out, or a reviewer may simply recognise passages from the scholarly literature. A person well trained in statistics should be able to recognise cases where an author may have violated the assumptions behind a statistical test, and reviewers can in theory run the data through their own analysis, as long as the data are available. Variance in results does not necessarily imply bad intentions or actual errors, since data are complex, though odd results certainly ought to trigger suspicion.

Such testing takes both time and expertise, and not all reviewers have either the expertise or the time. It is easy to say that journals should always pick reviewers who can do both, but the reality is (and probably always has been) that appropriate reviewers are hard to find and that they often feel so stretched that they simply lack the time to pursue problems that are not immediately obvious. In a sense, the role of reviewers may have become to serve as scapegoats. Most journals and most institutions provide too little time and resources for systematic investigation. Finding research integrity problems will also not enhance career opportunities, except occasionally when hunting for plagiarism in the writings of well-known persons, where software can do most of the work.

Doctoral dissertation advisors ought to understand the work that their students are doing, and most try to catch and correct any errors they see. Context matters here too. Advisors have a social relationship with their doctoral candidates from years of working with them, and a natural urge to protect them can outweigh suspicions. This does not mean that advisors willingly overlook problems, only that the urge to hunt for weaknesses may be weak. Other factors play a role too. Doctoral students are supposed to break new ground. In social science and humanities fields this can involve languages that the advisor may not know or knows imperfectly. While dissertation advisors ought to theoretically have access to all of a candidate's data, there are increasingly cases where the data may involve confidential information, and both the law and institutional practice may offer incomplete guidance about appropriate access. A more common problem is that advisors simply do not have the time (or do not take the time) to review all of the data or to reanalyse all of the results. It could seem like a failure of trust if the advisor insisted on redoing all of the analysis, and could even be seen as giving the doctoral candidate too much help. The norm today varies enormously from discipline to discipline, but in most fields today, redoing all of the data and the whole of the analysis is uncommon.

No one advisor can grant a doctorate today at most institutions, since they require either second readers or outside reviewers to guarantee quality. A second reader often serves also in an advisory capacity for the dissertation writer, and may have important social connections. It is rare that a second reader is as involved with the research and writing. A second reader may also feel less obligation to spend a lot of time re-examining the analysis. The goal of involving reviewers from outside of the department or the university is to get a truly objective opinion. The principle makes sense, but the fact is that the interconnections among people in the same discipline means that no one with the skills to evaluate a dissertation lies completely outside of the social context of the advisor or doctoral candidate. Getting someone totally and completely from the outside risks involving a person who does not really understand the research methods or goals. Complete outside objectivity represents a mythical and probably unrealistic ideal. In general, dissertations are not a major source of integrity problems, perhaps because the rewards of getting the degree are not worth the trouble or the risk. The positive aspect is that the research community cares enough about information integrity that most doctoral dissertations include no deliberate fraud.

Master's theses and works by bachelor's students rarely get the same degree of attention. In many European countries and some Asian countries a master's student must write a serious thesis and must make an oral defence. This is less common in the USA, where some schools do not even require a written thesis. The problem is that programmes with a large number of students lack the resources to handle substantial master's or bachelor's theses, and future employers may show little interest in a written thesis.

Students almost never accuse their professors of violating research integrity, except in very rare cases, such as happened to Leiden University psychology professor Diederik Stapel, when two doctoral students found the courage to go to their department head, who was himself a close friend of Stapel, and accused Stapel of research fraud (Bhattacharjee, 2013). The problem was that Stapel made up data. His 'explanation that editors wanted simplicity and elegance likely has an element of truth, but is also self-serving in shifting responsibility. He had enough experience with real data to be able to create a very plausible fictional account of the data gathering with situations and stories so plausible that there was no incentive to investigate too closely' (Seadle, 2017). Stapel's error was that he made mistakes about details. When he revisited the location where one experiment supposedly took place, the configuration of the chairs and other details simply did not match. Stapel admitted his fraud more readily than many.

Another scholar who apparently manufactured data was James Hunton, an accounting professor at Bentley University in Boston. The original problem that created suspicion appeared to be a simple mistake in the number of US offices a company had. Hunton used confidentiality agreements as the reason why he could not make the data available. When he could not provide convincing versions of the confidential agreements, suspicion grew. Hunton deleted all of the data on his work computer, which seems to have belonged to the university, and when the university hired experts they discovered a deliberate cover-up using an 'eraser utility' that had 'run multiple times in an attempt (only partially successful) to delete all of the files on the laptop – including the metadata manipulation utility' (Malone, 2014). Hunton vanished without a trace, and left behind many embarrassed colleagues, with whom he had shared the false data.

For the information scientist it is striking how difficult the discovery of integrity problems is, which means that chance plays a role in the discovery and makes it more likely that more undiscovered cases exist. Ivan Oransky's *Retraction Watch* blog documents many of the cases that come to light, and performs an invaluable service, but his function is to document known problems rather than to discover new ones.

Measuring information integrity

Not all integrity problems are alike in the amount of damage they do to the scholarly and scientific community. Two very different measurement problems arise: those that involve only ethical issues and those that change the substance of results. Not every integrity issue sorts perfectly into one of these categories, and they are unequal in their effect and the kind of long-term impact.

Plagiarism is only one form of ethical problem, and ought in a sense to be the easiest to measure by counting the number of duplicate words. The US government Office of Research Integrity (ORI) claims: 'As a general working definition, ORI considers plagiarism to include both the theft or misappropriation of intellectual property and the substantial unattributed textual copying of another's work. It does not include authorship or credit disputes' (ORI, 1994).

This is a common attitude but lacks nuanced measurement. A search for rules about exactly how many consecutive words count as plagiarism results in widely varying answers. One site that appears on a Google search suggests that more than three consecutive words (not counting function words) could be plagiarism. Under that rule, the phrase 'three consecutive words' would count as plagiarism. Other sites suggest five words, which runs into the same problem (Sefton, 2013).

In fact most sophisticated academic sites realise that the number of words matters less than the substance and originality of what an author is saying. King's College London makes students send their essays through the plagiarism checker Turnitin before submitting them, and it warns students that the 'plagiarism score will never be 0% and you should not aim for this. There will always be coincidental matches between your work and other submissions, and also "false" readings on quotations, footnotes etc.' (King's College London, 2016).

The VroniPlag website sets a standard that a work is suspicious when 10% of the pages contain text overlap. This only means that one or more phrases within the page appear to duplicate other works, not the whole page. For VroniPlag a significant issue is the reference: for them, an imperfect or distant reference can count as plagiarism. Under rules of this sort plagiarism is widespread. Stefan Senders (2008) takes a broader view of student plagiarism: 'Only by analyzing the way the relationship of plagiarism takes shape can we say whether it is best fit by paradigms of "theft," "fraud," "infidelity," or even excessive intimacy.'

Insofar as 'excessive intimacy' means an excellent memory, many established writers must plead guilty. Measuring plagiarism is as hard as defining it precisely.

Privacy has become an ethical problem that is less prominent than plagiarism, but violating confidentiality and privacy is a serious legal issue in many countries, especially within the European Union. It is as important to keep survey-type data confidential as interview data, and any data that someone could trace back to an individual respondent could be problematic. The issue is especially important with medical data. The reverse problem with privacy is the need for transparency about where the data came from and what they mean. Context matters greatly with all forms of data, and if a scholar so completely eliminates all context information that the background becomes obscure, that can also damage the integrity of the data. There is no easy solution other than being aware of the problem. When the options for discussing the context are clearly labelled, and when the reason is legal compliance, the ethical concern perhaps vanishes, but some unmeasurable uncertainty about the validity of the data can nonetheless remain.

Methodology represents another potential integrity problem. A public example comes from a paper where the authors needed additional data points and filled in the data using 'Excel's autofill function' on the argument that '[i]f we do not use imputation, such data is [sic] almost useless' (Smith, 2024). There are cases where the autofill function makes sense, but such data is merely an extrapolation, not original data, and should at the least be clearly designated as such. A more common problem is a broadcast survey where the researcher cannot know whether those answering are representative of the population. One common goal of a survey is to include as many respondents as possible to increase its reliability, but numbers alone do not guarantee reliability. Large numbers can skew the results if only an unrepresentative minority have answered. On 24 May 2024 Nate Cohn published an article in the *New York Times* in which he discusses why Donald Trump had appeared to have a lead in the polls for eight months. The problem was who, exactly, was responding to the polls. The answer appeared to be 'disengaged voters' who 'are far likelier to report getting their news from social media' (Cohn, 2024). If only a subset of people respond to a questionnaire, then the question becomes: how representative is that subset? The answer may be largely unknowable.

Information integrity is too dependent on context to be readily measurable, but falsification problems often come up in the literature, especially when young scholars feel so under pressure to publish that they take short cuts. Measuring integrity might ideally have an absolute scale, but the world is not so simple. There are small errors that may not really matter, and, historically, even Nobel prize winners make mistakes, such as when Fritz Haber based his theory about recovering gold from sea water on flawed data (see Chapter 2, section on 'Reliable information'). No researcher is perfect, and most attempt to get reliable results. What the scholarly world could ideally do is to ease some of the pressure on scholars young and old to produce a set number of published works per year. To some degree the pressure is social and internal, but institutions could also put less stress on short-term than on long-term results. Changes in the incentive system are needed, and that requires institutional political choices that are never quick.

Assuring information integrity

Assuring information integrity is particularly important for information scientists, and ought perhaps to be a core focus of information science research. Unfortunately it is also an area where information scientists generally lack training beyond general admonitions to be honest. Integrity problems in the historical past were often associated with mistaken assumptions about what sources counted as reliable, or with economic hopes for profiting from a solution that seemed plausible, even if it did not work reliably. Results based on information lacking integrity often failed in the marketplace, simply because widespread testing over time revealed flaws.

The same problem happens in modern times as well. In the long run, solutions based on flawed results will fail and will not reward their creators.

This is not to say that an open market for testing new ideas necessarily guarantees quality information. Darwin's theories did not find acceptance everywhere. One of the alternatives came from Lamarck at the beginning of the 19th century, whose ideas about the 'inheritance of acquired characteristics' offered an alternative mechanism that seemed plausible for many years (Wikipedia, 2025j). Lamarckism found support in the Soviet Union under Joseph Stalin, but once the Soviet Union came to an end, support for Lamarck ended as well. Lamarckism had an unusually long lifetime for a theory where the evidence remained unconvincing for most scientists, but attempts to resurrect it persisted nonetheless into the later part of the 20th century.

There are plenty of other examples of theories that failed more quickly, such as the cold fusion announcement in 1989 – that other scientists could not replicate. These failed theories sometimes inspire fresh attempts to reach the same results using different means, as in this case, since the social and economic desire to make nuclear fusion into a viable energy source remains strong. In 2023 scientists in California claimed success by 'shooting nearly 200 lasers at a cylinder holding a fuel capsule the size of a peppercorn … Now they say they have successfully replicated ignition at least three times this year …' (Paddison, 2023). The process produced only energy 'enough to boil around 10 kettles of water. But it was sufficient to make it a successful ignition and to prove that laser fusion could create energy' (Paddison, 2023).

Physics is an area where public testing can effectively discredit false theories. The marketplace for disproving theories functions less well in other fields. Medicine is an area where integrity matters to people's lives, but medical testing can also fail to catch problems, in part because the process of testing new medicines is complex and expensive, and in part because medical testing does not and perhaps cannot take into account all of the contextual factors that matter. A bigger problem is that ordinary citizens will sometimes try new and even magical cures on the strength of claims that regulators never saw or approved. The public does not invariably act in its own self-interest when faced with clever marketing. In the social sciences and especially the humanities it can be hard to discredit ideas that have a weak factual or logical basis, especially when the ideas are well presented and fit with existing preconceived ideas. Marketplace testing may work better for a field like economics, which is strongly data oriented, but even in economics genuine disproof can require years or decades and unproven ideas can persist for political or social reasons.

It is not clear that any reliable scholarly mechanism can ensure information integrity in the short term, despite contemporary publication requirements and editorial efforts. From a historical perspective, it is safe to say that the quality and reliability of information today is significantly better than it was hundreds of years ago, and a good information scientist should understand what an achievement that is, even if it is not an achievement for which the field can take any direct credit. Nonetheless, maintaining a public focus on the integrity of information should count as a contribution.

Conclusion

While the integrity of information represents a key focus of modern information science, scholars today should never imagine that contemporary circumstances and contemporary standards are any more eternal and persistent than those of the past. The artefacts of past authority systems remain, and one of the factors that seems particularly hard to escape is the advantage that well-funded organisations and well-to-do people have when making decisions about information reliability. Climate change offers a good example. The amount of reproducible scientific evidence about changes in the climate of the Earth faces no credible counter-evidence, but organisations and people with economic interest in the sources of climate change – such as major oil companies – discount their own role in the causes in order to continue their lucrative practices that make climate change worse. For the information scientist, this kind of context is an element in the integrity of information that cannot be ignored.

CHAPTER 9

Artificial Intelligence

What is artificial intelligence?

Artificial intelligence (AI) usually refers to systems that seem capable of solving problems in ways that resemble human thought. Christopher Manning (2020) provides one of the classic definitions: 'Artificial Intelligence …, a term coined by emeritus Stanford Professor John McCarthy in 1955, was defined by him as "the science and engineering of making intelligent machines".'

Like most descriptions, this one avoids defining what exactly 'intelligence' means. McCarthy's definition differs from more recent versions that link AI specifically with computers, as if people never thought about making machines behave intelligently before computers. Information scientists know that most systems with the means to make variable responses to external stimuli exhibit some measure of intelligence. The idea of AI is old, even if the current name and hype suggest otherwise.

People have long looked for ways to outsource human thinking, and an important element of AI today is the ability for people to interact with that new intelligence. AI proponents typically define that interaction as a form of verbal exchange, because people associate words with thinking, but in fact people get information from a range of non-verbal sources and can interact with those sources without necessarily using words. One example is the automatic clutch, which responds to changes in road conditions (slope, for example) in ways that make human intervention unnecessary. It is not intelligence of the same kind as belongs to a large language model (LLM) capable of writing essays, but the response of the automatic clutch can sometimes exhibit more intelligence than a human driver. Other of the standard sources of non-verbal intelligence that humans use are visual and auditory. These will be discussed later in this chapter.

The idea that AI embodies a general and independent intelligence with human levels of creativity that works completely independently from human input is still largely science fiction, though that could change as systems evolve. Every system so far relies on human-provided information input, including the newest LLMs which depend on people selecting appropriate sources and writing appropriate code. Current AI systems depend also on human judgement about the value of the results. None of these AI systems think or operate as independently as Isaac Asimov's robots. Science-fiction fears and expectations about AI have become so enmeshed in current discussions that they sometimes misrepresent what the current state of AI can do.

Artificial intelligence past and present

Identifying what the first forms of artificial intelligence were depends on the context in which people sought external help with making complex decisions. It is possible to argue that astrology was an early AI system, because many people believed that the movements of the planets told them how the world worked and how to respond to events. The scientific information behind astrological observations still holds up to a significant extent, though few today still take the stars seriously as a source of advice. The visible behaviours of planets and stars correspond largely to what ancient astronomers observed, but people today draw different conclusions from the movements and placements of the stars. In an information science sense the astrologers' answers had an accurate technical basis, even though the validity of the astrological interpretation is at odds with modern science. In the past many people trusted the economic and political recommendations of their star charts more than some trust AI today.

Examining entrails represented another early AI system that the ancient world relied on. This goes back to ancient Etruscan, Greek and Roman times. 'The fourth-century Athenian writer Xenophon describes an occasion when the mercenaries with whom he served were held up in hostile territory and short of food, and the entrails forbade them either to move on or even to go out foraging for supplies, for several days' (Bowden, 2005). Reading entrails required picking the right animal and an interpretation that fit the expectations of the time. Divination was also practised in pre-modern China. The important fact is how widespread the trust was in these tools as a means for making decisions.

Other non-magical examples exist for how pre-modern people used tools for advice. The abacus was an early device for calculating. An abacus did not communicate in words, as modern AI systems do, but used a visual arrangement of beads in a two-dimensional array. The abacus is itself quite ancient, and versions were used in China, India and the Middle East as well as in Europe. According to Wikipedia (2025k), both South and Central American cultures appear to have had a similar calculation tool. For information science, one of the important features of AI systems is the ability to make reliable recommendations, even if only on specific topics. The reliability of the abacus has held up for millennia.

Many other simple tools provided reliable information, often using standard mathematics. The sextant is an example. Wikipedia (2025l) explains how a sextant works:

> The estimation of this angle, the altitude, is known as sighting or shooting the object, or taking a sight. The angle, and the time when it was measured, can be used to calculate a position line on a nautical or aeronautical chart – for example, sighting the Sun at noon or Polaris at night (in the Northern Hemisphere) to estimate latitude (with sight reduction).

Isaac Newton may have been the first person to describe the way a sextant works (Liebman, 2019). By the 18th century the sextant had come into broad use for ships travelling long distances across the oceans, which meant that it was de facto an invaluable AI tool for both trade and military purposes.

In the mid-20th century car manufacturers began to use robots to make assembly lines more efficient. Mostly these were robots with flexible arms and the strength to handle parts that weighed more than a normal human being could manage. According to Wikipedia (2025m), the International Federation of Robotics estimated there were just under four million robots in 2022. Some were able to work without human control, and the earliest could react to external signals like light. These systems were consistent and replaced humans in tasks that were dangerous, repetitious and boring. Typically, a human supervisor would make sure that nothing went wrong. Factories were not the only place where semi-intelligent robots found work. Robotic cleaning systems for home use have been available for decades. Many can work around barriers, remember where they were in a room and recognise dirt. Their ability to interact with people is limited, but they can react to their environment when necessary.

Context awareness is a problem with most AI systems. Some investors use intelligent trading systems to buy or sell stocks based on an algorithm that embodies a trading strategy and sets trigger points for when buy or sell actions should take place. They analyse external data feeds using statistical tools to identify when to take action in the market. In general they do not interact with humans, unless someone stops the trading. The advantage of these systems is their speed in volatile market conditions. Their disadvantage is that their intelligence is limited to the set of instructions built into their algorithms, and, if circumstances change in unexpected ways, humans must intervene.

The context-awareness problem can also be seen in self-driving cars. In theory, self-driving cars could be safer because humans easily become distracted or make bad judgements, but the record of self-driving cars is far from perfect when conditions are abnormal:

> California has ordered the company Cruise to immediately stop operations of its driverless cars in the state.... The move comes after one of Cruise's driverless cars struck a pedestrian in downtown San Francisco earlier this month. The incident involved a woman who was first hit by a human driver and then thrown onto the road in front of a Cruise vehicle. The Cruise vehicle braked but then continued to roll over the pedestrian, pulling her forward, then coming to a final stop on top of her.
>
> (Kerr, 2023)

Cummings (2023) warns about the degree to which software is error prone, especially in complex systems: 'For example, if a self-driving car fleet operates in one city with one kind of bus, and then the fleet moves to another city with different bus types, the underlying model of bus detection will likely drift, which could lead to serious consequences.' The point is that information scientists need to remember that contemporary AI systems are as context dependent as all other systems that were used historically to make decisions. One advantage that humans continue to have over AI-driven cars is an awareness of their surroundings, which is not as easily imitated as developers have hoped.

Early computing efforts at AI

Computer scientists have been thinking about how to turn computers into AI tools for as long as computers have been around. John McCarthy first worked on the computer language Lisp from the summer of 1956 to the summer of 1958, 'when most of the key ideas were developed (some of which were implemented in the FORTRAN based FLPL)' (McCarthy, 1979). One of the problems at the time was the limited size of computer memory. Prolog was a newer AI language 'conceived by Alain Colmerauer at the University of Aix-Marseille, France, where the language was first implemented in 1973' (Copeland, 2018). Both languages continue to be used today, but neither succeeded in enabling computers to understand the nuances of human language.

One of the common tests for whether a computer can imitate humans in conversation is typically called the Turing test because Alan Turing conceived it as an imitation game: 'The interrogator is in a room separated from the other person and the machine. The object of the game is for the interrogator to determine which of the other two is the person, and which is the machine' (Oppy and Dowe, 2021). Turing believed that by roughly the year 2000 (50 years from when he was writing) computers would be able to 'play the imitation game so well that an average interrogator will not have more than 70 percent chance of making the right identification after five minutes of questioning' (Oppy and Dowe, 2021). This has not happened, but has long represented one of the goals of AI. The degree of sophistication and complexity of the questions add another challenge for the Turing test. The simple fact is that no single AI system has yet convincingly passed the Turing test.

Expert systems were an early approach to create systems that could give reasonable advice for real-world operations. They were supposed to resemble AI systems with limited reasoning capabilities. Although expert systems were popular in the 1980s, their focus was too narrow.

> What are 'expert systems'? They are programs which reproduce human decision-making from a set of precoded rules. They are the offspring of artificial intelligence research, but unlike artificial intelligence, the intellectual scope of expert systems is narrow. They do not attempt to think, but only repeat what humans have thought. They capture expertise instead of creating it, and are in many respects like the conventional programs that working computer people deal with every day.
>
> (Seadle, 1991, x)

The best expert systems could deal with some degree of uncertainty, but genuinely complex situations exceeded their capacity.

Programs could imitate certain kinds of intelligent human tasks. Among them were chess-playing programs, most of which failed when playing against top professionals,, until in 1996 when IBM's Deep Blue defeated Garry Kasparov, the top-ranked player at the time in two out of six games. This was the best that a chess program had ever done, and inspired IBM to work on the system further until it defeated Kasparov in a new match a year later (Wikipedia, 2025n). A computer could calculate the consequences of moves far faster than any human, but the best chess masters do not rely only on combinational logic and on a sense of how positions could evolve. Bobby Fischer famously defeated his opponents by doing the unexpected. Chess computers continued to evolve, until Google programmers tried a neural network approach that resulted in 2017 in AlphaZero, which used neural networks that in effect let the system learn chess on its own. In that sense, it was a true AI, though one whose scope was limited to a board with 64 squares and figures that had closely prescribed movements.

Games offer many possibilities for AI-like research under constrained conditions. The popular US television quiz game 'Jeopardy' is an example. The game required players to answer factual questions in competition with others. The first to offer a correct answer won the points for that question. The challenges for an AI were not merely to understand the question (which it received in text form instead of orally), but also to search its databases quickly enough to decide whether it had a correct answer. Some human players would signal an answer before they were quite ready, just to be the first. Watson's programming did not allow that, but over-fast responses did not always help the humans. Watson's success made an impression, but, as with chess, Watson did not have to deal with complex context shifts. The rules and the kinds of questions remained the same throughout the game. Except for parsing the questions, it was less of a genuine AI challenge than a database search issue.

One of the goals of AI developers has been to create tools called 'chatbots' that offer online help independent of humans. In terms of corporate finances, a chatbot pays for itself when it can substitute for a far more expensive human. This does not mean that people using chatbots always feel that they have received a satisfactory answer. Companies may consider the chatbot a success any time a question does not get escalated to a human operator. Chatbots can often respond well to very specific factual questions. A study from October 2023 rated the answers of chatbots to medical questions:

> In this cross-sectional study of 33 physicians across 17 specialties who generated 284 medical questions, chatbot generated predominantly accurate information in response to these diverse medical queries as judged by these academic physician specialists. The median accuracy score was 5.5 (between almost completely and completely correct), and the median completeness score was 3.0 (complete and comprehensive).
>
> (Goodman et al., 2023)

The reliability rate varied a lot, though. Metz (2023) reports somewhat different results: 'Now a new start-up called Vectara, founded by former Google employees, is trying to figure out how often chatbots veer from the truth. The company's research estimates that even in situations designed to prevent it from happening, chatbots invent information at least 3 percent of the time – and as high as 27 percent.'

Chatbots increasingly rely on LLMs.

Large language models

LLMs grew out of work on natural language processing, which has long interested computer scientists. 'In 1966, an MIT computer scientist, Joseph Weizenbaum, developed ELIZA, which is described as the first program using NLP [Natural Language Processing]' (Foote, 2023). ELIZA was able to give responses to people that seemed so real that Weizenbaum's secretary responded as if it were a real person. '[Weizenbaum] later added, "I had not realized … that extremely short exposures to a relatively simple computer program could induce powerful delusional thinking in quite normal people"' (Foote, 2023).

This reaction is symptomatic of the first impression that people who are neither computer scientists nor information scientists still have today when encountering modern AI systems. It speaks well for the quality of the systems that they can create such an impression. It also means that information scientists have an obligation to make the limitations of LLM responses clear.

The large language algorithms are typically not transparent. The models consist of two core components: the language source and the analytical engine that puts the data (mainly words) together into plausible words and paragraphs. The models currently work only with text-based vocabulary, which cuts them off from non-verbal context information surrounding the words. That will likely change as the AI tools behind these systems grow more sophisticated, but that would also mean adding capabilities to collect visual and tonal and other forms of information. Text can describe the information that people get via their senses, but a strictly verbal description may leave out important social and emotional details. At this point computers can capture sounds and visual information effectively, but lack many of the nuances that matter for processing that information.

The choices about where an LLM learns words determine what AI engines can do. Ideally the sources match the purpose. Even when the whole of the World Wide Web is the source of words, not all models handle unknown languages. Linguistic discrimination is a known challenge.

> LLMs can exhibit linguistic discrimination due to the uneven distribution of training data across languages.… We conduct this analysis with two datasets … The results show that LLMs exhibit stronger human alignment capabilities with queries in English, French, Russian, and Spanish … Moreover, for queries in English, Danish, Czech and Slovenian, LLMs tend to produce responses with a higher quality (with 0.1494 F1 score on average) compared to the other languages.
>
> (Dong et al., 2024)

The four languages in the test described above belong to two Western European language groups and belong to countries that share considerable intellectual overlap. Since much of the academic writing today is in English because of the dominance of English-language journals, it is not clear how much impact the other languages have.

The sources for LLMs matter, because the AI is not just pulling words from a dictionary but is trying to fit the words to a particular context. The right combination of words matters: in many sentences an LLM could pick adjectives that would be grammatically correct but would give the phrase a different meaning. This is one of the areas in which an AI needs some degree of contextual understanding to be effective. That is one reason why large collections of academic articles are a popular choice, because they provide not only a scholarly vocabulary but also context information about what words and phrases belong together.

LLM systems typically go through a pre-training phase. As Mehra (2023) explains, the purpose is to 'establish the fundamental language skills of LLMs'. In a sense, LLMs are like small children who must learn how to use words:

> Most LLMs use general data, such as web pages, books, and conversations, as their pre-training corpus because it is abundant, diverse, and easily accessible. This helps improve their language modeling and generalization skills.... It is important to preprocess the collected text data to create a pre-training corpus for LLMs to remove noise, redundancy, irrelevance, and potentially harmful content.
> (Mehra, 2023)

What to exclude from the pre-processing is as important as what to include. Removing duplicates matters too: 'At the sentence level, low-quality sentences that contain repetitive phrases or words should be removed to avoid introducing repetitive patterns into the model' (Mehra, 2023). Wikipedia, Google data and government data are commonly used as sources because they are large, diverse and tend to be free of copyright problems.

As with training children to speak, the training process for LLMs depends on teachers, in this case the models. 'During training, the model is presented with a sequence of words and is trained to predict the next word in the sequence. The model adjusts its weights based on the difference between its prediction and the actual next word. This process is repeated millions of times until the model reaches a satisfactory level of performance' (Dilmegani, 2024).

Size is a training issue: 'By dividing the model into smaller parts, each part can be trained in parallel, resulting in a faster training process compared to training the entire model on a single GPU or processor' (Dilmegani, 2024).

From an information science perspective, this is another reason why it is important for people to understand how AI systems using LLMs work, because their reliability depends directly on their training. This is another reason why training information and the algorithms need to be made public.

The language models do not actually use words and letters in the way that humans do. The process is called 'tokenisation'. 'Large language model' in Wikipedia (2025o) offers an explanation: 'Because machine learning algorithms process numbers rather than text, the text must be converted to numbers. In the first step, a vocabulary is decided upon, then integer indexes are arbitrarily but uniquely assigned to each vocabulary entry, and finally, an embedding is associated to the integer index.' The process of creating tokens varies from language to language. Wikipedia (2025o) claims that languages like German require 50% more tokens. Wiik (2024) explains: 'This process has traditionally been tailored to each language based on its unique linguistic rules. For instance, an English tokenizer might handle contractions like "don't" by recognizing them as single tokens, whereas a German tokenizer might split compound words to manage token size effectively.'

The tokenisation process adds context tags to indicate whether a word is a noun, verb or adjective. It also captures context elements by creating n-grams. 'N-grams are sequences of "n" consecutive words, which provide a context that single words in isolation do not (e.g. "not good") for capturing negations. They have been essential for building traditional language models that predict the probability of a word based on its preceding words' (Wiik, 2024).

One additional linguistic transformation is to 'stem' the word, which means removing endings, and to 'lemmatise' a word by reducing the various forms to a single word. One additional feature of how LLMs use words is called 'Byte-pair Encoding'. It 'originally started as a data compression technique and was later adapted for use in natural language processing as a tokenization technique for subwords.... The algorithm starts with a vocabulary of individual characters and repeatedly merges the most frequent adjacent pairs of tokens into single tokens.... This approach helps manage a language model's vocabulary size ...' (Wiik, 2024).

One of the common problems with LLM output is that they lose track of where particular sets of phrases came from, which is a reason why LLM-written essays can have plagiarism problems. How large this problem is remains an open question with very little reliable data, in part because most LLM-produced text have not undergone serious plagiarism checking. That is likely to change as more students and more researchers take advantage of the tools.

One solution is to build plagiarism control into the LLM output process. A disadvantage of that solution could be that detecting LLM-produced writing becomes harder. The broader ethical question is under what circumstances students and researchers should be allowed to submit work as their own intellectual product, when they relied on LLM to do the writing. It is too early to give a reliable answer to this question, because a great deal depends on our understanding of the degree to which authors can control LLM output. An important legal question has to do with copyright: 'The prerequisite for copyright protection for AI supervision and AI-generated content is that human creativity in the materials used to train AI systems can be distinguished, so as to further promote the implementation of more complete legal supervision' (Wu et al., 2024). This represents an area where information scientists can make useful contributions.

AI images and voice

AI systems can generate products other than text, and AI-generated images have become relatively common. There is nothing new about fake images. People and governments have been creating them for decades. The Soviet Union was especially known for doctoring photos when someone fell out of favour. What is new now is the ease with which AI can create convincingly authentic images, even without an original. The same process can be used to create fake audio and video. People create these 'deep fakes' for commercial or political purposes, or for blackmail and harassment. The following incident was described in a 2021 report by the US Department of Homeland Security about the risks of deep fakes:

> Three teenagers, members of a cheerleading program in Bucks County, Pa., received a series of harassing text messages over the course of last summer. So did their parents and the owners of the gym where they practiced. Some of the anonymous messages contained doctored images and videos that attempted to incriminate the teenagers with fake depictions showing some of them nude, drinking alcohol or vaping. At times, the text messages took an even darker turn, telling at least one girl to die by suicide.
>
> (Morales, 2021)

Information scientists should be aware of the degree to which deep fakes can be misused and abused.

The basic technology for creating these images resembles the way in which LLMs work: 'An AI text-to-image generator often makes use of a machine learning technique called artificial neural networks that can receive input in the form of words, which it then processes to generate an image.... However, before they can be reliably deployed, neural networks require a lot of training' ('Alex', 2024).

Images are broken down into tokens, much as is done with LLM. 'Visual tokens are generated through ingenious techniques such as image segmentation, object detection, and feature extraction. By breaking down images into these meaningful visual elements, AI models gain the ability to identify objects, track their movements, and even understand the context of entire scenes' (Kamali, 2023).

As with LLMs, the quality of the training process matters:

> When you enter your words in an AI image generator, you're feeding a computer algorithm (neural network) trained on thousands or millions of images from books, the internet, or other sources. This neural network then analyzes your request to understand the style, shape, color, and overall detail of what you want, relying on the dataset it was trained on to produce the final result. The higher the quality of the dataset, the better the quality of the results.
>
> (Linto, 2024)

Unfortunately, the transparency of the training data is often limited, so that users do not know whose images went into the model. This is an ethical problem for sites offering to make deep fake nudes. Samelson (2024) writes:

> At its core, the technology relies on algorithms that can detect patterns and features within a photograph, such as the outline of clothing and the human body's form beneath it. These algorithms are trained on vast datasets of nude images to understand and replicate the appearance of the human body accurately … Using the learned patterns from its training data, the AI predicts what the person might look like without clothes and generates a new image by replacing the clothing with artificial nudity.

The easy availability of such tools (a simple web search finds them) means that anyone can create nude pictures that look genuine. In societies where nudity is socially unacceptable, deep fake nudes become a basis for blackmail and harassment.

From an information science perspective, deep fakes mean that an image may not be a reliable information source. The same problem applies to video, which AI tools can also fake. In broad technical terms, the same process that is used for words and images works for sound. An algorithm captures voices whose characteristics are stored as tokens, which makes it possible to assemble and reassemble them in different forms. This means that the combination of a person's image, movements and voice can be reformatted in ways that the subject never intended or allowed. Controls on this kind of deep fake are currently as incomplete as copyright controls were earlier, but the consequences can be more embarrassing. Josh Butler (2024) reported in the *Guardian* about an instance in Australia: 'Images of the finance minister, Katy Gallagher, and the foreign minister, Penny Wong, have been used in deepfake investment scam videos in the latest examples of a concerning trend of politicians being used in online fraud.' The same problem can be seen in the USA. Zachary Wolf (2024) reported for CNN: 'One distressing headline out of New Hampshire as voters prepared to cast in-person primary ballots was that a fake version of President Joe Biden's voice had been used in automatically generated robocalls to discourage Democrats from taking part in the primary.'

Political abuse of the technology of deep fakes represents a dark side of AI.

Conclusion

For information scientists, AI can represent a valuable enhancement for analysing, retrieving and representing information when used in ethical and scholarly ways. The hype about AI capabilities will likely fade over time, as it has in the past, once people discovered that AI tools did not eliminate the need for human judgement. The job of the information scientist is not to debunk AI but to explain how to apply it reliably and ethically. In some ways, modern statistical packages represent an earlier form of AI, because they implement complex tasks faster and more reliably than humans, and even make some decisions based on the data. Their results are also more reliable than the calculations most humans do. Reliability is a technical goal to which many fields can and should contribute, but those working on AI technology should not forget the context issues that complicate solutions. Self-driving cars offer a good example. Truly reliable self-driving cars can and likely will save lives, but the AI controlling the car must have a level of environmental awareness that is better than the notoriously imperfect human attention span, whose lapses are common causes of car accidents.

The ethical issues involving AI are at least as complex as the technological issues, and many technicians working on AI have little philosophical training on ethical or legal issues. Deep fakes are just an example of some of the problems that the technology enables. From a programming viewpoint, there is no reason why those creating AI applications could not build controls into their systems to prevent abuses, and from a legal viewpoint there is no reason not to establish laws limiting some of the worst deep fake uses. These are issues where information scientists might reasonably paraphrase Isaac Asimov's famous first law of robotics: an AI may not harm a human or, through inaction, allow humans to come to harm (Wikipedia, 2025p).

CHAPTER 10

Information Behaviour

What is information behaviour?

Marcia Bates (2010) defined information behaviour as

> the currently preferred term used to describe the many ways in which human beings interact with information, in particular, the ways in which people seek and utilize information. Information behavior is also the term of art used in library and information science to refer to a sub-discipline that engages in a wide range of types of research conducted in order to understand the human relationship to information.

When discussing information behaviour, Greifeneder and Schlebbe (2022) also cite Tom Wilson's (2000) definition: 'the totality of human behaviour in relation to sources and channels of Information, including both active and passive information seeking, and information use'. These scholars are primarily describing a modern academic field. An information scientist could also consider the philosophical and historical implications.

The contemporary field of information behaviour focuses on how humans behave towards information. In the academic world information depends largely on language, and philosophers have long recognised that language is not a passive player. For example, Steiner (1987) cites Heidegger as saying: 'Man acts as though he were the shaper and master of language, while in fact language remains the master of man.' In plain terms this means that words as information carriers can have meanings beyond what the speaker or writer intends, since their connotations may express different meanings in different contexts, and because words from one language may not mean the same thing in another. A simple example is that the standard German word for a radiator (*Heizkörper*) does not imply something at all similar to a car radiator (*Kühler*). The former adds heat and the latter removes heat. Cross-language meanings challenge expectations.

How people behave towards information, and how information alters people's behaviour, has changed over time, and is not just a matter of words. Symbols embody complex and variable information that has radically different meanings in different contexts. The Sanskrit word for swastika (सस्वस्तिक) means something like 'conducive to well-being' (Wikipedia, 2025q). The right-facing form of the symbol is as ancient as the Indus Valley civilisations, but its positive meaning changed in the 20th century when the Nazi party adopted it as their symbol and made it synonymous with antisemitism. The symbol did not change, but its 20th-century usage imparted a message that few can look at without remembering its Nazi connotation. There are many other symbols with strong meanings that in some sense speak to people. A simple cross may look like a letter 'T' in some contexts, but can also represent the Christian cross, which has strong religious connotations for church members.

When people encounter new information, their emotional reactions vary. Casual evidence for this is available in the daily newspapers. In terms of classic information seeking, it should be reasonable to think that people look for information they like, but the reality is that people encounter a broad range of information in their daily lives that cannot always be avoided.

Pre-modern information behaviour

Human behaviour towards information in the pre-modern world was different than it is today, in part because modern mechanisms for seeking or understanding information did not exist. Facts sometimes confronted people in ways that did not fit existing intellectual schemes. A comet, for example. Essentially, seeing a comet evoked thoughts that had no relationship to contemporary explanations about an object composed of ice and dust. Today people can find some form of factual information to explain almost everything. The pre-modern world had to struggle with unexpected mysteries, and people had to invent explanations to make sense of what they encountered in a context that they could understand.

As Greifeneder and Schlebbe (2022) write: 'As part of information discovery, *intentional discovery* describes research that assumes that a conscious need for information exists, and that people pursue the information actively.... *Accidental discovery*, in contrast, is classified as the unstructured or unplanned discovery of information and refers to the accidental but useful finding of information.'

In the pre-modern world, accidental discovery was perhaps the norm. Greifeneder and Schlebbe also discuss information 'non-use' and 'non-seeking'. Non-use and non-seeking played a significant role in a world where written records were relatively rare. Information was often purely oral and was easily forgotten, and most people lacked a clear awareness of the formal existence of information sources. People reacted to events, which was the form of information they knew best. The intellectual context meant that people interpreted the information in a different social context than people would today.

Insofar as records exist today about information seeking in the ancient world, that world was so culturally different that people's reactions may seem illogical. Prayer was a common means for getting information, and some records exist about the prayers that people paid monasteries to repeat on their behalf. Some prayers took the form of information wishes, but the wording of the prayers tended to be formulaic. People might pray privately for foreknowledge about the weather, or pray for their crops, or for success in sporting events, or to know what their enemies were plotting – but much of what we think we know is speculation because private prayers were mostly not written down. The ancient military desperately wanted information to give them an advantage in battles, and they recognised the strategic value of information, but their sources tended to be imperfect, despite the best efforts of leaders and spies. Accurate maps represented a reliable information source, but historians know today that, despite the best efforts of commanders, Roman troops in places like England and Germany still lacked the detailed knowledge they needed about the terrain. In other words, the pre-modern world knew relatively little about information seeking and lacked key intellectual mechanisms to improve results.

When people do not understand the causes of events, they try to explain them in terms of their culture. This is a case where facts speak to people in ways that they so poorly comprehend that they have to translate them into something that makes sense. For example, ancient Roman society made no effort to address the Antonine plague of 165–180 CE, despite the huge number of deaths. They had no way of recognising the cause or (in modern terms) the real nature of a disease that was disrupting their society and killing up to one third of the population. They could only react to the plague in terms that made sense to them, and misconceptions about the consequences of the plague persisted for centuries. When William McNeill wrote his book on *Plagues and Peoples* (1976) a common assumption was still that Rome's decline resulted from a form of internal (or moral) 'decadence', rather than as a consequence of depopulation due to the plague. Deaths from diseases like the bubonic plague in the 14th century represented another form of information that was practically invisible to people because they had no mechanism to understand the role of the fleas that carried the bacterium *Yersinia pestis*. The population's behaviour when faced with the fact of the deaths led survivors to self-damaging behaviour such as self-flagellation to purge sins, and pogroms against Jews for causing the deaths (Britannica, 2025d).

Disease was not the only information that people misunderstood and misinterpreted. Today historians believe that the personal political interests of rulers led to wars in early modern times, but at the time the vital importance of religious issues seemed paramount. The Thirty Years' War devastated the core of Europe, much as the fall of the Ming dynasty devastated China. One of the conventional causes of the Ming's fall was the Mongol invasion that overthrew the Ming dynasty, but the fall may also have been a consequence of something less conventionally visible, because the Mongol invasion came at the time of 'the deadliest phase of the Little Ice Age, when temperatures and rainfall plunged and world economies buckled' (Brook, 2023). Recognising the information value of something like an ice age would have taken a level of careful record keeping, combined with the science to understand the consequences of climate change.

Anticipating the consequences of events was hard for people living in an era without systematic record keeping and reliable information sources in libraries or archives. They had little chance to address problems. Today people have better tools and more accurate information to deal with events, but even in modern times people have shown a remarkable ability to ignore factual information when it conflicts with their personal preferences or short-term economic and social interests. Climate change is only one example.

Role of language in information behaviour

Language is not the only means by which people create or communicate information. People need to remember that words often have an information value separate from their dictionary meaning and that language is more than just an information carrier. Steiner (1987) cites Heidegger as saying, 'Language remains the master of man'. The connotations of words themselves provide forms of information that are often intransparent. Words can also change their meanings over time, sometimes in dramatic ways. A common example is the English word 'beauty'. This concept has over the centuries implied quite different body forms in Western culture. The female body type that exemplified beauty in the 17th century can be seen in the paintings of Peter Paul Rubens: the women had a broad expanse of soft white flesh. Three centuries later the model Twiggy presented a very different standard of beauty that emphasised extreme leanness and thinness. The excess flesh of a Rubens nude would today imply overweight and no longer fits an ideal body type. The amount of visible fat on the women could also imply health consequences, even though it was considered healthy at a time when leanness implied poverty. The excessive thinness of the 20th century model Twiggy might have inspired modern young women to anorexia, which is itself dangerously unhealthy.

Even closely related languages like German and English have words that have different connotations and therefore carry different information, which can make translations challenging. An example comes from George Steiner's (1987) discussion of Heidegger's language: '"Innermost basic feature" is an honest attempt at rendering *Grundzug*. In German, and most notably in Heideggerian German, Grund portends intensely concrete but also numerous strains of rootedness, of earthly ancientness and provenance.' The conventional dictionary meaning for the German word '*Grund*' is 'ground' or 'cause' or 'reason', which leaves open many of the implications that Steiner is discussing. A more conventional variation in meaning can be found in the German word for 'dinner'. A dinner is generally a large meal often but not invariably served in the evening. The German dictionary word for dinner is typically '*Abendessen*', which explicitly means evening meal and generally implies a substantial one. A lighter evening meal is often called '*Abendbrot*' (evening bread), which could correspond with the English word 'supper', which often suggests a light meal but does not imply having bread. The English word 'dinner' actually comes from the French term '*dîner*'.

Less closely related languages may have more divergent meanings and connotations. For example, in (simplified) Chinese the characters 火车 mean 'train', but someone who knows Chinese will realise that the first character of the two-character set means 'fire', which is a reminder of the origin of trains as coal-fired vehicles. The combinations of meanings in words often gives a clue to subconscious implications. The traditional version of the character 车 (車) gives a clue to its meaning: the four squares in the centre represent wheels for the classical Chinese chariots. Word etymology often gives a clue as to meaning. Even when the early meanings of words are largely forgotten, they can influence contemporary understanding. Examples of this abound. The game that Americans call 'soccer' is called football in most of the rest of the world, and the reason is historical. Cunningham (2023) explains: 'Linguistically creative students at the University of Oxford in the 1880s distinguished between the sports of "rugger" (rugby football) and "assoccer" (association football).... By the 20th century, rugby football was more commonly called rugby, while association football had earned the right to be known as just plain football.' Why the Americans and Canadians adopted the British term is apparently unknown. Football can literally just be any ball game played with the foot. Associations play a key role in both football (soccer) and rugby because it is the associations that determine the rules.

Words involving politics were especially subject to divergent meetings in the early 20th century. When the Soviets spoke about democracy, they meant a political system with elections controlled by the Communist Party, which many observers from Western countries called a dictatorship, even though voting rights were (technically at least) widespread. At this point, there is no special word for countries that allow large amounts of corporate spending to influence the results of voting. The cultural context in the West sees a meaningful difference between party influence and financial influence, and might even be shocked if someone equated the two. For Western Europe, democracy has often meant voting for members of a parliament, who in turn elect a prime minister, whose role is generally more important than that of the country's president. The only major European country with a strong president is France.

At the beginning of the 20th century, democracy primarily meant voting rights only for men. It took decades of political pressure before women received the right to vote, and the expansion of voting rights changed at different times in different countries. Women first received the right to vote in the Soviet Union (1917), followed by Germany in 1918, the UK in 1918 (but only for women over 30, and not until a decade later for women over 21), the United States in 1920, France in 1944 and China in 1954 once the People's Republic was firmly established. Insofar as the word democracy implies voting rights, its practical meaning depends on the local context and its traditions. Nonetheless, some historians and commentators act as if the word has a clear fixed meaning.

Information reliability

Information excess does not necessarily imply an overabundance of usable information, but an overabundance of distractions that are labelled as information and are sometimes even false. An important aspect of human information behaviour is learning how to distinguish unimportant or even wrong information from information that is genuinely (at least partly) useful. Ideally, people never seek flawed or dubious information, but it is often hard to avoid, perhaps especially in societies with limited information sources, where every form of news can seem interesting. Gossip may seem like a good source of local information, even though it is not always reliable. Proper information behaviour means learning how to distinguish between the fake and the real, especially when fake news seems more attractive.

In pre-modern times, excess information often came from gossip, both because there were few other sources and because people naturally took an interest in the people and events surrounding them. There was no way to check the reliability of local gossip, except to ask more neighbours, which could lead to rumours. Accusations of witchcraft in the form of gossip were common in Europe in medieval and early modern times, and could result in persecutions, trials, even burning women to death. Gossip could cause other forms of panic too, especially if times were bad and leading local figures believed the gossip. In a local context sometimes people with social 'standing' could serve as a reliability check, but measures of plausibility and reliability often had more to do with preserving order than with truth. In other words, mechanisms for testing the reliability of information relied less on facts than on people, except in cases where information that would count today as facts was too obvious to ignore.

Once newspapers became widely available, people had access to an external source of information that was not always reliable but was mostly better than neighbourhood gossip. On a modest scale, newspapers had been around in China since the Tang dynasty and in Germany and the Netherlands since the early 17th century (Britannica, 2025e). The Chinese version largely contained official news from the imperial court. The European newspapers were not official and often faced official censorship, which may have had a modestly positive effect in making publishers cautious. In later 19th-century Germany, publishers often named someone to be a '*Sitzredaktur*', that is, an editor whose job it was to sit in prison when the authorities wanted to crack down on publications they disliked. The truth of a newspaper's claims did not necessarily prevent the arrest, because many governments disliked reliable information that exposed their own failings.

The political opinions of so-called tabloid newspapers have tended to be right wing and nationalist, insofar as the tabloids offer any actual news with factual substance. Mostly they have focused on selling their papers to an audience that would not read complex stories with unfamiliar vocabulary, and have made their content as sensational as possible. Sexual innuendo was an especially popular way of attracting readers, as in this American example: 'Sometimes the publishers wanted to inflame a situation such as during the weeks before the Spanish-American war of 1898. The famous Hearst newspaper drawing of male Spanish authorities strip searching a woman was successfully inflammatory, but was wrong in several respects: the woman was Cuban, not American, and the searchers were women, not men' (Campbell, 2014, cited in Seadle, 2022, 33).

The best-known German tabloid, *Bild Zeitung*, was famous for headlines like that of 9 July 1984 on its 40th anniversary: '80 naked women locked up' (Bild Zeitung, 1984). Vicki Barker (2015) reported on the US National Public Radio that 'Britain's most popular newspaper will reportedly stop featuring photos of topless women on its pages. *The Sun* began its "Page 3" pictures 44 years ago …'. The sensationalism represented a form of information excess that drove out more serious sources.

The same has happened since the advent of social media on the internet. The Pew Research Center's 'Social Media and News Fact Sheet' (2023) stated: 'Today, half of U.S. adults get news at least sometimes from social media.' In the decades after World War 2, a few well-established newspapers and news broadcasters served as the main respectable sources for the educated middle class. A common criticism was that they represented the 'establishment' and deliberately excluded some kinds of information. This criticism was especially common among American students opposed to the war in Vietnam. Ben Kamisar (2024) reports that 'Among registered voters, 54% described themselves as primarily traditional news consumers, while 40% described themselves as primarily digital media consumers.' This split affects voting preferences.

It could be that news preferences determine election results. Polls involving people who rely on social media for news could affect the reliability of election predictions, even in a relatively traditional country like India. *Guardian* reporter Ellis-Petersen (2024) wrote: 'According to a flurry of exit polls released on Saturday night, Modi and his Bharatiya Janata party (BJP) are looking at a decisive win and may even gain seats to win a two-thirds majority in parliament, which would allow the government to make far-reaching amendments to the constitution.' In fact Modi did significantly less well than expected and did not get a majority in the Loc Saba (parliament). He had to rely on coalition partners to remain prime minister.

Some problems with information excess are traceable to unreliable popular sources. Fears about vaccines during the COVID-19 pandemic represent just one well-documented way in which unfounded reports cost lives, and many of those fears persist. Reports that discount climate change evidence offer another example. The problem is not just that multiple conflicting sources of information exist, but the very human inclination to disbelieve inconvenient news.

Information gaps

Information gaps represent the reverse of information excess. The gaps make people seek answers as best they can. Information seeking represents a standard topic in information behaviour and there is substantial research about it. Medical information seeking is typical and may account for as many as half of the searches on Google. However, the scholarly literature is not a source that the general public searches with much regularity, perhaps because the formal language of academic journals can seem opaque to ordinary readers. In other words, there are at least two forms of information gaps that information scientists need to consider: gaps for scholars, and those for the broader public.

The gaps for scholars cause fewer problems, because most scholars are accustomed to searching for information, and many electronic tools make the process easier, among them Google Scholar. There is no official measure of how large Google Scholar is, but a somewhat outdated estimate by Orduna-Malea et al. (2015) is 'around 170–175 million unique records (regardless the number of versions of each record)'. Some estimates of the various scholarly databases put the numbers higher: 'The results show that based on QHC [Query Hit Count], Google Scholar, WorldWideScience, and ProQuest ... are by far the largest systems providing scholarly information, with each containing about 300 million records' (Gusenbauer, 2019).

It is reasonable to assume that many of the entries in these databases are duplicates. This means from an information science perspective that the problem of scholarly information gaps begins to resemble the problem of information excess, with the important difference being that the information in these databases ought to be reliable.

The fact that articles appear in these respectable databases does not guarantee their reliability. The *Retraction Watch* blog reports regularly on problems in the academic journal literature. Anna Abalkina (2024) wrote in *Retraction Watch*, 'I've cataloged 67 cases since 2013 of hijacked journals penetrating the [Scopus] database. I found 23 profiles of journals that contained links to a cloned version, and 33 cases of content from the cloned version of a journal that had not been peer reviewed appearing in the profile of the legitimate journal, while 11 did both.' This represents only one example of the availability of hijacked journals in trusted databases, and the expectation is generally that such content may be untrustworthy. In other words, the hijacked journals may actually exacerbate the information gaps, since their review processes fail to catch errors or deliberate falsification. Instead of filling an information gap, they mask it.

Filling information gaps can be especially challenging for non-academics, because the range of tools and resources is more limited. Google and Bing provide answers to many common questions, but even their answers have flaws. One of the most common problems is not the fault of Google or Bing, but of the people who manage the websites they index. Searches for restaurant menus occur commonly, but not every restaurant keeps its online menus up to date, and the restaurant reviews that appear as part of these searches lack reliability. Anyone can fill out a reviewer form, but the sites make no attempt to ensure a random sample of reviews. This means that any customer with strong opinions could mislead readers. Professional restaurant reviewers mostly write for established journals or newspapers, but sites like TripAdvisor allow almost anyone to write a review. Tony Naylor (2013) wrote in the *Guardian*: 'You can't just look at the scores. And to read it in a way that is rewarding, you need to develop a set of personal idiot filters, far more powerful than anything TA could develop to police the site.'

Wikipedia can be a useful source for filling information gaps, but some caution is needed. Wikipedia does not use professional peer-reviewers, but lets any reader correct and update articles. In 2005 Jim Giles wrote in *Nature* that a comparison of Wikipedia and Britannica found that 'Wikipedia comes close to Britannica in terms of the accuracy of its science entries'. Academic assessments are often more cautious, such as this from Harvard College Writing Program (2024):

> There's nothing more convenient than Wikipedia if you're looking for some quick information, and when the stakes are low … Nevertheless, when you're doing academic research, you should be extremely cautious about using Wikipedia. As its own disclaimer states, information on Wikipedia is contributed by anyone who wants to post material … If you do start with Wikipedia, you should make sure articles you read contain citations – and then go read the cited articles to check the accuracy of what you read on Wikipedia.

The *Encyclopedia Britannica* is another readily available general source of information that covers less than Wikipedia, but the Britannica editors often name the authors of articles and do enough fact-checking to protect their brand.

Fake information

Fake information has become a research area for information scientists because of its long-term damaging effects on scholarship and on rational political discourse. Identifying fake information requires a classic set of intellectual tools that have developed over the millennia and that the library community has long cherished as a means of guaranteeing the long-term quality of their collections. Fake information has a long history, especially in medicine, where claims about unproven cures have long found gullible consumers. Claims about cures generate non-trivial amounts of fake information, especially when they seem to have a small element of truth. Virtually every form of inoculation against diseases like smallpox or polio or COVID-19 carries a risk of negative side-effects. Such risks are not fake, but some people publicise the risks so loudly that they gain salience in some communities.

The first wide-scale use of inoculation against a specific disease was against smallpox, and it became available in the UK in the 19th century. The vaccination involved using pus from infected cows. Jess McHugh (2021) wrote:

> Just as quickly as doctors heralded Edward Jenner's revolutionary 1796 discovery that the deadly smallpox virus could be prevented with a cowpox vaccine, some Brits met the news with a superstitious distrust that bordered on hysteria. Opposition to vaccination would grow and evolve over the next 100 years to become one of the largest mass movements of 19th-century Britain. People refused the vaccine for medical, religious and even political reasons …

The opposition came also from within the medical establishment, and reflects some of the differences in the nature of medical training then and now:

> In an 1805 pamphlet, William Rowley, a member of the Royal College of Physicians, warned against vaccination, threatening the direst possible side effects. Rowley (among others) went so far as to suggest that the injection of cow material into a human body could cause a person to begin to resemble a cow, sprouting actual horns out of his head and hoofs in place of feet.
>
> (McHugh, 2021)

Medical research responded to the COVID pandemic with vaccines that provided protection against the worst effects of COVID-19, but a non-trivial portion of the American public expressed concerns, as Funk et al. (2023) reported: 'A majority of those who have not been vaccinated say it makes them angry when COVID-19 vaccines are required (67% say this describes their views very well) and nearly as many (60%) say the idea that public health officials are not telling us everything they know about the vaccines describes their views very well.' Political leadership can play a role: 'Democrats are about twice as likely as Republicans to say the benefits of coronavirus vaccines outweigh the risks (84% vs. 40%).' (Funk et al., 2023). Smith (2022) wrote about Donald Trump in the *Guardian*: 'The ex-president's customary applause turned to jeers when he encouraged supporters to get vaccinated and told O'Reilly that he received a booster himself.'

Information scientists can do little to combat fake information except to expose it with cogent and convincing facts, and to teach everyone how to distinguish fake from real information. The latter is especially hard because convincing people does not just involve academic logic but also the logic of readers, which invariably depends on their context. Context for fake information can involve education or scientific background, but more often involves what people's friends and neighbours believe, what their sources of news are and their political leanings. Ivan Oransky's *Retraction Watch* plays an important role in exposing fake information in the scholarly world, but it is just one voice – not quite a small voice in the wilderness, since many scholars (and information scientists) follow his posts, but not all publishers or universities take sufficient or appropriate action. Information scientists must always remember that economic interests and personal lifestyle can have a more decisive influence than science or pure logic.

Conclusion

If information behaviour is, as Marcia Bates wrote, the way that people interact with information, then the scope is enormous, and those interactions change constantly over time as new information and new needs arise. In the ancient world people trusted different information sources than scholars accept today. The trust mechanisms in their context relied on authorities for advice that lacked scientific reliability, which from a modern perspective meant that they had more fake information to deal with.

One of the key points in this chapter is that information itself is a player in how people behave towards concepts of information. The choice of language matters because words count as a chief information source and languages express a range of implicit meanings and connotations that can shift how people understand the information they read or hear. Oral communication is especially sensitive to the tone of voice and accent. A person with a lower-class accent may have less credibility with an academic audience, and more with a group that itself identifies with the way the person speaks. Songs can give words important subliminal information, as can images and smell. Smell is not one of the senses that humans rely on heavily for information, especially not in the modern world where electronic information sanitises any direct signals of smell or taste or feel, which must then be conveyed indirectly with words or images or not at all. Information scientists need to take all of this into account when considering people's information behaviour.

CHAPTER 11
Data Science

What is data science?

IBM's corporate website (IBM Corp., 2021) provides the following definition of data science: 'Data science combines math and statistics, specialized programming, advanced analytics, artificial intelligence (AI) and machine learning with specific subject matter expertise to uncover actionable insights hidden in an organization's data. These insights can be used to guide decision making and strategic planning.' This is a relatively neutral definition that reflects how many academic programmes understand data science, and the resemblance to computer science is not accidental. For US programmes especially the market implications for graduates play a role in why data science has become popular. Some see it as a soft form of computer science with lower maths requirements and no pressure to learn the more difficult computing languages. If a data science programme actually offered everything in the IBM definition, it could compete well with the average computer science programmes, but the reality is that many programmes offer much less serious technical training and rely on the marketing value of the name.

At present the term 'data science' appears in 112,000 entries in Google Scholar, but few attempt to define it clearly. One example is Nasution et al. (2023), who wrote a chapter called 'What Is Data Science' in a book on *Data Science with Semantic Technologies*. The authors begin by saying, 'Without realizing it, data have been companions to humans throughout their existence'. Information scientists can readily agree, since data is a form of information. Understanding data 'across various scientific fields – such as medicine and health, agriculture and production, engineering and industry, etc. – requires transformation into one general concept that is systematic and organized' (Nasution et al., 2023). A key question is whether a single general concept can include all the nuances of the fields they list.

A more critical description of data science can be found in a 2023 article by Seadle and Havelka: 'Data are the eunuchs of the information world because data and data sets are functionally sterile and meaningless without reference to the intellectual, spatial, temporal, and social environment that represents their context. A serious researcher can prove nothing with data without knowing where they came from and what they mean.' The point of this description is that the strong focus on processing data leaves out essential questions about the meaning of data in the broader intellectual and social context. Anyone who has worked in a corporate computing environment at more than entry level should know that processing data is effective only when the purpose, the nature and the use of the data are clear. Useful data cannot be reduced to meaningless lumps of bits and bytes. Understanding the mechanics of how to process data matters only when the value of data is understood and the purpose is clear.

Of course the best data science programmes do not ignore the meaning and purpose of data, but those elements are core to information science. The University of California's Berkeley School of Information (2024) has a well-regarded data science programme which describes itself as 'A Rigorous, Holistic Curriculum: The multidisciplinary online data science master's curriculum draws upon computer science, social sciences, statistics, management, and law. Students use the latest tools and analytical methods to work with data at scale, derive insights from complex and unstructured data, and solve real-world problems.' It also includes 'Information ethics and privacy' and 'Machine learning' (Berkeley School of Information, 2024). The breadth of this programme may reflect the iSchools connection in addition to Berkeley's long-standing intellectual tradition.

The Ludwig Maximilian University in Munich (LMU) has a programme that describes data science as:

> the science of extracting knowledge and information from data and requires competencies in both statistical and computer-based data analysis. Students learn statistical and computational methods for collecting, managing, and analysing large and complex data sets and how to extract knowledge and information from these data sets. The program also comprises courses on data security, data confidentiality, and data ethics.
>
> (LMU Munich, 2024)

A third example of a data science programme is the School of Information at Sheffield University (UK). Sheffield offers students 'a set of fundamental principles that support ethical extraction of information and knowledge from data. Case studies will help to show the practical application of these principles to real life problems' (Sheffield University, 2024). The description goes on to include 'practical skills in handling structured and unstructured data, analysing and visualising data, data mining, as well as gaining hands-on experience of software tools used and their use in real-world settings'.

These are only three examples of the many international institutions that offer data science programmes. Common elements in these programmes are topics like statistics, ethics and privacy or confidentiality. What is striking is not only the overlap with computer science and statistics but the absence of topics not directly relevant to the job market. For many schools of information science, data science offers a way to re-envision their library science past in order to improve their job-market appeal by discarding much of the old humanist content.

A goal of this chapter is to describe where data science and information science converge, and what elements a data science programme ought to consider.

Data before 1800

Knowledge about units of information that would today be called 'data' certainly existed in pre-modern times, well before there were digital computers to process them. Some of the oldest Sumerian records were accounting records, and the information recorded in the clay tablets was a form of financial data by any modern definition. Ashley Huang (2017) describes a Sumerian abacus that 'had a clay board that was scored with columns. The columns were numbered from right to left in increasing magnitudes of 10s or 60s. They had shaped clay tokens that were assigned numeric values, in units of 1s, 10s, 60s, 600s, and 3600s. To represent a number, they place the tokens in the board columns (Wikipedia, 2025k).' This abacus has a different appearance than the Chinese suanpan (算盘) from the Han dynasty, and also from the modern abacus, but intellectually the principle was essentially identical (Norman, 2004). Neither Sumaria nor Han China used a decimal system, but results from calculations were comprehensible and reliable, which made them ideal numerical data-processing tools.

Financial records were not the only form of data that needed processing in the pre-modern world. Almost every person and physical object counted as data that needed to be allocated into categories to become useful. For example, the military needed information about how many soldiers were available in what location at what time. Their training mattered, as well as the arms that were available and how well the soldiers could use them. Information about transportation was equally important in a world where getting from one place to another involved keeping track of shoes, horses, ox carts, and boats or ships for longer journeys. In the modern world it is easy to discount the importance not only of knowing these data points but of allocating them to categories that made sense, even though precision was hard. In the time of Julius Caesar the Roman army structured its military in units called 'centuries' because the centuries were supposed to have 100 men with a 'centurion' to command them. In fact the units rarely stayed at full strength. However, the weapons were standardised. They included a shield, a short sword and a spear, and no army could remain effective without some reserve of these standard-issue items.

An important form of data in earlier eras was the status of people. For example, the Roman and Greek societies included slaves, who had obligations towards their owners but also had more rights than did American slaves in later centuries, and keeping track of those rights mattered. Knowing the skill sets of a slave mattered too, since they were not used only for hard labour in the fields. In the ancient world they might be teachers or skilled in a particular craft. Records about a person's religion represented another form of information that mattered in a society with a range of greater and lesser gods and cults. Roman emperors before Constantine regarded Christianity as potentially dangerous, and the government periodically attempted to eliminate them, which for the Christians increased the importance of keeping track (often secretly) of who their members were and where they were.

In the ancient and medieval worlds, the only way to handle most forms of non-numerical data was to record it in appropriate categories. Often this organisation occurred orally by repeating facts about people, places and things. Poetry was a good memory tool. The degree to which memory worked varied widely. Literate people kept written records, but there is no clear agreement on the level of literacy in the Roman Empire, and likely it varied over time. Generous estimates suggest 15%, but without a clear scholarly basis. Leonard Curchin (1995), writing about Spain, suggests at most 5–10%, which may be low for urban centres like Rome. From an information science viewpoint this means simply that data science, insofar as it could exist at the time, had limited capacity for analysis.

Smaller communities could sometimes cope better with data just because fewer details were involved. Specialisation helped, of course. Those responsible for a particular landholding needed only to remember the traditional implements and people and crops. Military commanders needed only to remember how their units worked. Since major changes were rare, memory functioned moderately well. The farming technology tended to remain the same in particular locations in most societies, in part because no one invented new tools or planted new crops as long as the old ones served the purpose and markets remained stable. That is not to suggest that no change occurred. Weather problems, invasions, illnesses all disrupted the mechanisms for categorising the data of the time. The market changes occurred mostly because of external circumstances, not because entrepreneurs had ideas. Entrepreneurs mostly did not exist. This meant that the aspects of modern data science which are focused on analysing change had little relevance.

The situation changed in the medieval world, not because new forms of processing data came into being but because growing literacy and the invention of printing increased the number of people who could handle more and more complex data. The situation in China was not fundamentally different, though literacy probably remained very limited until after the Communist revolution. A UNESCO report by Tiedao Zhang (2005) suggests that '[t]he fifth national census in 2000 shows that, the illiterate population of above 15 years of age has decreased to 86 million, that is, a 100 million reduction of illiterate population during the last 10 years …'. Printing was of course well established in China by European medieval times, which meant that Chinese institutions had the means for recording data.

Data 1800–1950

From an information science viewpoint, the situation began to change in the 17th century, due to factors such as a substantial increase in international trade. Trade meant more information about a range of unfamiliar foods, objects and cultures, and that meant that the 'data science' of the time needed new categories. Contact with India meant, for example, new religions, new spices, and new ways of thinking mapped imperfectly to existing ways of organising knowledge.

Unfamiliar languages counted as a new form of data, and linguistic scholars worked hard on understanding their roots and linkages. Fellmann (1978) writes: 'It is customary in the linguistic literature to date the first scientific Sanskrit grammar written by a European to the Grammar of the Sankrita Language of Sir Charles Wilkens, published in London in 1808 …' Fellmann (1978) also notes that in fact the earliest Sanskrit grammar 'may be dated ca. 1660, being composed by the German missionary Heinrich Roth, a native of Augsburg … His work, it is true, was never published, and thus had no effect in Europe …'

The main spoken language in northern India is called Hindustani and includes both modern Hindi (written in the Devanagari script) and Urdu (written in the Persian script). Anna Pytlowany (2018) wrote: 'To any Indologist, *Instructie off Onderwijsinge der Hindoustanse en Persiaanse talen*

(1698) is instantly recognizable as the iconic "first grammar of Hindustani" – just as the name of its author, Joan Josua Ketelaar, is familiar to scholars of Dutch colonial history.' Recognition for the southern Indian languages came slightly later. Krishnamurti (2024) wrote: 'In 1816, Englishman Francis Whyte Ellis of the Indian Civil Service (at the time a division of the East India Company) introduced the notion of a Dravidian family.'

Merchants in the 18th century understood the importance of language for their business, not just to sell their products but to understand the meaning of new foods or objects or tools or anything quantifiable. Data ideally included metadata to explain meaning and context, which was no less important than it is today. Before 1950 language was the chief analytical tool to let people analyse and categorise valuable discoveries. A simple example was the American fruit called tomato and the vegetable called potato, both of which grew to have culinary value in Europe. When travellers encountered them, they had to learn from the natives what they were. It took decades before their popularity reached a point where counting them had commercial value. According to Giulia Bortolotti (2023), 'It wasn't until 1694 that the first recipe using tomatoes was published in the Bel Paese – courtesy of Neapolitan chef Antonio Latini and his book "Lo Scalco alla Moderna" ("The Modern Steward"). It was not until the nineteenth century that the tomato found its way across Italian kitchens beyond Naples.' The potato arrived in Europe with the Spanish explorers, but, as a potentially poisonous nightshade, the plant did not gain acceptance until the 17th century. It became important as a food source once the population exploded and potatoes were needed as a cheap source of nutrition (Wikipedia, 2025r).

The Industrial Revolution occurred at quite different times in different countries. Generally, historians talk about it starting in the UK, which is true for certain aspects like coal mining and iron smelting, and people often associate trains with the Industrial Revolution, but Iowa State University (2016) claims that 'Railways existed as early as 1550, in Germany. These pathways of wooden rails called "wagonways" were the beginning of modern rail transport, making it easier for horse-drawn wagons or carts to move along dirt roads.' Data about maintenance needs was critical. In the early 19th century data about railway tracks, the condition of the engines, the number of passengers mattered, and could only be managed using ink and paper tools, plus a good understanding of what information mattered. Ticket sales in particular required a level of social organisation to take in money, give out paper tickets and to make sure that only legitimate passengers boarded the trains.

Today data scientists might care about the algorithms for calculating ticket prices, for which there was no precedent except by analogy with travel by horse-powered carriages. The price was within the reach of many citizens, including those willing to ride in discomfort on the carriage roof. Speed was a major attraction of the railway in its earliest days. Increasingly, people also valued the distance they could travel in a comparatively short time. The data for calculating what a middle-class traveller might pay was not available in any modern sense. The railways substituted a broad range of information including expectations, needs and the subtle attraction of modern technology, all of which an information scientist understands as part of the context of the time.

Data in context

As noted earlier, one of the key differences between information science and data science is an awareness of context as a decisive factor. Descriptions of data science focus relentlessly on modern applications. While the context for data science is largely contemporary business and operational needs, this will likely change over time, as long as data science graduates from top schools remember the librarian's and the information scientist's awareness of the importance of contextual breadth. A focus on the present is typical of technical fields trying to make an impact, and it is only after they mature that they remember the past. The path is not always straightforward. A century ago, economics had a strong historical sense, which economists later rejected in favour of a belief in timeless mathematical models. Once the algorithms ceased to appear to solve all problems, the interest in history revived. It is hard to reduce something as complex as human behaviour to an algorithm. Change over time is typical. When computer science was new, its training emphasised pragmatic technical aspects such as writing programs. It was not unusual for a doctoral project to deal with compilers. Today, sophisticated computer science dissertations discuss behavioural as well as technical issues. Doubtless, data science will change too.

One of the most data-centric professions is actuarial science, and those who want to become actuaries need proficiency in mathematics because risk analysis depends heavily on probability calculations. For decades, computers have done most of the actual calculating. An actuary must understand the math, but must also understand the nature of the risks. Life insurance is a typical example. It matters whether the person or persons in question are male, because the risk factors are different for men than for women. It is also important whether they smoke, or are overweight, or have a history of high blood pressure. Understanding the meaning of the data matters more than the simple processing of the data points. The best universities do not generally offer programmes explicitly called actuarial science. Future actuaries at top universities generally get degrees in mathematics or perhaps in business. One of the future risks for data science could be that it becomes so narrowly focused on the processing aspects that top universities lose interest.

Data science programmes often mention topics on data ethics and confidentiality, and the legal issues surrounding data have received more attention in recent years as the EU's General Data Protection Regulations (GDPR) have come into legal force in most EU countries, which means that companies wanting to do business in the EU must comply. Karthik Kashyap (2022) reported in the *Spiceworks* blog that a 'study found that 94% of [US] companies that must comply with GDPR were partially or [completely] non-complian[t] with the requirements'. Here is an example: 'Ireland's Data Protection Commission (DPC) yesterday announced the conclusion of an ongoing investigation involving WhatsApp regarding the violation of GDPR laws. Accordingly, DPC slapped the instant messaging service provider with a record €225 million fine' (Kashyap, 2021). It is certainly true that many people do not understand GDPR compliance, partly because the regulations are complex, but perhaps also because the US corporate world shows little interest in non-US regulation. An interesting question will be to what degree US data science programmes cover GDPR and other foreign laws.

China also has data protection laws. Arendse Huld (2023) wrote: '2023 saw the implementation of several new regulations on data protection and cybersecurity in China, with a particular focus on cross-border data transfer and personal information protection. However, in an effort to improve the business environment, China's cybersecurity authorities are also considering easing some requirements on multinationals and foreign companies.'

Different legal frameworks add complications to teaching students about data ethics and confidentiality, because it is not always clear what the laws may or may not allow, especially for those who cannot read the laws in the original language. Context issues force themselves on data science programmes more and more, which may well mean in the end that these programmes resemble information science with a name that seems more marketable in some locations.

Types of data

The argument of this section is that data are too complex to pretend to have any inherent uniformity. Data science, no less than information science, always needs to deal with a range of information types and formats. If all data were simple units representing something concrete, managing data would be relatively straightforward, but even data durability represents a complex topic. Simple examples abound: canned foods are not unchanging things, and now always have expiration dates. Clothes go out of fashion, and computers age at variable speeds, depending partly on the manufacturer, but their useful lifetime rarely exceeds a decade. Financial data are even less immune to change. The amount of money in a bank account may seem to represent something stable, but inflation can erode its value, as can bank charges. Interest payments may increase, which is also a value change. The point is that managing data of almost every sort means looking beyond the data themselves. Any good data science programme, like every good information science programme, must take these complicating factors into account.

Perhaps the simplest types of data include counts of what is happening at any one time. Countries with speed limits often have devices that track the speed of vehicles in a particular location at a particular time. The number of cars violating the speed limit represents concrete data points, which data scientists could compare to similar numbers at similar locations, assuming the measurements were all done using the exact same numerical speed limit rather than ones with a grace period calibrated to accept variations. Even then, true standardisation is hard, given cultural and other variables: a tolerance for speeding is greater in some countries and in some US states than in others. That does not make the data wrong, but it can and probably should influence any analysis.

Voter surveys are an area where counting may seem standardised, but answers to surveys vary depending on the reliability of the sample and on how honestly respondents answer. David Dutwin (2024), writing in *Scientific American*, explains that one problem with election polls is that people change their minds. Further:

> Second, polls have real margins of error, which are reported too modestly. True ranges of error in election polls average around 5 percent, and many elections are won and lost with much smaller margins. Third, election polls have a unique characteristic not encountered in any other survey: they survey a population that does not (yet) exist. Election pollsters must predict who will actually vote. Their likely-voter models tend to be 80 percent accurate, leaving quite a bit of imprecision in deciding who among those polled should actually count in a 'horse race' estimate.
>
> (Dutwin 2024)

Predicting outcomes represents an attractive goal for any form of scholarship, but the most reliable analysts are cautious. Elliott Morris (2024) wrote on *FiveThirtyEight* that '538 uses polling, economic and demographic data to explore likely election outcomes'. He adds the caveat: 'It's not meant to "call" a winner, but rather to give you a sense of how likely each candidate is to win.'

In theory, data from natural sciences like physics ought to generally be unambiguous, which is how scientists understood 'atoms' at one time, but even the true nature of an atom has become complicated since the early 20th century, when Niels Bohr proposed a new model for the structure of an atom that included electrons, protons and neutrons. The model became more complex over time as Max Planck developed the concept known today as Planck's Constant and Albert Einstein described the nature of special and general relativity. Further research into the nature of elementary particles continues to refine how scientists understand their interactions. Even at the most atomic level, data are rarely just data, though there are occasions when it makes sense to treat them as if they were, in order to discover something new.

Biological data are even more varied than physics data. Even one-celled organisms have considerable variety and structure and can have very different effects on human bodies, depending on their genetic make-up. The complexity of living data means most forms of processing such data need to take factors into account that could affect the meaning of the result. Cattle ranchers, for example, need data about the herd they are bringing to the market, and that data needs to include not only the number but the types of cattle, their health and, ideally, their weight to be sure that the dealers who buy them do not cheat.

For human medicine the data issues are more involved, and over-simplification can be dangerous. When the World Health Organization (WHO) collects data, it must rely on its members. WHO (2024) writes that 'A core component of WHO's support to Member States is to strengthen their capacity to collect, compile, manage, analyze and use health data mainly derived from population-based sources (household surveys, civil registration systems of vital events) and institution-based sources (administrative and operational activities of institutions, such as health facilities).'

Unfortunately, the quality criteria for these data are not always transparent, and agencies must make do with what they can get. Collecting health data even in a developed country can involve politics. An example comes from the COVID-19 pandemic, when then US President Donald Trump 'encouraged his top health officials to study the injection of bleach into the human body as a means of fighting Covid' (McGraw and Stein, 2021). His suggestion appears to have had no basis in fact, but may well have sent researchers on a quest for worthless data. The US National Institute on Aging (2023) put together a set of criteria when checking sites. What they do not say is how to know whether the data in the recommendations are trustworthy, only that they should come from experts.

Public and private data

Rules about data privacy are both legal and cultural. Some extremes are clear: access to data about state secrets, especially military secrets, are generally restricted. Julian Assange 'spent nearly seven years in the Ecuadorian embassy in London in an effort to avoid prosecution and an additional five years in British prison fighting extradition to the United States' (Ray, 2023). The data that Assange exposed had a level of protection that showed it was clearly not for public consumption: 'Numerous independent cybersecurity experts and U.S. law enforcement agencies confirmed that the data had been obtained by hackers associated with Russian intelligence agencies' (Ray, 2023).

Most data exposure cases do not result in imprisonment, but some end up in law suits. A British website run by the registered charity Protect writes on its blog: 'Under the DPA [Data Protection Act], there are a number of civil and criminal offences relating to the breach of personal data. However, the broadest, most serious, and most likely to apply is that of "unlawfully obtaining personal data" (section 170(1))' (Protect, 2024). The rules vary from country to country, but many corporations are ready to take legal action against people exposing their data.

The risks for exposing personal information depend on the kind of information and the circumstances. Most universities today have rules about what questions their researchers can ask in a survey, and what steps they must take to protect any data that subjects give them. The University of Sheffield, for example, has a policy that 'covers any staff or students who may be involved in research or other activity that requires them to process or have access to personal data (see section 2.2), for instance as part of a research project or as part of professional practice activities' (Thompson, 2024). The policy goes on to list exactly what is included: 'Personal data is any information relating to a living individual who can be directly or indirectly identified, by reference to an identifier, such as a name, an identification number, location data, or an on-line identifier or to one or more factors specific to the physical, physiological, genetic, mental, economic, cultural or social identity of that person' (Thompson, 2024). This means that scholars doing social research must know how to make the data they collect as anonymous as possible, and must have ways of keeping it secure. Many universities now have secure sites where researchers may (and ought to) store any form of confidential information.

Some data is meant to be public. Health statistics provide an example, and most countries make the information available at a high level of granularity. These data matter for people who are making travel plans or taking jobs in an unfamiliar location. Physicians often use public health statistics to recommend what inoculations a patient should have when travelling. They must also consider environmental data for patients who have conditions like asthma. Data for travellers can also mean information about public safety, and the differences between purse snatching, armed robbery and rape or murder. One of the problems with public data is that the different levels of aggregation matter, depending on the degree to which aggregation is in fact concealing problems by grouping them. In the US, state legislatures use census data about race and ethnic background to influence where to draw congressional boundaries. The US census data is public, and the details about race, age and location feed into efforts that fit the negative term 'gerrymandering', which is illegal in some locations. One of the reasons for protecting private data is how easily the data can be abused, even in the aggregate.

Conclusion

Data science is not the same as information science, although the two have much in common. Data science today defines itself as a technology field. One of the reasons for this may be that data science is trying to make itself more attractive for corporate recruiters, who want people with strong technical backgrounds. Some corporate recruiters seem to regard information science as being too closely related to the humanist side of library science to fit the needs of their organisations. Data science is a new field that is likely to develop differently in different contexts and different countries as the interest in it grows.

In the 1990s, when universities began to recognise information science as an official academic field, it seemed like an attractive technical specialisation for many students in library schools. At that time the term 'information processing' referred broadly to computing activities, and many of the new information science programmes contained strong technical aspects, such as teaching programming languages to their students. In that sense, information science had a strong resemblance to data science today. It seems reasonable to imagine that the two fields will grow to become indistinguishable in time, regardless of which name takes priority.

CHAPTER 12

Non-verbal Information

What is non-verbal information?

Non-verbal information includes all sources that do not primarily rely on the use of words. One of the advantages of a face-to-face meeting, as opposed to written messages, is that there is more nuanced information in human expressions and in the tone of voice than most people are capable of putting in words. This form of non-verbal information may not count as data in a conventional sense, but it is certainly information that can influence how people understand the meaning of an oral message. The non-verbal information is quintessentially context based, and has strong cultural aspects that do not appear in written form. A facial expression such as a smile or a frown can indicate whether a person takes the information seriously or positively and whether or not the speaker trusts the information. Most people have relatively poor control over their facial expressions, unless they are trained actors. This means that impressions that the speakers might not intend to convey can also be read into their words. Something as simple as a raised eyebrow can make clear how a listener is reacting to a verbal message. A person chairing a meeting, or a teacher leading a class, is generally able to see the listeners' faces and to judge their reactions by reading their expressions.

Tone of voice is another important factor in communicating information. A person who speaks forcefully and clearly gives an impression of control that matters both in politics and in the classroom. The quality of pronunciation also gives a clue about background, and especially about class background for communities where such assumptions matter. Grammar may matter less, but it serves as another indication of educational background and bad grammar can undermine credibility. The degree to which grammar and accent matter varies enormously with the situation. The ability to project one's voice was a factor in public speaking, especially before microphones became ubiquitously available. Even speaking into a microphone requires training, because of the way microphones are tuned. Speaking too loudly into a microphone gives the impression of yelling.

Body language is another indicator of attitudes. Crossed arms may indicate defiance. A person holding both hands up may indicate surrender. A head tilted to one side can indicate doubt. Hand gestures are particularly important: the middle finger raised is the equivalent of an obscenity. 'As in Western cultures, giving someone your middle finger is offensive in Chinese culture, signifying disrespect' (Chairman's BAO, 2024). A hand that is clutching the thumb means wishing someone good luck in German, much as touching wood or knocking on wood represents the same wish in British or American English. In China, wrapping a hand around a fist can signal a good luck wish as well. A handshake is generally seen around the world as a friendly sign. In some cultures it is appropriate for a man to offer a hand to the woman first, and in other cultures that is inappropriate unless the woman herself makes the offer. In Chinese culture, it is typical to let the highest-ranked person go through a door first. In many Western cultures, a polite man always lets the woman go first.

This chapter will look beyond human expressions and practices to discuss the kind of information that images and music embody, as well as the information that smell conveys, even though it is generally the least discussed of the human senses in academic writing.

Pre-modern non-verbal information

Since animals have no formal vocabulary, they must rely entirely on non-verbal channels for information, and the situation was probably similar for early humanoid species. The discovery of language made sharing sensory information easier insofar as the vocabulary sufficed. We know that cultures develop words for things that matter to them. Snow serves as a good example. There is a widespread claim that Eskimos have up to 100 words for snow, because the different types of snow matter to them.

> Even if we exclude the sorts of terms that some have suggested should not count in our tally of snow terms, it still appears that Inupiaq at least has an extensive vocabulary for snow and ice. It would surely be a surprise if Inuit people did not pay special attention to snow and ice, which are important features of the landscape throughout most of the year.
>
> (Kaplan, 2003)

The role of language serves here to confirm the importance of the tactile aspects of snow. It is only through vocabulary that scholars today gain insight into the non-verbal information that has played a role in people's lives.

Sounds certainly played an important role in the lives of early hominids, and play an equally important role once modern humans begin to explore new territories and encounter new phenomena. The roar of a lion can serve as a warning. For hunters, the sound of sheep might indicate where the next meal might come from. The sound of water could have been important to early travellers who had limited means for carrying liquids. Anyone who tends animals will recognise that some sounds express fear, or hunger, or even pleasure. Interpreting these sounds is part of caring for the animal. Some animals communicate with humans using sound in ways that are more effective than others. Cats do not have a vocabulary per se, but purring conveys positive emotion. The domestication of animals may indicate one of the important ways in which people use non-verbal information to understand their environment. Animals communicate without words.

Smell is often an undervalued sense, and yet for early humans it was important because it allowed them to make judgements about the quality and freshness of their food. Rancid meat has a distinct warning smell, and the scent of a flower like belladona can indicate whether it is poisonous. Scent also indicates whether a piece of fruit is ripe enough to eat. Modern vocabulary does a poor job of distinguishing various scents. Yet there are businesses such as restaurants where a good sense of smell is central for the person cooking. Distinct odours from exotic cuisines can give a clear indication of their cultural origin. There is plenty of information available via smell, but most humans either classify it vaguely or ignore it. Some Western organisations make use of certain smells for ceremonial purposes. Incense in a religious service is one clear example. Smell is also a sign that something is no longer fresh and clean. In early modern times people perfumed themselves to hide body odours that modern deodorants disguise. People have often used scents such as sandalwood, or lavender, or jasmine to give the sense that a room is fresh and clean.

In the medieval world, bells had an important social significance that lingers to this day. Arnold and Goodson (2012) wrote: 'By Innocent III's time, bells had long been established at the core of Christian observance. Indeed some historians have thought that the ecclesiastical use of bells stretches back to late antiquity, and various writers have noted the conjunction of bells, liturgy, and community.' The role of bells in telling the time lasted well into the 20th century. For example, alarm clocks use bells to indicate when a person should wake up. In many countries, a bell is used to indicate when classes start in a school, or when there is a recess, or lunchtime, or when it is time to go home. Other uses include doorbells that indicate the arrival of a visitor. Bells also indicate when food is ready to come out of an oven or microwave.

Many other non-verbal sounds play a role in modern life. Honking a car horn in a traffic jam indicates impatience. Distinctive noise makers are often used as part of a New Year's celebration. The sound of a smart phone vibrating is not just a tactile signal, but also an aural one that lets people know someone is trying to reach them. In the American Midwest, people treat the first chirping of a robin as a reliable indication that spring is starting. The importance of hearing sounds can perhaps best be understood through the role that being able to hear appears to have in dementia. A Johns Hopkins University (2022) website reports that 'In a study that tracked 639 adults for nearly 12 years, Johns Hopkins expert Frank Lin, M.D., Ph.D., and his colleagues found that mild hearing loss doubled dementia risk. Moderate loss tripled risk, and people with a severe hearing impairment were five times more likely to develop dementia.' This represents one of many indications of how important sounds are as a source of human information.

Information in paintings

Humans, like most land-based animals, depend heavily on visual information about their surroundings, which is one reason why paintings matter to scholars. Much of what we know today about the life of the ancient Cro-Magnon people comes from the paintings they left in caves in France. The scenes depicted animals that the Cro-Magnon people knew or hunted, and they were not the only early painters. Oktaviana et al. (2024) found Indonesian cave paintings that may be as much as 51,200 years old and depict 'human-like figures interacting with a pig, [which] is now the earliest known surviving example of representational art, and visual storytelling, in the world'.

Such paintings effectively transmitted information well before writing existed. Egyptian pyramids have paintings that survived because the buildings protected them from the weather. China has a long tradition of landscape and other painting that goes back at least to the Zhou and Han dynasties (Wikipedia, 2025s). The wall paintings that the volcanic ash preserved in Pompeii give a vivid picture of Roman life in 79 CE. It was typical that these paintings told stories, such as in a surviving double fresco where 'the god Apollo is seen trying to seduce the priestess Cassandra. Her rejection of him, according to legend, resulted in her prophecies being ignored. The tragic consequence is told in the second painting, in which Prince Paris meets the beautiful Helen – a union Cassandra knows will doom them all in the resulting Trojan War' (Amos et al., 2024).

Paintings played a similar narrative role in the medieval world, especially for those who could not read or write. They often told stories about lives of the saints for whom local churches were named. Paintings played a similar narrative role for Buddhism, both in India and in China. The purpose of painting was often to give concrete shape to figures in stories. Perhaps the most common stories in the Christian world were the birth and crucifixion of Jesus, which painters reproduced again and again. Icons played a significant role in Byzantium, which inherited elements of style from ancient Greek painting. As a general rule, medieval paintings did not produce plausibly accurate human portraits until approximately the 15th century. In the 16th century painters like Pieter Bruegel the Elder began to paint peasant festivals and everyday scenes that continue to serve as valuable sources of information about the social life of the time. Lucas Cranach the Elder produced exceptionally lifelike portraits in roughly the same era. Rembrandt followed in the same tradition with images that continue to be valued in the modern world for their realism. Rembrandt also painted scenes out of the Bible, but with a different tone than the medieval iconography. The visual horror of Rembrandt's painting of the blinding of Samson still upsets some modern viewers. While northern European painters focused on realistic depictions, artists in Italy during the Renaissance favoured images of beauty in idealised portraits. Leonardo da Vinci's *Mona Lisa* is an often admired example of Renaissance portraiture.

Paintings served also to educate people about the ancient Classics. Many paintings reproduced legends that most educated people found familiar. Sandro Botticelli's much-reproduced painting of the *Birth of Venus* in the 1480s is just one example of a story out of Greek mythology. Other popular topics included *Bacchus* (Caravaggio, 1596), *Narcissus* (Caravaggio, 1597–99), *Romulus and Remus Suckled by the Wolf* (Carracci, 1590) and *Venus and Cupid at Vulcan's Forge* (Negretti, 1610).

Northern European paintings also showed changes in social norms. Peter Paul Rubens's paintings offered vast amounts of naked female flesh at a time when public nudity was largely unacceptable, and yet the churches were among his main customers. The historical context of the paintings mattered. Rubens painted many non-religious scenes as well. Rembrandt painted fewer nudes, but the number of his genuine works is widely disputed and has recently been researched by the Staatliche Museen zu Berlin (2016) and the Netherlands Institute for Art History.

Painting is a technically complex activity that involves more than a good eye and manual skill. The key ingredients to make oil paint are pigment and some form of oil like linseed, and an emulsifier, which can be as simple as beeswax. Basic tools are a mortar and pestle to grind the pigment and spread it, a glass base to mix the ingredients and a scale to measure the amounts. Details matter, such as the consistency of the paste that turns into the base for the paint and the exact choice of pigments so that the colour comes out correctly. Drawing is technically simpler because it involves fewer tools, like charcoal or graphite or a carbon ink, plus a surface to draw on, which can be anything that is moderately absorbent. Etching is more complex because it involves incising an image into a metal plate using acid. Wikipedia (2025z) explains: 'In traditional pure etching, a metal plate (usually of copper, zinc or steel) is covered with a waxy ground which is resistant to acid. The artist then scratches off the ground with a pointed etching needle where the artist wants a line to appear in the finished piece, exposing the bare metal.' One use of etching has been in printmaking, which allows the images to be reproduced for a larger audience. Making prints from etchings began in the 16th century in Europe. Printing images using wood blocks was well established in China, but etching did not come to that part of the world until the 17th century. 'While copper-printing can be traced back to the Yuan Dynasty in China, the art of copper-engraving was introduced by the Italian missionary, Matteo Ripa, in 1711' (Walravens, 1997).

Painters do not always try to reproduce exact images, and increasingly in the 19th and 20th centuries Western painters wanted to create an 'impression' or to give 'expression' to ideas they wanted to share. This form of information was not easily reduced to words. The 1884–86 painting by the French artist George Seurat titled *A Sunday Afternoon on the Island of La Grande Jatte* was meant to create a particular mood that is both tranquil but also intentionally somewhat stiff, as were social relationships at the time. The 1881 painting of *Two Sisters (on the Terrace)* by Seurat's contemporary, Pierre-Auguste Renoir, conveys a very different sense of harmony and tranquillity. Pablo Picasso, a Spanish painter who belonged to a somewhat later generation, presented a harsher view of the world, as in his 1937 painting *Guernica,* which described his feelings about the aerial bombing of the city of Guernica during the Spanish Civil war, a painting that remains vivid even after the greater slaughter through bombing in the following decade. Edward Hopper's 1942 painting *Nighthawks,* which shows two lone people at the counter of an all-night New York diner, offers an image of urban loneliness, and Andy Warhol's 1962 painting of variations of *Campbell's Soup* represents a critical commentary on American commercial advertising.

Information in photographs

Photography first became available in 19th-century Europe, after coinciding with a number of other innovations. The ability to project an image on a wall, known as a 'camera obscura', was 'probably known to the Chinese and to ancient Greeks such as Aristotle more than 2,000 years ago. Late in the 16th century, the Italian scientist and writer Giambattista della Porta demonstrated and described in detail the use of a "camera obscura" with a lens' (Grundberg and Gernsheim, 2025). From the viewpoint of an information scientist, this provided little new information, except insofar as people used the projection to record images in greater detail. The lens made details sharper, but the image was fleeting until a more permanent recording technology became available based on the reaction of silver salts to light, as demonstrated by Johann Heinrich Schulze in the 18th century. A French inventor named Nicéphore Niépce began producing something that could be called a photograph in the 1820s. Louis-Jacques-Mandé Daguerre took the process further by using mercury vapour as a catalyst to speed the development process.

From an information science perspective, the importance of photography grew as its audience broadened to include scholars who wanted to record reactions under conditions where words did not suffice to give a full and detailed account. Early cameras were large and heavy and could not be used for most purposes outside of a studio, but by the time of the American Civil War that had changed substantially. Jeff Rosenheim, who organised an exhibition of American Civil War photography at the Metropolitan Museum in New York, writes: 'The Civil War created an incredible demand for photography. It was used by the Union and Confederate armies and of course by regular Americans who wanted photographs of their family members heading into danger, and of the battle scenes themselves' (Hansen and Becker, 2013).

The American Civil War also represents the start of photojournalism. Taking photographs remained a cumbersome operation with cameras that were neither light nor easily transported, and with photographic media that needed careful handling. George Eastman did not develop his highly portable camera and roll film until the 1880s. This technology changed the nature of the information that people could get about distant places or events. Painting and drawing could not compete with the speed and detailed accuracy of cameras. This is one reason why newspapers began to include photographs as early as possible, because they brought an immediacy to the reporting that words could not achieve,

One of the problems with photography was the need to develop the film, which required the right set of chemicals and a 'dark room' where the film could develop. Once roll-based film became available, more professionals began developing their own pictures because it gave them control over the final image and because it allowed both editing and control over brightness.

Black and white film was easier to develop than colour film, because it required fewer chemicals. Small portable cameras made by manufacturers like Kodak and Agfa created a demand for businesses that would create prints at a moderate price. The popularity of portable cameras meant that middle-class people who could afford a camera and the means to go on a vacation could record new sights and later show them to family and friends. This change enabled people to share information not only about new locations but also about children, pets and friends. The 'Polaroid Land' camera appeared in the USA in 1948 and grew in popularity in the 1950s and 1960s as economies improved and people could afford the luxury of instant images. From an information science viewpoint, this was virtually a revolution because it enabled individuals with no special training to capture visual image information almost instantly.

Digital photography represented a further revolution in how people could record information in image form. Early digital cameras were cumbersome and the images they created were larger than most people could easily process with their home computers. Affordable digital cameras did not really become available until the 1990s at the earliest, and even then the quality of the images was significantly less than those from film-based cameras. Early in the 21st century virtually all smart phones could capture digital images. The ability to edit digital images grew simultaneously, and the necessary software became widely available, so that by the early decades of the 21st century everyone could edit pictures. This editing ability also opened up a greater risk of falsification and manipulation. Since digital images were now widely used in scientific experiments as a form of evidence, the ability to manipulate that evidence became a concern for scholarly integrity, and image manipulation has become one of the reasons for the retraction of some academic papers.

Information in theatre and video

Theatre is an ancient art that people have used since the beginning of recorded time to tell stories important to their society, and an important part of those stories includes non-verbal information. For an information scientist, theatre represents a communications tool that is technology independent because it requires nothing more than hearing, vision and the physical presence of an audience. The demands on good actors include the ability to project their voices (which is different than merely speaking loudly) and, ideally, a degree of facial control because expression plays a role in the way people understand the words. Formal theatre can be traced back to the Shang dynasty in China and to the ancient Egyptians in the West. India appears also to have had theatre since the first millennium BCE (Wikipedia, 2025t). In the Western world, Greek theatre has a long and well-respected tradition:

> The first plays were performed with just one actor (called a protagonist) and a chorus of people who helped him to tell the story. However, throughout the 5th century BC playwrights continued to innovate. The playwright Aeschylus added a second speaking role, called the antagonist, and reduced the chorus from 50 to 12. His play 'The Persians', first performed in 472 BC, is the oldest surviving of all Greek plays.
>
> (PBS, 2024)

The information in these early plays mainly recounted history and religion, presumably with the goal that people would learn the stories and ideas that made up the social context of their cultural past. The Trojan War played a particularly large role in the Greek world, thanks to plays like *The Trojan Women* by Euripides. Rome also had an active theatrical life. The comic dramatist Plautus was famous in the second century BCE, but many of his works have not survived to modern times. Terence was an equally popular contemporary, many of whose works are available today. Roman theatre tended to follow Greek models, including a chorus and prologue.

Christianity disapproved of the lewdness of Roman theatre and increasingly took measures to discourage attendance. Theatre survived longer in Byzantium, but eventually vanished because of church opposition. Islam did not ban theatre, but regulated it. According to Wikipedia (2025u), 'The most popular forms of theatre in the medieval Islamic world were puppet theatre (which included hand puppets, shadow plays and marionette productions) and live passion plays known as ta'ziya, where actors re-enact episodes from Muslim history.' Passion plays also became popular in Christian countries. The city of Oberammergau in Germany has repeated a passion play decennially since the 17th century, and visitors come from a wide range of countries. The point of the passion plays was to remind often illiterate people of notable religious events in the past.

Theatre was already widespread in Europe in early modern times, but its popularity grew as more dedicated theatre buildings were built and as authors like William Shakespeare grew in popularity. Shakespeare's plays educated the people of his time in histories that were not always quite accurate, but made the events vivid. His plays about British kings gave information about the conflicts that shaped his own Elizabethan age, and served as a legitimation for the Tudor dynasty. French theatre in the 17th century performed a similar educational role. Molière's plays provide a picture of the social life of 17th-century France and, like Shakespeare's, continue to be performed. Eighteenth-century German theatre also had historical dramas by writers like Schiller, who, in 1784, described theatre as a means to help the highly splintered German 'nation' to unite (Hinderer, 2009). Goethe's *Faust* ventured into topics that included religion and philosophy. High schools and universities sometimes include theatrical performances in their activities, not only as a way to teach students about the literature, but to educate them about the past.

Movies did not eliminate theatre, but opened access to drama at prices that more people could afford. Movies became commercially successful even while they were still relatively crude. The 1903 film *The Great Train Robbery* was an American silent film by Edwin S. Porter produced by the Edison Manufacturing Company, and helped to establish the genre of American 'Westerns'. Talking movies and colour films established the dominance of film as a means to reach a large number of people, including the newsreels that were at one time a staple of the movie-theatre experience. Television dramas began to replace movies as the way in which most people received stories about new social worlds. A comedy like *I Love Lucy* gave many Americans their first intimate view of life in the apartment world of New York City in the 1950s. Viewers saw the rooms, heard the complaints and learned about managing such buildings from the characters Fred and Ethel Mertz. It was more effective than a sociological treatise – which typical viewers would never have opened.

More recent examples of the power of video come from social media, where smart phones or computers are used to record opinions by people who want to become 'influencers' and speak to people of their own age and generation. Sparsh Sadhu (2024) writes: 'A social media influencer is an expert who has established credibility in a specific industry and has built a large following on social media. By regularly creating insightful and engaging content, creators leverage their influence to promote products, services or causes to their followers.'

Influencers do not necessarily focus only on products, but may also engage in politics. 'Key to the success of influencers is their ability to convey authenticity. Conceptually, authenticity has different connotations: (a) being true to oneself, (b) being real (vis-à-vis being fake), and (c) being original (Syvertsen & Enli, 2020)' (Goodwin et al., 2023). The difference between traditional celebrity endorsements and political influencers mainly involves the platform. 'Though influencers are sometimes perceived as a new phenomenon, their activity follows a history of celebrity endorsements in marketing' (Goodwin et al., 2023). The messages of influencers involve many non-verbal factors such as tone, facial expression and body language, which play a key role in establishing their 'authenticity'.

Information in taste and smell

Taste is one of the most hidden sources of information, mainly because no current media can effectively communicate the sensation of taste, except through words, images and sounds. The human ability to smell is surprisingly sensitive. Steven Shapin (2024) wrote in the *London Review of Books*: 'It's said that we can detect as many as a trillion distinct odours, even if we haven't got the language to describe them.' There is no way for anyone to get genuine information about taste online. It can be obtained only by putting something onto the tongue or into the mouth. Many people may not consider the information value of taste to be important, but it does matter for anyone who wants to discuss professional cooking, or someone who wants to give information about the actual taste of potentially dangerous foods such as poisonous mushrooms. The same problem exists for the sense of smell, for which modern media have no means for communication. There is a close relationship between taste and smell, as professional cooks know. Video conferencing has become good enough to eliminate some of the need for face-to-face communication, but it is still impossible to share the taste of a meal via video, except indirectly.

The ACM Digital Library describes a research project whose goal is to enable the transfer of taste and smell via the internet, but the success of such experiments depends on special equipment that is currently very rare. Ranasinghe et al. (2011) write: 'As the initial step, we developed a control system, an actuator, which could digitally stimulate the sense of taste remotely. The system uses two approaches to stimulate taste sensations digitally: the electrical and thermal stimulations on tongue. Primary results suggested that sourness and saltiness are the main sensations that could be evoked through this device.' The fact that their article was written 14 years ago (at the time of this writing) suggests a lack of progress, which may be due to a lack of funding.

Conclusion

The relative lack of discussion about non-verbal information indicates how frequently scholars ignore it. For information scientists non-verbal information plays a special role because it is context rich, but even information scientists lack any unique vocabulary to describe the role of non-verbal information. The increasing reliance on images and diagrams in scholarly articles is one way that scholars try to circumvent their reliance on words alone. Many journals encourage diagrams, even though they may limit their number, and diagrams rarely play the same role as word counts do. In the mid-20th century, when publishers still relied on paper, diagrams required special handling and special printing, which was expensive. Even after the costs came down, publishers remained cautious about encouraging too many diagrams.

One of the information problems with diagrams in academic papers is that while they show connections between topics effectively, they often lose the detail. The value of many diagrams is precisely that they cut through the verbiage of long explanations, but in some cases they are so complex that they become hard to follow, which weakens their role as an information source. Academic journals could include more pictures or photographs, but scholarly tradition favours text. Electronic journals could also easily include sound recordings, but those are rare.

CHAPTER 13

Information Retrieval for Technology

What is information's role in creating technology?

All technologies are creations of information. Without retrieving the right information, it is hard to develop viable technologies. Of course, non-technological tools exist. A club lying on the ground in a forest is a simple example. But most modern technologies require active design, involving information. Once a new technology comes into existence it becomes an independent entity that has a role and a context that is different from its components. A simple example is a train, which is a technologically complex travel technology. Most train riders have only a vague idea about what makes it run, and they know even less about how to build one. The core information value of a functioning train is its ability to travel along tracks from one place to another. It is typical of technology that products involve so much complex information that what people understand is only an abstraction of its capabilities.

Technology always has a purpose and context, even though that context may be forgotten once the technology becomes part of everyday life. Technologies can have multiple purposes, depending on the context – sometimes one at their time of creation and another after they become standard. Trousers offer a simple example. Their original purpose was to make it easier to ride horses: 'Trousers were first invented because robes are uncomfortable to wear on horseback. In fact, those who wore trousers in battle had the upper hand over those who wore robes' (King and Allen Limited, 2016). Today trousers are not even considered technology but clothing, and until relatively recently as clothing appropriate chiefly for males. Their technological value for riding horses and engaging in battle has faded from popular consciousness.

This means the information that formed a technology shifts over time as circumstances change, as an awareness of the initial purpose of a technology fades. Technologies like chariots, or carriages, or cars replaced the need for riding horses. Information about technology obsolescence takes on a new purpose because it changes the user base, and can serve as an incentive to develop new technologies. The problem is often to get enough information about an old technology to judge which aspects to keep and which to replace.

Reliable information about the limits of technologies is so various that simple explanations cannot always be trusted. Scholars have a tendency to assume that new technologies will create new social conditions that override what went before. The hype about AI offers examples. 'Expert systems' had a similar hype some decades ago, and in their time they served a useful purpose for dealing with complex technical matters, without changing the social environments of workplaces. Too often, people imagine science-fiction scenarios where a new technology transforms the world. Of course some science-fiction scenarios do eventually turn into something resembling reality. Space travel became a reality in the 1960s mainly because of its military value, but popular notions from science fiction probably helped to sell the investment costs.

Jules Verne's stories about space travel made no substantive contribution other than to exploit a well-established interest in exploration, which was important in the social and political context. Verne never tried to explain how space travel could become realistic. The same was true of Ray Bradbury, whose *Martian Chronicles* continue to inspire an interest in finding life on Mars. Information scientists should know that these fictional works established an interest that contributed indirectly to building a technology for space travel, even while it remained unrealistic. Establishing goals is an important element in new technology development, and the importance of such goals should never be forgotten.

Information retrieval in past technologies

For much of human history sheer necessity drove the need for technological development. Knowing that one is hungry is a form of information, but knowing how to find animals that could be killed and eaten, or knowing which plants satisfy hunger without being poisonous required information retrieval via persons or groups. Necessity probably also led to inventing ways for cutting animal flesh with sharpened stones. Sharpening a stone is not a simple and obvious skill. A person needs to recognise the right kind of stone, and it is a technological skill to learn how to hit the stone at exactly the right angle to make a sharp edge. This is not easy. Retrieving information about where to find the right kind of stones for chipping meant that tribes had to store this knowledge over many years and maintain it within the community.

In all likelihood this information was passed along visually and physically by showing others, and perhaps verbally once language was sufficiently developed for this purpose.

Creating fire in order to cook and to stay warm was a life-enhancing technological development whose significance Greek mythology enshrined in the legends of Prometheus, the bringer of fire. Equally important was learning how to keep fires going, which meant finding the right kind of burnable materials, which could include things like dry wood or peat, and learning how to dry them out if they were too moist to begin to burn. It was equally important to learn how to restart a fire after it had gone out, which could mean finding a lightning strike or discovering how to steal fire from neighbours. People also had to invent means to cook meats or vegetables other than just holding them in the flame. Soup was an important new technology that required inventing a watertight vessel that would not break on contact with fire and could hold hot or boiling water for long enough to allow the food to cook.

Similar examples of the use of information to develop technology exist at all times. The development of trains in the 19th century required information that was readily available but needed retrieval because it did not always seem immediately relevant for travel. The early steam-powered trains were technologically complex compared to hitching a horse to a wagon. The information that people needed to begin to develop the locomotive technology grew out of years of experimenting with iron and with steam pressure. Iron-smelting technology had to be capable of producing plates strong enough to handle pressure, which meant assembling metallurgical information. This information had to be combined with information about how to produce high-pressure steam. The developers also needed engineering skills to design boiler plates to contain the steam, and to control the steam to keep the boiler functioning. This may seem simple today, but retrieving and applying the right information to do that was non-trivial at the time. Even knowing how to put metal plates together to contain the steam required discovering information about when to use bolts or to weld the plates. At the time of the first steam locomotive, the social co-ordination of a workforce to complete the complex task was new, and it was necessary to train people to do the work correctly. It is worth remembering that large engineering projects were new when steam engines first appeared.

Technology depends on organisational skills that often took centuries to develop. Historical information about how to co-ordinate working groups has many roots, among them the military. Even the earliest military units required a greater degree of co-operation and co-ordination than was common. The classic technique to enable people to work together was to impose a high level of discipline. Soldiers marching together helped to train men in ways that also had a future social value in factory work. The Prussian military was one of the first to recognise the value not merely of following orders but of having educated soldiers capable of making intelligent decisions even when not under direct orders. Zinkina et al. (2013) write that 'for Frederick the Great the role of primary education was closely connected with the military needs. Literate officers and soldiers could increase the capability of the army (Melton 1988: 173–175)'. This form of social engineering mattered increasingly over the centuries.

The growth of libraries in the 19th century was symbolic of the need for information in order to support new technologies. The class of British tinkerers who contributed many small inventions to the Industrial Revolution probably did visit libraries, but it may be that the information they needed was available anyway, thanks to others who read books and consulted libraries. The social diffusion of information mattered, even if individual inventors were relatively uneducated. Becker et al. (2011) write:

> The main existing evidence on the role of human capital during the Industrial Revolution refers to the technological leader country, Britain, where the established view is that formal education did not play a prominent role in the emergence of new industries (David Mitch 1999). However, surprisingly little attention has been paid to the role of education in the industrial catch-up of the technological follower nations …This paper provides evidence that initially better-educated regions within Prussia responded more successfully to the opportunities created by the outside technological changes from Britain …

Within a laboratory environment, having trained personnel has always been important, and working laboratories often had a nearby library available for the staff in the days before online access. From an information science perspective, the interrelation of information and technology is unmistakable.

Information retrieval for technology today

The role of information in developing modern technology may be clear, but the mechanisms by which developers keep up to date on the information are less transparent. Some people today may assume that everything developers need today is available online, if only they search for it. This is an oversimplification, despite the effectiveness of search engines like Google and Bing which can help in finding online information for those who know how to use them. Very specific and very technical information retrieval searches can be effective when key words are particularly technical, because a high level of specificity makes it less likely that search engines will offer too many false hits, though that does not guarantee that the items the search engines have found are correct. Non-expert searchers risk getting information that seems plausible, but is false or misleading.

Another problem with web-based information for technological development is that paywalls may block important information. For developers at well-funded corporations, a paywall may not matter, but a start-up may lack sufficient funds. Start-ups in developing countries may have even greater financial problems in accessing paywall-protected information, which is one reason why information scientists have been active in promoting open access. Some publishers have moved to 'gold', 'diamond' or 'platinum' open access, which means that readers do not have to pay, but authors must, or their institutions or their grant-funders must. Sometimes the advertising revenue pays instead. Open access has significant benefits for anyone doing technical development work, because community members share the articles with colleagues.

One of the unfortunate consequences is that journals have sprung up whose apparent purpose is to get author fees without any serious scholarly reviewing. The result has been that some of the information that they publish is dubious or fake. What makes the situation worse is that simplistic ranking services may use algorithms that give the impression that scholars regard these articles as valuable because they are widely read. Sites like the *Retraction Watch* blog do an excellent job of flagging the problem articles in these journals, but people developing new technologies do not necessarily take the time or have a desire to check the quality of the information. Many scholars fail to check too, which becomes a problem for information retrieval, when the errors multiply.

Assumptions about language play a role in accessing technological information. A great deal of such information online is in English, and searchers may assume that a search in English suffices. In certain technological areas that may be true, since publishing in English in the natural sciences is almost standard, but searching in only one language opens the risk of information gaps. A complex explanation in English may also include passages that suffer from linguistic unclarity. In a very mathematical field, the unclarity may matter less, so long as the math is correct, but not all technical information is purely mathematical. Information about how to assemble a tool, for example, is likely to be verbal and may not necessarily include diagrams. A search for diagrams can also require specialised vocabulary. For an information scientist, these issues are well known, but developers without search training may get poor results.

Another important information retrieval issue for technological development is access to patent and copyright databases. The patent records for established technologies can serve as a roadmap for designing alternatives that accomplish the same tasks without violating the legal protection. Patents matter, especially for physical devices. Knowing when to file a patent matters. The lawyer Daniel Tysver (2022) writes:

> Under current U.S. law (as of the 2011 America Invents Act), patents are awarded to the first inventor that files for patent protection. This differs from the manner in which United States law used to operate, which would award the patent to the individual that first invented the invention, even if they were not the first to file for patent protection.

This means that the inventor needs to know exactly how the new technology will work when filing, but risks not getting the patent by waiting too long to work out extra details. Tysver (2022) advises that '[m]any valuable inventions are protected by patents even before the first working prototype is constructed'. The caveat is that the explanation of the product must be 'in sufficient detail that a person having ordinary skill in your technology is able to create your product "without undue experimentation"' (Tysver, 2022).

Patent applicants without a legal department to help them must retrieve the legal forms on their own. The rules are different in the EU. People have the choice of registering in only one country or at the European Patent Office, which also requires country-level validation. Nothing is simple. Searching for legal advice may not occur to technology developers, but in a Western society it may be necessary to retain control of the product.

Developers in fields such as computing may choose not to get patents, because the ideas behind the technology matter more than the implementation details. A good programmer can often effectively imitate the effect of lines of code using different but equally effective command sequences. For this reason some programmers prefer to rely on copyright protection that requires no registration. This means that the best way to protect the code-base of a new technology is to keep it hidden, which is also hard because compiled code can be disassembled or reverse-engineered. A quick search can retrieve a number of reverse-engineering tools. That does not mean that reverse-engineering is easy. Assembly language is highly context dependent. It is not just the differences among computing chips, but how the chips interact with the whole machine configuration, including its input–output devices, that can lead to reverse-engineering mistakes. The goal of reverse-engineering is often not to reproduce a product exactly, but to understand more specifically how it works in order to imitate it. For the information scientist, information retrieval is not just about database searching, but about retrieving a range of information that is sometimes almost invisible.

Information retrieval for future technologies

One of the best ways to retrieve information is via a library, with help from trained staff. Digital retrieval works only if the information is on a website or accessible in a database. The 'dark web' may also have sources that claim to have information about future and cutting-edge technologies, but it may not be reliable or readily available. Some future-oriented technologies generate a lot of news, such as AI systems, but details about the algorithms and data sources are kept deliberately obscure to protect investments. Other technologies offer less public information and focus mainly on what they do or may be able to do, in order to avoid explaining how they actually work. This means that a developer who wants to retrieve information for future technologies must have a good-enough technology understanding to formulate a plausible search. For someone starting out with little experience, this means a two-step search, where the first step involves background information. Those without natural science or engineering training may find future-oriented information retrieval hard without help.

A logical place to begin an information retrieval search is with public announcements about related technologies. Finding the right technical key words for a search can enable discoveries that give more search terms. Large Language Models offer an example. IBM has a record of providing reliably accurate explanations for readers without broad technical training. On its website IBM writes that 'LLMs are a class of foundation models, which are trained on enormous amounts of data to provide the foundational capabilities needed to drive multiple use cases and applications, as well as resolve a multitude of tasks. This is in stark contrast to the idea of building and training domain specific models for each of these use cases individually …' (IBM Corp., 2022).

IBM also provides a link to the phrase 'foundational models', which explains that the term comes from the Stanford Institute for Human-Centered Artificial Intelligence and implies something that can 'be the foundation for many applications of the AI model' (IBM Corp., 2021). The flaw in this explanation is that it uses the word 'foundation' to explain foundational. Readers new to discussions about LLMs may rightly find tautological explanations unenlightening.

The IBM article focuses on the benefits of LLMs and AI systems, rather than discussing how they actually work or the algorithms behind them. The IBM site offers a useful explanation about why earlier systems (including their own) cannot do what LLM systems can. 'The domain-specific foundation model can be used for many tasks as opposed to the previous technologies that required building models from scratch in each use case' (IBM Corp., 2023). The article leaves out details that might give away technical secrets, and demonstrates the difficulty in retrieving information about cutting-edge developments. Other searches about LLM systems may give more detailed answers, but those doing such searches need to be able to evaluate the reliability of the results. Information retrieval is no solution for would-be inventors with limited modern mathematical, engineering or other technical backgrounds.

It should be obvious that retrieving cutting-edge information requires the right technical background knowledge, which will vary with the field. In well-established scholarly fields like physics or chemistry, the best sources are still likely to be the leading scholarly journals, conferences, and scholars who are active in both. Nonetheless, there are fields where less academic preparation and formal training is needed. One of the best ways to learn about new developments in such fields is to talk with people at conferences that are open to non-specialists. Of course, discovering the right conferences to attend is itself a challenging information retrieval project.

Once developers are ready to begin working on a new project and believe they have the necessary information, they will likely need information about funding. Ideas and the technical knowledge to execute them are just first steps. Funding sources for technical development break down into several categories. The easiest is of course self-funding, which means having the financial means to begin the work on one's own, but this is rare for those who do not come from rich families. A rich family offers other advantages in the form of introductions and models for how to approach funders. Connections matter. Elon Musk had the advantage of attending Stanford University, where he could meet more monied people. Information retrieval does little to help with this funding model without the right starting point, but with it, retrieving information about fruitful sources becomes realistic.

Companies with an established interest in technology development and an established willingness to fund outsiders is an option for those who can explain their ideas convincingly. Retrieving information about such companies is easy, because many large corporations like Apple and Google and venture capital firms are open to people with profitable ideas. Getting this kind of support takes a level of verbal persuasiveness that balances technical details with plausible marketing. Finding the right contacts within those companies matters for success. Good MBA programmes can help their graduates make such contacts, but this form of information retrieval relies mainly on personal networks. The criteria that corporations use to fund start-ups are typically not publicly available information.

Government grants represent a potential source for funding technical development, and a number of countries have special programmes for the kinds of start-up they want to encourage. Some universities have programmes that help start-ups by matching them with academics in technical areas who have experience in getting grant money. Germany has a wide range of programmes for start-ups, which vary from German state to German state. The USA also has many small-business programmes that provide seed-money and some level of management and technical advice. This is an area where online searches can provide genuine practical assistance. Searches for start-ups that successfully used these programmes can be especially useful by providing contacts who can give practical advice about how these programmes work. In the end, connections matter.

Retrieving information about obsolescence

Obsolescence matters even for new technologies, for two reasons. The first is that knowing which technologies are at risk of obsolescence shows where new ideas can find a market share. The second is that understanding the causes of obsolescence can help developers to avoid unnecessary risks.

Computing technologies are among those most at risk, because the field evolves so quickly. For an information scientist, understanding the answer depends both on the context and on the timeframe. Computers have been around for about 80 years, counting from the development of ENIAC (Electronic Numerical Integrator and Computer) in 1945, or slightly longer, since Konrad Zuse developed a computer in 1941, which never went into commercial use because of World War 2. Within the first 20 years after ENIAC (1945–65), two new languages began to compete with programming in the alphanumeric version of native machine languages called assembly languages. The first of these new languages were Fortran (Formula Translation) in 1958 and COBOL (Common Business-Oriented Language) in 1959. They were called third-generation languages, whose processing involved two steps in order to 'compile' executable code. Early compilers did not always work perfectly, which meant that assembly language experts occasionally had to fix the output.

These new languages did not render assembly languages obsolete, in part because assembly/machine language remains basic to every sort of computing at the operating system level, but assembly language is essentially obsolete for everyday use, and few computer science students learn it. Both Fortran and COBOL have continued to evolve. Fortran 90 remains important for certain kinds of natural science programming, since it can operate efficiently in a parallel computing environment. In 2021 the ByteScout Team wrote that

'Many people widely regard COBOL as "dead" or "outdated." ... [But] considering the amount of effort put into the toolchains and the quantity of code currently produced in it, it is far from dead. ... However, many businesses are already looking to replace their old code base with new ones.' Many businesses still rely on COBOL code, in part because the cost of replacing code that works is prohibitive, though this is an area where AI may offer substantial help (see below).

Languages like C or C++ (the object-oriented version of C), Pascal and Python are popular today. The C language dates from the early 1970s and was used in creating the Unix operating system. C is capable of some low-level operations like memory management that third-generation languages like COBOL and Fortran cannot do, but many beginners consider C difficult, because the code is cryptic. Pascal also dates from the early 1970s and is a highly structured language with a formal (and largely inescapable) if-then-else control flow that was meant to enhance readability, but could also seem less flexible to programmers accustomed to other languages. Python is a significantly newer language that appeared in the 1990s. It is an interpreted language, meaning that the Python environment translates the code immediately into executable machine language, which became possible with improvements in processor speed. Python is easy for anyone who knows English to read, thanks to Python's Dutch developer, Guido van Rossum. Python's use is currently widespread, especially for beginning programming classes, but it may not be ideal for computationally intensive operations. BASIC (Beginners' All-purpose Symbolic Instruction Code) is a computing language that had widespread use on early microcomputers, but has lost much of its market share to languages like Python.

Many other computer languages have come and gone. REXX was an interpreted language on IBM Virtual Machine systems and later on other IBM mainframe operating systems. REXX still exists, but has grown obscure. There are too many other computing languages to list or discuss here. Not all programming languages have commands that resemble English, but most appear to use similar command structures. Obsolescence of a computing language can mean that it no longer handles some operations, but more often means that the language's popularity has waned. AI systems can create effective computer programs. IBM Education wrote:

> Programmers enter plain text prompts describing what they want the code to do. Generative AI tools suggest code snippets or full functions, streamlining the coding process by handling repetitive tasks and reducing manual coding. Generative AI can also translate code from one language to another, streamlining

> code conversion or modernization projects, such as updating legacy applications by transforming COBOL to Java.
>
> (IBM, 2023)

IBM Education (IBM, 2023) also lists three benefits of using AI code generators: it saves time, it helps to test and debug, and it makes coding 'accessible to non-developers'.

There is nothing new about claims that a new programming tool will be so user friendly that it will replace professional programmers, as some claimed when COBOL first appeared. (Hacker News, 2014) The flaw in these claims is not that newer and more human-friendly languages cannot or have not replaced existing languages, but that every computer program needs proofreading and testing. In that sense, an AI system that creates reliable computer programs is just another higher-level language. In the end, someone (or perhaps another AI) needs to specify what exactly the program should do. Many generations of AI systems have come and gone, and some, like Expert Systems, are no longer considered to be real AI. Obsolescence is endemic in computing technology, and the rate of change may only increase. Developers need information retrieval skills so as to learn what is changing and what is not.

Conclusion

Developers need to consider what information they need in order to create new technologies, and then to think how to retrieve that information. In the past, this might have been as simple as observing what others were doing and thinking about how to improve it. That is not so easy in the modern world, in part because of the complexity of modern technology and the number of people who want to do something similar. Developers need to remember that the key information is not always discoverable in an article or available via a database, because so much depends on the exact context in which a new technology is being developed and exactly what new purpose it will have. Technical details certainly matter, and in the modern world many such details should be available in the scholarly literature, but the key technical information may be secret, and that is unavoidable. The competition over new versions of AI offers an example.

One of the challenges for technology developers is to uncover exactly what information they need, without revealing why there is a balance between the marketing propaganda about what a new tool will be able to accomplish and reliable information about how it will accomplish that purpose. AI developers find themselves in that position at present. There is an enormous amount of speculation about what AI in general can do, but few developers want to expose specific algorithms for specific applications to a competitive public. A related example is the sensors that allow for self-driving cars, which means that developers need to retrieve both AI and engineering information. The sensors need sufficient sensitivity and sophistication to recognise environmental changes quickly, since that affects what the car needs to do. A sensor must, for example, be able to distinguish between a small child who suddenly dashes out into the street and a ball whose size may seem to resemble the head of a child. Simply slamming on the car's brakes if a child is in danger makes sense, but braking too suddenly for a ball could cause an accident if a second car were too close behind. AI alone is not sufficient to allow autonomous driving, because the AI needs to be able to perceive the whole complex environment around the car, and to make decisions based on that. That is a reason why self-driving cars are not allowed on all streets in all countries at present.

CHAPTER 14

Information Curation

What is information curation?

Information curation involves preserving information and making it usable over time. Curation is arguably as old as the first written records, which would make clay tablets the earliest curation medium, and some of those clay tablets have lasted to present times. Oral traditions also helped to curate information. In the ancient world, poetry was a preservation mechanism because the formal structure of poetry made it easier for people to remember long strings of words. The *Iliad* is an example of this form of curation, since it survived in purely oral form for generations. Chinese poetry has an equally ancient tradition. Curation often involves both organisation and access in addition to simple preservation, and the earliest libraries provided a greater degree of curation than had existed previously, even though they lacked clear policies and the technical expertise to preserve the storage media (papyrus or vellum or, later, paper). All they could do was to put content in a safe location, which was itself a non-trivial contribution.

Librarians have traditionally emphasised systematic organisation as an element of curation, and such access depends on rules about filing and locating works reliably over time. Today these rules are generally part of cataloguing or classification systems. In the past, libraries sometimes just kept materials in accession order with sequence numbers often based on the date of acquisition. One of the hallmarks of a good librarian in past centuries was the ability to find (often simply to remember) where a particular work was on a shelf. In a small collection, memory might suffice, but as collections grew, that ceased to work. Curation as a principle applies to all forms of information, not just words on paper, and it is equally important in museums and archives. Curating museum objects represents a particularly challenging task because of their non-verbal nature, since most classification systems depend on some form of written description. This leads to descriptive metadata for museums that is long and complex and less standardised than that of libraries, since the information objects are less uniform. Archives should, in theory, have fewer challenges in creating reliable organisation schemes, but the contents of archives are sometimes so idiosyncratic that outsiders find them intransparent.

Digital curation is newer because computers are newer. Digital curation has in some sense been around since the first computer operators began to store data on external media such as magnetic tape in the 1950s. Tape was a flawed medium because it was too vulnerable to physical damage, especially when being loaded onto a machine by an inexperienced operator, but tape was at least readily available and was arguably more reliable than punched cards or using disk storage, which was in the early years both unreliable and prohibitively expensive. Cassette tapes instead of open-reel tapes became more common in the 1990s and largely replaced reel-to-reel tape readers, not only because of their greater reliability but because loading them took less skill. In recent decades other forms of digital storage have emerged, including optical disk. The reliability of storage media has increased over recent decades, but media is only part of the consideration. All media deteriorates eventually, and the important question for information scientists is how to make sure that the information survives when the medium breaks down.

In their 2016 book, Gillian Oliver and Ross Harvey cite Daisy Abbott from the University of Glasgow for her concise definition of digital curation: 'the management and preservation of digital material to ensure accessibility over the long-term' (Abbott, 2008). The definition is true, but ignores the urgency. Victoria Reich, one of the founders of the LOCKSS project (Lots of Copies Keep Stuff Safe), expressed the urgency in 2012: 'If you don't preserve digital content then it won't exist. Most of society's culture and commercial assets are now digital but, generally, the move from print to electronic is about access rather than preservation' (Reich and Kiefer, 2012). Her point is clear: effective digital preservation is essential for passing the current cultural heritage on to other generations, otherwise it will not exist. There are people who believe that paper copies are the best form of curation, but even if that were true of written works, it would not suffice for the full range of contemporary digital information that needs curation and preservation.

Pre-1800 curation

The pre-modern world was never perfectly successful in preserving texts or objects, but some incomplete information has come down to us today. Curation efforts in the pre-modern world were not systematic, and were often limited to things with a clear economic value at the time, which meant that many popular tales and everyday playthings have been lost. Insofar as they were preserved, it was mainly by chance. China and parts of the Middle East may have preserved more information content, but that is hard to measure, since the whole pre-modern world suffered from wars, invasions, conquests and levels of violence that did not respect any form of information. The Christian West and the Islamic Middle East cared about preserving sacred religious texts and relics, and China had a proud literary tradition that gave an incentive for preserving a wide range of literary works, but no one knows how much was lost. From an information science perspective the problem was the lack of any concept of systematic curation or physical mechanism for saving information that was not immediately necessary.

Curating information was a luxury in pre-modern times, when people had few resources for anything except the necessities of everyday life, but many Christians viewed sacred texts as a necessity for their afterlife. Copyists in monasteries contributed materially to saving a wealth of information that had only tangential religious value, including some legends that could be treated as cases of divine intervention. Historians often credit the monasteries for their efforts to preserve manuscripts. The sheer number of monasteries meant the creation of multiple copies, which was also important for longer-term preservation, on the same principle of LOCKSS (Lots of Copies Keep Stuff Safe) (see below).

Error rates were a problem. The monastic workers made plenty of writing errors and often used abbreviations in order to avoid writing out full words. Literacy levels among the copiers were highly variable. Many copyists had a limited knowledge of Latin, and may not have understood all of the words they were writing. Proofreading was at best irregular, and there was no clean way to replace false words or incorrect spellings after they were discovered. Storage for the texts often meant putting the pages on a desk or shelf for later binding. The codex form of books existed and had replaced scrolls by the fourth century CE in the West, but scrolls had a longer life in China. One problem with scrolls was their relative fragility as compared to the solid mass of a codex, and people sometimes compensated for this by storing them in protective cases. Some media were also more robust than others. Vellum made from animal hides was expensive, but did not easily deteriorate. The types of ink varied too, with a wide range of recipes for the pigments and the materials used to bind the pigments, such as gum arabic or other resins.

The art world feels strongly about preserving the original, but text preservation is more focused on content preservation via copies. Printing matters for content curation, both in Europe and China, because it radically increased the number of copies of any given work. Printing did nothing to improve the curation of museum content, but the increasing wealth of society made a difference because more people could buy art and other image-based forms of information, and any increase in numbers helps preservation. If the goal of preservation is saving the information, not just the object, copies of museum works also matter.

In the 16th century Pieter Breugel the Elder painted many scenes of peasant life. Among the most famous were his paintings *The Wedding Dance* (1566, now in the Detroit Institute of Arts) and *Dutch Proverbs* (1559, now in the Berlin Gemäldegalerie). These paintings preserved social information not otherwise easily available, and the popularity of his works meant that others imitated him, including his sons. Italian Renaissance paintings were often rich in background detail, even though they gave less attention to the life of the poor.

One of the advantages of oil paintings was their relative robustness over time, because the colours did not fade and the canvas or wood base tended to survive. Frescoes were more vulnerable, depending on the environmental conditions. The frescoes of Pompeii survived the eruption of Vesuvius in 79 CE, thanks to the volcanic ash that covered the city. They depict details of everyday life, including fruit, fish, vases, banquets and scrolls as well as mythological scenes, and are one of the richest sources of social information about first-century Rome. The fact that this information survived to modern times was due in large part to its long burial and slow rediscovery by professionals wanting to preserve it.

Buildings serve also as lasting information sources. Many ancient sports arenas have left archaeological records because they were so solidly built that they could be used for other purposes. The amphitheatre at Arles, France, is an example: 'In the Middle Ages, the monument served as a home and refuge for the people during troubled times. The ancient amphitheater was transformed into a real walled and fortified city with 212 houses, streets, squares and even churches. The walls of the amphitheater were used as defensive ramparts during the sieges led by the barbarians' (Arles Tourism Board, 2024). The surviving baths and villas of Roman Britain provide information about heating systems, hygiene and places to wash. The same can be said of medieval castles and palaces, which survived better than peasant huts. What historians know today about peasant life comes mostly from archaeological investigations.

Throughout the era before 1800 systematic attempts at curation mainly involved things of religious value. This was also broadly true for all cultures and regions, with the exception of certain kinds of official documents, treaties or deeds, and even they could be lost or forgotten. Preserving access worked only when interest in doing so was high enough, but discovery aids such as metadata, insofar as they existed, were local and themselves needed curation.

Curation: 1700 to the computer age

Libraries and museums are key to information curation. Libraries existed well before 1700, but tended to be private and local. An exception is the Bibliothèque nationale de France, which grew from the 900 volumes of King Charles V in the Louvre palace in 1368. King Francis I guaranteed the library's growth by requiring legal deposit for all printed works at the Château de Blois, a collection that moved to Paris in the mid-17th century (Bibliothèque nationale de France, 2024). Many other libraries became established in roughly the same period. For example, the Bavarian court library dates from 1571 and began benefiting from legal deposit in 1663. The collection expanded significantly in 1803, when it acquired the Bavarian cloister libraries (Bayerische Staatsbibliothek, 2024). The British Museum (which housed the British Library) was founded in 1753 and quickly grew into a repository for information of every sort, thanks to the wealth of the British Empire. At about the same time the Prussian government established the institution that became the Prussian State Library (today the Staatsbibliothek zu Berlin): 'As of 1701 it was known as the Königliche Bibliothek (Royal Library) and was the court library of the absolute ruler. The ruler regarded this institution as his own private library – accessible to the public …' (Staatsbibliothek zu Berlin, 2025b). Other Western European libraries also grew during the centuries before the French Revolution. Substantial libraries also existed in China from the time of the Shang dynasty, but remained largely private collections until modern times.

The first librarian at the Bibliothèque nationale de France entered into office in 1719. His name was Abbé Bignon and he was 'appointed librarian to the King in 1719, [and] gave the library unprecedented brilliance. He organized it into departments: Printed Material, Manuscripts, Medals and Engraved Stones, Engraved Plates and Collections of Prints, Titles and Genealogies. He also continued the work of his predecessors in terms of acquiring documents, very concerned with bringing in all the important works of learned Europe' (Bibliothèque nationale de France, 2024).

From an information science perspective collecting and organising the physical materials that contain information is part of curation, and contributes indirectly to preservation because it prevents their loss. The abstract intellectual task of separating intellectual content from its physical carrier took longer, in part because of a lingering sense that the original object had a special economic value. First editions of notable works still continue to fetch high prices. Physically reproducing a printed work grew much easier because of the printing press, which meant accurate copies of intellectual contents became more widely available.

An important question is what responsibilities Abbé Bignon undertook beyond collection building. There is evidence that he created five departments that separated printed works from manuscripts and other information sources. In information science terms that separation was intellectually important because the information contents of manuscripts are often different even if the book began originally as a manuscript. At the time of Abbé Bignon many documents were only in handwritten form, such as treaties and legal agreements between two parties. Museums especially needed to focus on curating physical objects, because there was no tool for making copies. Until top museums are ready to accept digital copies as adequate, they have many of the same curation problems in the digital age that they had in the 19th century,

Organising, classifying and protecting museum works was all that most curation efforts could do, because the problems were greater for museums than for libraries due to the range of physical materials as well as the intellectual complexity of the contents, for which verbal descriptions were often inadequate. The profession of museum curator was also slower to develop the kinds of standards that have become common for librarians. There is no specific degree requirement for museum curators comparable to those for librarians. University degrees in history or art history are common, but the field is less regulated and often less well paid, though that varies by institution and country. In the pre-digital world, curating the information in museum objects depended on physical preservation, combined with detailed descriptions and photographs for situations when the object had deteriorated beyond repair or (more commonly) was stolen. The range of physical materials in museums is broader than for books and manuscripts, and the effect of aging could mean that in order to address preservation needs museum curators need to understand the chemistry involved in long-term environmental effects for a wide range of materials. Different types of wood age at different rates, and humidity is often a factor. Metal is relatively robust, but will also interact with a range of environmental factors over time so that it discolours or becomes brittle. Physical curation has no simple solutions.

Museums and libraries in the 19th century took curation seriously, but could only curate the materials they had on hand. World War 2 involved serious looting and physical damage to buildings from bombing. War zones around the world have seen even more deliberate damage. The aerial bombing of Coventry Cathedral in 1940 largely destroyed the 14th-century cathedral and its treasures. Despite the best efforts of the community, 'it was clear that little had been saved' (Historic England, 2024). The firebombing of Dresden in 1945 not only destroyed the cathedral but destroyed large portions of the inner city: 'Before World War II, Dresden was called "Florence on the Elbe" and was considered one of the world's most beautiful cities because of its architecture and art treasures' (Britannica, 2025f). A few European cities, including Rome and Paris, escaped major destruction. Post-war Berlin and London showed the scale of the war damage for decades afterwards. No curation efforts can protect against this kind of deliberate violence, and the best that anyone at the time could do was to remove anything capable of being moved, such as the art collections in both London and Berlin. However, the Berlin collections were not safe from theft by invading soldiers.

Major European wars offer only one example of the problem. During the Cambodian civil war in the early 1970s, most of the ancient temples of Angkor Wat survived thanks to collaborative efforts between the armies, but restoration work had to stop (News CNE, 2021).

> Camping Khmer Rouge forces used whatever wood remained in the building structures for firewood, and a shoot-out between Khmer Rouge and Vietnamese forces caused a few bullet holes in bas reliefs. In the late 1980s and early 1990s, far more damage was done to the reliefs by art thieves working out of Thailand who lopped off many sculptures and other structures, including earlier reconstructions.
>
> (Wikipedia, 2025v)

The efforts to save famous artefacts from notable sites should not be undervalued, even though they are often later forgotten. Perhaps the most common curation problem is simply negligence. For example, students often throw away notes from lectures, which is generally no problem, since such notes may neither be complete nor completely accurate, but such ephemeral information can have significant informational value.

> In the winter of 1830 the later Utrecht professor in Economics Jan Ackerdijck arrived in Berlin, where he followed lectures by Hegel, the most famous philosopher of his time. In Ackerdijck's diary we read that he met Hegel several times, and had his lecture notes on Hegel's first series of lectures copied in a notebook.
>
> (Utrecht University, 2022)

> [Hegel's] notes were subjected to perpetual revisions and additions. It is possible to form an idea of them from the shape in which they appear in his published writings. Those on *Aesthetics*, on the *Philosophy of Religion*, on the *Philosophy of History*, and on the *History of Philosophy* have been published by his editors, mainly from the notes of his students …
>
> (Knox, 2024)

Philosophy is not the only case where lecture notes became the basis for a significant publication. Based on the lectures and the tape recordings, a team of physicists and graduate students put together a manuscript that would become *The Feynman Lectures on Physics* (Wikipedia, 2025w). The content of these lectures was challenging:

> Caltech's educators aim high. They wanted to stop using textbooks as the primary material for the first two years of college physics and instead teach it through a series of original lectures … Audio (but not video) recordings were made, and other faculty transcribed the lectures, intending to edit them into a new textbook. Things did not go as planned. The editing process was grueling and required, as the editors reported in their foreword, 'the close attention of a professional physicist for from 10 to 20 hours per lecture'. Even then, the editors were dissatisfied with the 'completeness, smoothness, or logical organization' of their product. But they decided to publish anyway.
>
> (Crease, 2014)

The point is that curation does not only involve finished products, but can involve intermediaries with a significance of their own.

Librarians and museum staff generally do their best to curate materials by preserving them and by making them accessible. Microfilm was seen as a preservation option in the mid-20th century, but microfilm was neither user friendly nor entirely error free, as users discovered.

Digital curation

Digital storage was long seen as risky, and for good reasons. At the beginning of the digital era, the early mechanisms for preserving digital information were more fragile than for paper. Typical offline digital storage solutions at the time were punched cards or reel-to-reel magnetic tape, but cardboard punched cards had the same weakness as any paper products. The card decks lacked any structure to keep them in order. Punched cards were popular for data entry until companies like IBM developed online systems like TSO (Time Sharing Option) in the early 1970s that allowed programmers to enter lines of code directly without relying on punched card operators, but many companies had invested in punched card typing pools. The process was also time consuming. A programmer had to write the code on a paper form, which then went to the data-entry department. Typically, the punched cards came back to the programmer, who then needed to get them to a card-reader device to load into the computer. If the programmer discovered an error, then the process had to be repeated.

Each company had its own way to preserve card decks, and that depended on filing systems ill designed for retrieval. Often they looked like oversized card catalogue drawers, but with little to indicate what the individual cards meant. Professional punched card typists were efficient for general data-entry tasks, but the quantity of punched cards quickly became a storage problem, in part because containers for the cards were poorly adapted to storing corporate-level quantities, and were even more poorly designed for retrieval. Punched cards presented a space problem too, since the containers took up significantly more room than reel-to-reel tapes. Many companies that relied on large amounts of data gave up on punched cards relatively early.

Storing data long term on 'spinning discs' was simply too costly until the 1990s, when the reliability of computer discs improved and the costs went down. As a general rule, organisations only kept data on spinning disks when they needed to have it readily accessible. In the early days there were removable discs, which operators could put on a shelf and retrieve when necessary. These removable disks were somewhat less expensive, but were themselves a storage problem and had vulnerabilities. Later versions of spinning discs were faster, did not allow removal and were generally more reliable. Operating systems determined where data was stored on the discs. Data was generally not stored sequentially. Instead, the operating system stored data on particular tracks of a disk and set up a reference to know what data could be found where. This means when a disc 'crashed' it could be possible to reconstruct some of the missing data by searching through undamaged tracks on the disk. As a rule this was done only in emergencies, but it was possible when the data were so valuable that recovering them was worth the trouble.

Serious long-term digital preservation and curation began in the late 1990s and early 2000s. The basic approach built on converting paper-based texts into digital images and using the newer generation of reliable discs to store content and to make it accessible. By this time reliability presented fewer problems than legal issues like copyright, which introduced the additional complication that copyright laws differ somewhat from one country to another. Storage itself eventually became less of an issue than formats, because the format affected usability. In simple terms, an image provided less accessibility than machine-readable content, but the reliability of optical character scanning processes left something to be desired, especially in the early years. Some form of human correction was often necessary. However, the important first step was to make sure that text-based content was in digital form.

Most of the current digital long-term archiving solutions grew out of the years between 1996 and 2004. Three countries made active contributions: the

USA, Germany and the UK, and the leaders of these efforts quickly came to know each other, or were already in contact. The first project was the Internet Archive, which Brewster Kahle founded in 1996 after successfully selling his WAIS system. One of the key focuses for the Internet Archive has long been to harvest web content, much of which could vanish completely. The Internet Archive uses its own harvesting tool called Heretrix and a tool called Alexa. Heretrix respects flags that indicate a site does not want to be crawled, which is important for copyright reasons, and it stores the harvested data in WARC (Web Archive) files. The Wayback Machine provides access to Internet Archive content.

In 1997 the German Research Foundation (Deutsche Forschungsgemeinschaft) funded two major digitisation projects, one at Göttingen University and the other at the Bavarian State Library. Those libraries had a substantial number of important works, including a Gutenberg Bible in Göttingen and a wealth of medieval manuscripts at the Bavarian State library. Visiting scholars used both collections heavily, and digitising content made them much more available to the scholarly world. Only shortly thereafter, Peter Schirmbacher implemented Humboldt Universität zu Berlin's edoc-Server in 1999, which was the first institutional repository. The edoc-Server did not harvest content, but was available for people with appropriate authorisation to store academic content, including doctoral dissertations, journals and other kinds of publications. The edoc-Server never sought to be a universal solution to digital archiving and curation, but provided an example of how to manage digital content and make that content freely available.

When the US National Science Foundation's 'Digital Library Initiative' project went into its second phase, one of the projects that it funded in 1999 was 'Lots of Copies Keep Stuff Safe' (LOCKSS) by Dr David Rosenthal and Victoria Reich of Stanford University. As the name suggests, content was scanned and stored on servers in multiple locations in order to ensure sufficient redundant capacity in case of disasters or system failures. The users of member libraries always have access to content in LOCKSS. This project was explicitly intended for long-term digital preservation and access, and it involves a number of networks in different locations, including the LOCKSS global network and various private LOCKSS networks, including one in Canada. CLOCKSS (Controlled LOCKSS) also began officially in 1999. The CLOCKSS website describes the service as 'Digital content is stored in the CLOCKSS archive with no user access unless a "trigger" event occurs' (CLOCKSS, 2024).

JSTOR did not begin as a long-term archiving project, but as a means for freeing physical storage in libraries. The goal was to

> convert printed scholarly journals into electronic form and store them in a centralized digital archive. Participating libraries and their institutions could free physical space, reduce capital and other costs associated with collection storage, and vastly improve access to scholarly research.... In 1995, following a pilot launched under the direction of the University of Michigan, JSTOR was established as an independent not-for-profit organization.
>
> (JSTOR, 2024)

The Michigan staff realised that digitisation was also a way to preserve the contents, and launched Portico in 2002 as a tool for the copyright-compliant preservation of digital content. Initially, Portico offered contracts to publishers that excluded recent issues of journals. The length of the exclusion period varied over time and became shorter as publishers discovered that it did not affect their sales. Portico has been part of the Mellon Foundation-funded ITHAKA organisation since 2005 (Portico, 2024). Since Portico focuses almost exclusively on English-language publications, Elmar Mittler at Göttingen University established 'DigiZeitschriften: das deutsche digitale Zeitschriftarchiv' [the German digital journal archive], which serves a purpose similar to Portico for scholarly journals in German.

Massachusetts Institute of Technology (MIT) and HP Labs unveiled the DSpace institutional repository in 2002, three years after the edoc-Server began operating in Berlin, but with far more publicity. DSpace was meant to be sold to other institutions that would want to customise it. DSpace secured a long list of academic and commercial customers around the world, thanks to active marketing. This meant that digital curation became almost mainstream. Other digitisation projects followed, most notably the Google Books project, which began in 2004. The University of Michigan and Stanford University libraries were the primary initial partners, with contributions also from Harvard, New York Public Library and the Bodleian Library at Oxford University and, after 2007, the Bavarian State Library. Michigan insisted that partner libraries should receive digital copies of the works and persuaded Google to accept higher quality standards for the scans and underlying text. In 2008 management of the digital copies in the libraries shifted to a new entity called HathiTrust, under the leadership of the Committee on Institutional Cooperation (which included Michigan) and the libraries of the University of California system.

There is at present no entity that actively co-ordinates this broad range of digital creation projects. The projects are in general loosely in touch with each other, in part because the community working on long-term digital creation is relatively small. Participants from the various projects talk with each other via a wide range of academic organisations including the US-based Coalition for Networked Information and the Digital Creation Centre at the University of Edinburgh.

Conclusion

Information curation has seen considerable progress in recent decades as many have accepted the fact that preserving only the physical original does not suffice, and that for text-based information a digital copy provides better access than physical copies. Digital representations of physical information sources have also become more standard. Digital imagery can capture three-dimensional works in enough detail to be a viewing option, even if viewers prefer the original. Digital music has not replaced the enjoyment of a live concert, but has effectively replaced the earlier physical means of recording music, such as long-playing records.

For the information scientist better training in long-term preservation remains a priority. Information still remains fragile, perhaps for the old reason that people forget about everything not immediately urgent. Every information source requires active curation, and costs are a factor. Justifying the cost is hard for those who see no immediate value. The question arises: how much redundancy is necessary? LOCKSS typically uses seven well-separated servers to guarantee the safety of digital content because the statistical likelihood of all seven failing at once is low. People often feel that a physical copy is more authentic than a digital one, which makes less sense for text than for physical objects. Museums have discovered that people still want to see the original painting, even if high-quality digital reproductions are available on the internet. For many people, digital solutions have not eliminated the need to curate physical originals.

CHAPTER 15

Information for Education

What is information for education?

Education is about imparting information to prepare younger people for their working life and their ongoing role in society. The difference between formal education and informal education depends on the social organisation of schooling and the availability of other learning opportunities. Separating information from education is practically impossible. Children begin learning from birth, and one of the first things they learn is their parents' language, which lets them communicate their needs and enables them to understand adults. A substantial literature exists on all stages of education, including the very earliest stages between parents and children, and those very early years may be the most important for later information acquisition. Early education is a topic that information science programmes have rarely emphasised, but recent research has taken an interest in the information behaviour of young children (Schlebbe, 2023).

There is ongoing interest in how older persons learn to make use of online information (Hillebrand, 2024). For the information scientist, looking at how people learn cannot be confined to early years or school-based training. Anyone who has had jobs involving modern technology must be aware that the rate of change is high, and learning new information represents an essential part of work life. The same is true for every kind of job, except perhaps completely mechanical ones under close supervision. People working as waiters in restaurants must, for example, interact regularly with new technologies to take orders and to accept payments.

The trouble is that new information arises constantly, so people must re-educate themselves. Learning is not identical with education, but learning is an educational goal that is often measured formally. Education is not exclusively academic or abstract. People who learn how to drive a car not only need information about how the vehicle operates and about the laws governing driving; they need to also acquire physical skills for steering, braking, shifting gears (on cars without automatic transmission), parking and, perhaps above all, the skill to remain aware of the surroundings. These physical skills are all forms of information and need refreshing over time because circumstances change.

For the information scientist, an important issue is how different the kinds of learning are. Language learning offers an example because it varies substantially from country to country and person to person. There is evidence that 'A child's brain seems to benefit from growing up multilingually. Advantages are not only seen in language skills but also in other areas. Several studies have shown that children who grow up speaking more than one language are more likely to put themselves in someone else's position' (NeuroNation, 2017).

The physical effects are also noted: 'Brain imaging studies in bilingualism using various tasks have suggested that bilinguals may employ at least some different brain regions depending on the language used in the task' (Kobayashi et al., 2008).

There is still much that no one really understands about how the brain processes information.

Education before 1700

Education before 1700 in Europe was mainly a private matter. It was somewhat more formal in China at the time: 'The roots of a system of formal education in China can be traced back at least as far as the 16th century B.C. later Shang Dynasty (1523–1027 B.C.) Throughout this period education was the privilege of the elite few, and for the most part existed for no other purpose than to produce government officials' (Surowski, 2000).

Entry into the bureaucracy depended on passing rigorous exams. The students could prepare for these examinations based largely on the Chinese classics by enrolling in the private institutions 'which existed for no other reason than to prepare students for the civil service examinations' (Surowski, 2000). This was probably the earliest form of required education and it emphasised both humanities topics and legal learning. The examination system lasted for centuries. It was required in the sense that the information needed to pass examinations was formalised to a degree that may have discouraged learning at home.

The closest Roman counterpart was training in rhetoric, for which there were formal schools such as Augustine described in his *Confessions*. Rhetoric was important both for a political career and for law. It was not general education, any more than was the Chinese examination system. It is unclear in the pre-Christian era how much learning mechanisms became formalised into what one might call schools, but learning was certainly needed for those working with law. The fact is that people had to learn to read and write in order to discuss political and philosophical issues. Family members were not the only teachers. The wealthy could hire tutors (Greek slaves were popular tutors for a time in the Roman Empire), and older children could contribute. Education focused largely on males, but women in well-to-do families frequently learned along with their brothers. Many sources emphasise that the main goal of education for women was to prepare them for marriage and for running a household, which needed some level of literacy: 'some important literature written by women during this period has survived, and many other women writers published work that has not been preserved' (Plant, 2004). Plant lists 55 known female writers during the Roman period. It is hard to say how many works by women were lost because no one felt they were important enough to save.

The situation for women in ancient China was similar. Wang, van Leeuwen and Li (2020) wrote that 'women were given the opportunity to learn to read and write', though they note that education may have promoted obedience as a female virtue. The authors note, however, that '[i]t was not uncommon that, when a male who earned the money to support his family was unable to work due to disability or had died, educated women would either run the business by themselves or generate other income by selling their paintings or calligraphy, or serving as private teachers in wealthy households' (Wang, van Leeuwen and Li, 2020). Literacy in ancient China, as in pre-modern Europe, was low even among the elite, but that does not mean that women did not find ways of educating themselves in areas that mattered. Running a household and feeding a family required a broad range of information-based skills, even for the illiterate or barely literate, and it is entirely possible that (mostly male) professional historians have underrated how much practical and abstract information women learned.

The situation in India was somewhat different. Yasin and Hina (2023) write that even though the 'primary duty of women was to take care of the home and children', ancient Hindu sources 'strengthen the claim that the women in ancient India were educated, intelligent and an important part of the society'. Religious books formed the basis of education in India, as in Europe. Yasin and Hina (2023) make the argument that 'As far as general education among Hindus is concerned, the education system of ancient India was unique in its nature and aims. Not only philosophical subjects were taught there but general subjects like literature (religious and secular) arts and sciences were also taught.'

Little reliable factual information exists about women's education in the ancient and pre-modern world, presumably because it took place outside of official notice, and mostly must be extrapolated from the writings of women themselves, insofar as any survive.

Formal education in Europe existed mainly in the context of the Church, which needed moderately literate clergy, and people to support them. Even leaders like Charlemagne wanted a scholar to help with official documents. His most famous assistant was Alcuin, who grew up in the ninth century in Northumbria and attended a church school at York, where he learned the trivium, which included grammar, logic and rhetoric, and the quadrivium, which included arithmetic, geometry, music and astronomy, which played a long-term role in medieval education. Charlemagne may have learned to read, but likely he had people read to him and dictated written communications. The evidence is unclear, but it is clear that his court attracted people who were literate, that he respected them and that they played important roles in running the empire.

A group of students founded the first medieval university at Bologna in 1088, and hired scholars to teach them, which is a reverse of the current practice. It is not completely certain that Bologna was the first university: Charles Homer Haskins (1957) notes that Salerno may have had an earlier medical school, but Bologna and, two years later, Padua were among the earliest to resemble a modern university in teaching a range of subjects. The students had organisations like the guilds that gave them a measure of power. Haskins (1957) also explains the origin of professors and examinations:

> Excluded from the 'universities' of students, the professors also formed a gild or 'college,' requiring for admission thereto certain qualifications which were ascertained by examination, so that no student could enter save by the gild's consent. And, as much as ability to teach a subject is a good test of knowing it, the student came to seek the professor's license as a certificate of attainment, regardless of his future career. This certificate, the license to teach (licentia docendi), thus became the earliest form of academic degree.

Paris was different: 'Paris, in contrast to Bologna, was a university of masters' and it received a royal charter in 1200 (Haskins, 1957). Paris also set up different faculties, each with a dean, which is an ecclesiastical title that has remained in active use.

The next-earliest European university was probably Oxford. There is general agreement that its foundation by Alfred the Great in the tenth century was likely apocryphal. 'There is no clear date of foundation, but teaching existed at Oxford in some form in 1096 and developed rapidly from 1167, when Henry II banned English students from attending the University of Paris' (Oxford University, 2014). Those early students went to Oxford, where there was already a church school. Cambridge University was founded only slightly later in 1209, probably by students from Oxford. For an information scientist it matters that young people who wanted to learn appear to have taken the initiative in starting these universities. The information that students at these early institutions acquired mattered for their careers, especially in law or theology, and did not so clearly represent the same social or family pressures that are common in modern times.

Other universities also soon came into being. For example, Charles University in Prague 'was founded in 1348 during the rule of King of Bohemia and Holy Roman Emperor Charles IV. It became the first Studium generale north of the Alps and east of Paris. Modelled on universities in Bologna and Paris it quickly gained international renown. Originally, it had four faculties: theology, liberal arts, law, and medicine' (Charles University, 2024). The university soon faced an era of religious upheaval, in part because 'the religious reformer Master Jan Hus was rector of the university at the time' (Charles University, 2024). The language of the university was German until 1882, when the Czech National Revival led to dividing it into a Czech and German university. The founding of the University of Heidelberg took place in 1386 with papal permission, and '[t]he Dutch scholar Marsilius of Inghen who came to Heidelberg from the Paris University became the new university's first rector' (Heidelberg University, 2024). Paris represented the model for northern European universities.

Universities were not the only model for formal education in Europe. The British public schools appeared in the 15th and 16th centuries. The first 'was Winchester College ... with other resonant names following over the next two centuries, including Eton (1440), St Paul's (1509) and Westminster (1560)' (Kynaston, 2015). They were called 'public schools' in contrast to more local 'private' schools, and 'tended to have a much broader geographical intake, educating the children of wealthy families from across the nation' (Kynaston, 2015). The number of students at these and similar schools was comparatively small. The number of secondary schools in German-speaking areas before 1500 was surprisingly large and includes some that still exist. France also had a well-established secondary education system which, as in Britain, mainly served the upper classes.

Home schooling was the norm in most countries around the world, and of course the quality of the education depended on factors such as the educational attainments of the parents or the tutors they hired. The information resources available to the students generally meant those books the household owned. The reward system for learning for boys could mean a job and for girls a good husband. Reliable factual information about early secondary education is sparse and much of the information comes from personal accounts and diaries. Formal education was required for certain leadership positions in the Indian subcontinent, especially after British rule began. Often, access to the information needed for learning depended on caste, and one of the attractions of Islam was the ability to escape the caste system to some degree. For the information scientist it is important to remember how limited access to information was in eras with limited literacy. A Wikipedia (2025x) article on 'literacy' claims that 'in pre-modern times, it is unlikely that literacy was found in more than about 30–40% of the population'. The claim has no citation and represents at best a guess.

Education at universities up to 1900

Universities changed so substantially in the 19th century that the students and faculty of a university in 1700 would hardly recognise the curriculum or expectations in 1900. From an information science perspective, this resulted from the simultaneous increase in information creation and availability, and a recognition of the economic value of information. The transformation of universities from professional schools into information factories was arguably the real first information revolution.

External factors mattered as well. The Industrial Revolution affected European universities indirectly because European society became richer and because the ever-growing number of books, newspapers and journals improved information distribution. The mechanical effectiveness of the Gutenberg press and later improvements mattered, but so did changes in the publishing industry, which focused less on religious topics and more on political and social news. Without these changes, information availability and the creation of new information might have taken longer. The universities did not directly cause any of these changes, but reflected them and used them to a degree that differentiated them from the rest of society. They ceased to be the organs of established religions and almost became competitors. The same educational structure did not develop at the same time in other societies, even though some, like China, put a higher value on education.

No one university can reasonably claim to be the first real research university. Most information creation in the early 18th century often took place outside of any kind of formal educational structure and relied more on social interactions among people who were sufficiently socially elite to have good reading and mathematical skills. Nonetheless, in some countries the universities played the role of a good social club, where people could share ideas with each other, regardless of whether those ideas had any direct connection to the curriculum. Jena offers a good example. 'It became the centre of classical German philosophy with professors such as J. G. Fichte, C. L. Reinhold, F. W. Schelling, G. W. F. Hegel and J. F. Fries' (Jena University, 2024). Goethe also came regularly, after 1799, in official capacities to inspect the natural history collections, the palace museum and the library (JenaKultur, 2017). The University of Oxford also had its 'own lively and independent culture of debate and scholarship including two long-running research seminars' (Oxford University Faculty of English, 2018). The situation was different at the University of Paris, which had become more focused on theology. It had slowly been shrinking in the 18th century and closed in 1792 during the Revolution, though not necessarily because of the Revolution. The French Revolution brought about social and political changes that opened boundaries and ended most of the restrictions on Jews. Fighting during the Napoleonic wars, such as the battles at Jena and Auerstedt which took place near the University of Jena, made academic work difficult as did damage to the facilities:

> Jena's exhilarating intellectual atmosphere had disappeared. 'The scholarly exchange that existed when you were here is absolutely gone', one young professor wrote to Schelling, reporting how he ate alone at home and that there were no social gatherings. When the student numbers dropped from almost 900 in the 1790s to less than two hundred in 1806, the town's tradesmen lost their customers and shops closed.
>
> (Wulf, 2022, 325)

Most universities escaped with less damage, and the conservative reaction after Napoleon's fall did not end the culture of discussion that flourished, but made it more cautious. Censorship, which was never entirely absent, became more prevalent, with the result that people like the poet Heinrich Heine fled to France in 1831.

A number of new and strongly research-oriented universities trace their founding to the 19th century, among them the University of Berlin in 1810 and the University of Chicago in 1891. Wilhelm von Humboldt, who was a key founder of Berlin University was also the Minister for Culture and Teaching. Humboldt 'envisaged a "Universitas litterarum" which would achieve a unity of teaching and research and provide students with an all-round humanist education. This concept spread throughout the world and gave rise to the foundation of many universities of the same type over the following 150 years' (Humboldt-Universität zu Berlin, 2016).

Wilhelm's brother Alexander, himself a noted natural scientist, also influenced the new University, especially in the natural sciences. The 'unity of teaching and research' meant that professors were expected to engage in research that would enrich and expand the curriculum. Professors were no longer just responsible for transmitting information, but for creating it through research. The Prussian government funded the University sufficiently to enable natural science research. Hegel was among the notable scholars who researched and taught in Berlin, and figures like Karl Marx came to listen to his lectures. After the establishment of the Nobel prize in 1900, 30 Berlin professors became winners, including Albert Einstein.

The University of Chicago followed this model in emphasising research, and put unusual emphasis on the importance of having a depth of information available. William Rainey Harper, the first president of the University, believed that the University had to have a library that included more than just new works. He travelled to what he considered to be the best university of the time, walked down Unter-den-Linden where the University of Berlin had its main building, and bought the largest antiquarian bookstore he could find. This collection continues to be called 'the Berlin Collection', although it was quickly integrated into the library's general holdings. 'The University Library became the largest in the city, and by 1896 it was the second-largest university collection in the United States with 340,000 volumes, the Berlin Collection contributing its uncertain but dominant share. This rapidly achieved status was used by Harper to lure faculty and also to give a sense of stability to the University' (University of Chicago Library, 2024).

Many other universities followed the research model, including Johns Hopkins, Wisconsin and Michigan. The traditional Ivy League universities also became more research oriented, as did the newest member, Cornell, which was founded in 1865 with a mix of private and public funding.

From the information science perspective, what mattered most was the transmission and creation of information. Recognising the economic value of information did not lag far behind. This was particularly seen in natural science areas. The economic value of information became even clearer in the 20th century.

Technology research and education up to 1950

The world changed radically between 1900 and 1950. It was not just the two world wars that caused the changes, but also the sense of people in the West that they had achieved mastery over the limitations of nature. Ease of travel improved for everyone, even the poor. Of course the physical distance between continents had not changed, but travel times fell from weeks, to days, to hours. This was a direct consequence of the use of information in ship building, railway building, automobiles and, above all, air travel. These developments combined information about topics as diverse as metalworking, power sources, electronics and communication. Information and its applications expanded faster than at any time in the past, which inspired a certain arrogance about what people could do with scientific knowledge.

Businesses learned how to use information to create these new tools, and they began to set up their own research and development operations to create information that they could apply directly to saleable products. Their goal was money, not knowledge per se, and to achieve this they needed people with enough of the right kind of education. They included people from both traditional academic institutions and the newer technical schools that focused more on commercial application. It is no accident that many technical programmes started at this time. The founding date of the Massachusetts Institute of Technology was 1861 and the Technical University of Berlin was founded in 1879. There is no reliable date for the first corporate research and development operations, but General Electric set up such a unit in 1890. Mercedes-Benz began working on research and development in the 1880s and Ford Motor Company did so at the start of the 20th century.

Research on drugs has a long history and produced reliable commercial products at this time. Bayer, for example, started its pharmaceutical research programmes at the end of the 19th century: 'Hoffmann, a chemist in the pharmaceutical laboratory of the German dye manufacturer Friedrich Bayer & Co in Elberfeld, consulted the chemical literature and came across the synthesis of acetylsalicylic acid and then prepared the first sample of pure acetylsalicylic acid on 10 August 1897. This was marketed in 1899 under the registered trademark of Aspirin' (Sneader, 2000).

American pharmaceutical companies were also active, but not always with ideal results. For example, 'In 1937 over 100 people died after ingesting "Elixir Sulfanilamide" manufactured by S. E. Massengill Company of Tennessee. The product was formulated in diethylene glycol, a highly toxic solvent that is now widely used as antifreeze' (Wikipedia, 2025y). In the USA after World War 2 partnerships between corporations and universities grew. An example is streptomycin, which was 'discovered during a Merck-funded research program in Selman Waksman's laboratory at Rutgers in 1943, [and] became the first effective treatment for tuberculosis' (Wikipedia, 2025y).

A significant research area for information science was of course computing. The first digital computer was Konrad Zuse's 1941 Z3, which he developed independently and which was destroyed in the bombing of Berlin. People in both Britain and the USA were also working on early computers, among them 'the Small-Scale Experimental Machine (SSEM) at Manchester University, which first ran a program on 21 June 1948.... The first computer to undertake business data processing was probably LEO (Lyons Electronic Office), based on the design of the Cambridge University EDSAC. LEO ran its first simple clerical program in April 1951' (Lavington, 2010).

In the USA in 1944 the Harvard Mark I ran its first program. It was an electro-mechanical machine whose architecture was less advanced than Zuse's Z3. It was not until the Mark IV that newer generations of the Harvard machine became fully digital. ENIAC (Electronic Numerical Integrator and Computer) at the University of Pennsylvania was the first truly digital American computer, and became the model for corporations like IBM. A number of universities also became involved in computer development. The University of Illinois developed its own machine, the ILLIAC (Illinois Automatic Computer), which 'went online on September 22, 1952. Originally, it was available for use only eight hours a day' (Grainger College of Engineering, 2024). Hardware was not the only important aspect of computer development. The University of Michigan developed the 'Michigan Terminal System (MTS) – a time sharing operating system featuring a shared-access file system, message facility (i.e. e-mail), file editor and comprehensive set of language processors' (University of Michigan, 2004). MTS used IBM 360 hardware and offered more services than IBM systems did at the time.

Technology education after 1950

Corporations needed people with a level of technical education that was only available at universities. This is one of the reasons why corporate partnerships with universities mattered. This symbiosis benefited both sides, and universities soon recognised the economic value of training people to be able to handle this kind of technological development. This led to programmes such as those at Purdue University and Georgia Tech, which turned computer science into a serious academic field. It also led to the existence of a number of specialised commercial training programmes for people who lacked a university computing degree but wanted highly paid high-tech jobs.

These university graduates were key to the development of new computing technologies, since the corporate world itself lacked sophisticated training programmes. One example is Romney White from the University of Waterloo in Canada, whose consulting company specialised in modifications that allowed computer centres to run a single IBM Virtual Machine (VM) operating system simultaneously on multiple computers. This was attractive for non-profits that did not want to buy a new and more powerful machine and yet needed more processing power. Eventually IBM hired Romney White. Another individual was Melinda Varian at Princeton, who had international recognition as a VM software expert and contributed substantially, supporting an international community of systems programmers who used the system (Varian, 1991).

Both Unix and Linux have become key parts of the corporate computing environment. The Unix operating system was itself originally a product of Bell Labs in the late 1960s, which then licensed it to the University of California (Berkeley) The Berkeley standard distribution, often called 'BSD Unix', was written in the C programming language, which made it highly portable. Unix was notable for its modular design that allowed stability and flexibility. Over time it became the basis of other operating systems more closely tied to corporations like AIX (IBM), SunOS and, eventually, NeXTSTEP, the operating system of Steve Jobs's 'Next' computer, which he eventually transformed into MacOS. Unix was also the model for the operating system that Linus Torwalds, a graduate of the University of Helsinki, named Linux. Today that operating system is among the most widely used. According to Alexander Eser (2024), 'Over 70% of web servers run on Linux … [and] Linux holds a share of around 25% in the global server operating system market.'

Children today do not necessarily wait for school to learn how to use computers. Middle-class children often have access to a computer at an early age, even if access only means learning how to manipulate a touch screen to get a favourite song or cartoon. Juhaňák et al. (2019) write:

> The development of ICT competence in students is traditionally addressed in the context of school and formal education. However, recent studies suggest that students use modern technology much more often in the home environment than in the school … [The study used] data from the Program for International Student Assessment (PISA) 2015, which provides representative samples of fifteen year-old students in dozens of countries around the world …

It is not surprising that the home environment plays a significant role in technology interest, but the word 'competence' in this article is vague and appears mainly to mean the ability to enter commands. Writing computer code is primarily a language and information skill that may best be learned early in life. Aptitude varies with all forms of language learning, but the opportunity for learning also needs to be available. That is one of the goals of education. Rankin (2023) writes: 'A decade ago, tech powerhouses the likes of Microsoft, Google, and Amazon helped boost the non-profit Code.org, a learn-to-code program with a vision: "That every student in every school has the opportunity to learn computer science as part of their core K–12 education."' The degree to which this has succeeded has been somewhat limited: 'only eight states – Arkansas, Nebraska, Nevada, North Carolina,

North Dakota, Rhode Island, South Carolina and Tennessee – have legislation requiring public school students to pass a computer science course in order to graduate high school. There are 14 states where less than half of high schools offer computer science instruction' (Gifford, 2023).

Reliable figures about requirements for students to learn coding in school are not always available. 'Coding became part of the national curriculum in England in 2014 as part of the new Computing subject that replaced ICT' (Gruppetta, 2022). According to the *Frankfurter Allgemeine Zeitung* (2017), 'every tenth child can write his or her own program or construct an internet page according to a survey by Digitalverbandes Bitkom of those between 10 and 18' [translated from the German]. China also appears to have serious computer training programmes for students. Computer education for students is an economically important form of information science.

Conclusion

Information and education are so closely linked that separating them is hard. The focus of this chapter has been to look at how people over the years have used education to improve their understanding of information and their ability to create it. The focus of educational topics has changed over the centuries, but information has always had an economic value, and the awareness of this economic value has increased as the engagement with computing technology has grown. Formal education for all levels of society is relatively new, and the focus on research came into being only during the last few hundred years as more universities accepted the concept of 'the unity of teaching and research' as the best approach for transmitting and creating new information.

Recent centuries have been especially productive in creating new forms of information that have found their way into the economic life of societies. It is easy for those not directly engaged in research to forget the degree to which new information enables others to build tools that transform societies. Today is not merely an information age but belongs to an era that accepts the fundamental importance of learning. Precisely when the full promise of this principle will be realised is harder to say.

CHAPTER 16

Information and Politics

What is the role of information in politics?

In his book on *Information Politics: Liberation and Exploitation in the Digital Society*, Tim Jordan (2024) writes: 'Conflict over information has become a central part of modern politics and culture.' This conflict is particularly evident in cases where military force and personal claims often matter more than facts. In 1740 Frederick the Great of Prussia claimed ownership of the province of Silesia on the shadowy basis of a 1537 inheritance treaty and his more factual estimation that Maria Theresa's Austrian army could not stop him. He was right about the Austrian army. His invasion created a new 'fact' that Silesia was German, and it remained so until 1945, when it became Polish after Soviet forces drove out most ethnic Germans. The inhabitants had no say in either case.

Sometimes a 'moral' justification counts for more than facts, regardless of how doubtful that justification might seem. Southern politicians in America justified slavery on the basis of arguments that Africans were less human than white Europeans. The arguments of the pro-slavery politicians seem absurd today to most people. People often have trouble distinguishing what evidence is true, when their social environment favours one claim over another. The US Scopes trial of 1925 offers an example: 'high-school teacher, John T. Scopes, [was] charged with violating state law by teaching Charles Darwin's theory of evolution' (Britannica, 2025h). By today's standards Scopes was correct and the court was wrong, but the racist social climate of the time influenced the outcome. In Germany in the 1930s and 1940s the Nazis made similar claims about Jews being subhuman, and they cited pseudo-scholarly evidence that everyone except their supporters found absurd.

A problem with how information is used in political discourse is the weakness of reliable authenticity standards. Scholarly evidence does not always convince people outside of the academic world in the short term, even though it may influence people over longer periods of time when the evidence is presented in ways that people can understand.

Pre-modern times

Information has long played an important role in politics, when describing power relationships. Thucydides recounted the blunt Athenian justification for conquering Melos in his *History of the Peloponnesian War*: 'you know as well as we do that right, as the world goes, is only in question between equals in power, while the strong do what they can and the weak suffer what they must' (Thucydides, 2019).

Raw power has long served as a fact of political information. The Roman Empire was blunt in just taking territories that it wanted, and political power in the Roman Republic depended often on personal wealth. At a trial in 81 BCE, in a speech entitled 'Pro Quinctio', the young Marcus Tullius Cicero emphasised the treachery and wealth of his legal opponent, in contrast to the honesty of the hard-working man he was defending. Cicero's oratorical skills made the argument work, but few had someone as talented as Cicero as their lawyer.

In pre-modern society, information about personal power was not difficult to get because it was generally obvious. The rich did not hide their wealth, military leaders did not go about incognito and those who had power had no incentive to disguise it. The situation was no different in China or in India. This made political decisions straightforward, because power relationships were clear. A skilled speaker like Cicero had a modern kind of power because he could influence others, which may be one of the reasons for his assassination:

> Cicero was killed on December 7, 43 BC, aged sixty-three, his head and hands (having penned the Philippics) hacked off.... [The Philippics was named] after the speeches given by Demosthenes against Philip II of Macedonia more than three centuries earlier (Juvenal later called them divina Philippica, Satires IV.10.125), they argued against tyranny and for the restoration of the Republic.
>
> (Grout, 2024)

Cicero's speeches represented a form of power that the new dictators found intolerable. It seems likely that Cicero knew the risk and took his chances anyway. Mark Antony especially seems to have disliked and feared Cicero and wanted him dead.

In the medieval world it was normal to accept the fact of the political power of rulers, as had Charlemagne in Europe and William the Conqueror in

England, but the Church offered a source of power that was more subtle than the sword. The question of who had the right to appoint bishops led to disputes between emperors and popes. These 'Investiture controversies' lasted several centuries across multiple countries. The Concordat of Worms in 1122 provided a compromise in which the secular powers recognised the pope's right to appoint bishops and abbots, and the pope recognised that rulers had some rights to intervene when there was a controversy. Military power played a role, but equally important were the information-based arguments by those who knew both theology and church law, which eventually prevailed. Theology was a form of power broadly discussed among the laity in Byzantium: 'The Greek Emperor, in collaboration with the patriarch, was in a much weaker position: there was an active body of lay theological opinion and even more active and infirmly entrenched monastic opinion and a profound danger of popular disturbance' (Southern, 1970, 76).

From an information science viewpoint, the Protestant Reformation counts as a time when information transformed societies that primarily respected military force. Martin Luther was not a military commander but, like Cicero, he was a powerful writer and speaker whose opinions led a portion of the European population to rethink their allegiance to the Catholic Church and its hierarchy. He was more successful than earlier reformers like Jan Hus, not only because his preachings convinced secular leaders that his biblical interpretations were correct but because he gave them a basis for indulging their own wishes in ignoring the pope and emperor. The Protestant Reformation brought about major political changes to the map of Europe.

Islam also changed the political landscape. No information scientist today should doubt that religion tells people how to understand the world about them, and no one can reasonably doubt that Islam represented and still represents a potent political force. Religion defines truth and how its adherents should think about a broad range of political issues. The armies in the original small states where Islam first appeared could not have conquered territories as large or populous as Egypt, or North Africa, or portions of the Byzantine Empire without the passion of its new converts and its radical new way of seeing the world. Islam also offered a potential means of escaping the control of the Roman church. Even British kings like John were not immune from the temptation to convert, when he had a conflict with the Church: 'A contemporary chronicler says that the king thought of becoming a Muslim, and he gives a detailed account of the steps he took in this direction' (Southern, 1970, 20–1).

Buddhism offered another radical way of interpreting the world. Buddha's teaching in the fifth century BCE eventually separated into two versions: Mahayana, literally the great way, and Theravada, which more closely resembled the more monastic relationship of early Buddhism to the world. 'The Mahayana school has spread to China, where it has developed an eschatology that has inspired rebellions through history' (Laliberté, 2019). Nonetheless, there are few instances of major political disruptions in Asian society due to Buddhism, compared to the consequences of religion in Western Europe and in the Middle East. Islam played a significant political role in India, thanks to the explicitly Muslim Mogul emperors and to the opportunity that conversion to Islam offered for low-caste Indians to escape the stigma of their birth.

Information and politics since 1789

Historians do not typically regard the French Revolution as an information revolution, but it was in the sense that it changed how people understood the structure of society. The storming of the Bastille is typically counted as the beginning of the French Revolution, but many changes had already started, including an awareness of the financial problems of the French monarchy, which was the reason why Louis XVI needed to call for assistance from the Estates General. Information about the events in France spread rapidly throughout Europe and raised fears among traditional rulers, which is one reason why the anti-revolutionary coalition came together quickly. The counter-revolutionary forces soon learned to respect the effectiveness of the *levée en masse*, a form of national conscription. Although the new soldiers had minimal training, they had a level of passion that made a difference in battle. The Revolution also opened the military to those with talent and technical capabilities, despite their social background. Napoleon Bonaparte profited from this. He understood how to use artillery effectively for political purposes, and rose quickly to become emperor of France.

People quickly recognised the significance of the French Revolution, but today people forget how important it was and how hard it was to get information about it. The famously punctual Immanuel Kant began his walk late one day in order to get the latest news about what was happening in France. Although Kant was generally sympathetic towards the Revolution, his position was typically complicated: 'Kant sympathises with the commoners' deputies in 1789 because, unlike the rabble-rousers on the streets of Paris in 1792, they did not use force against an existing regime.... Several authors have followed Marx in claiming that Kant's turn to politics in the 1790s was a direct response to the revolution' (Maliks, 2022, 2).

The French Revolution influenced a range of other writers, including Karl Marx, for whom information about ongoing consequences with Louis Napoleon in 1848 influenced one of his most read-works: 'Hegel remarks somewhere that all facts and personages of great importance in world history occur, as it were, twice. He forgot to add: the first time as tragedy, the second as farce' (Marx, 1963, 15). The political philosophy of Karl Marx became the orthodox belief of the leaders of the Russian Revolution in 1917, and continues to be a key philosophical source in the People's Republic of China and many other countries. The longer-term influence of the French Revolution on the information world has not withered away.

World War 1 began with a series of information-based errors. When the assassination of Franz Ferdinand took place in Sarajevo in Bosnia, little was known about the 19-year-old assassin Gavrilo Princip and the Black Hand organisation, and officials did not immediately understand that Princip had probably just seized the opportunity. Austria-Hungary waited almost a month to react and then ignored the fact that Serbia had already begun investigating the assassination. Military escalation started with no real information about whether other countries would respect their treaty obligations. In Germany, people responded with joy and with no understanding of the potential consequences. The situation was similar in France, where people saw the war as a chance to recover the provinces of Alsace and Lorraine.

The political situation at the start of World War 2 was different, partly because of a widespread underestimate of the German army and the French army's disdain for Charles De Gaulle's advice about the use of tanks and the weakness of the Maginot line. One information error piled on another, and France fell quickly. Information failures mattered in the Pacific theatre as well. All that the attack on Pearl Harbor achieved was to demonstrate the uselessness of the battleships that the attack destroyed. Battleships played only a minor role in the rest of the war. Tactical bombing was effective in all theatres, but the strategic bombing raids in Europe and Japan failed to alter the military balance and engendered hatred among the survivors. It was not until later, during the Vietnam War, that 'a ceaseless and relentless bombing campaign against North Vietnam, was ultimately regarded as ineffective' (Britannica, 2023g).

Economic issues required serious information analysis in order to prevent what people in the 19th century called 'crises', and which today are labelled as depressions or recessions. Economic issues involved not only the stock markets but also inflation. Inflation has existed as long as currency has. In the medieval world the cause of inflation was often the physical adulteration of coinage with base metals, which was tempting for any ruler short of cash. Inflation fears increased with paper currency, because printing more currency was easy. However, in the absence of adequate information, governments might not print enough currency: in Britain in the late 19th century, the production of goods grew more rapidly than the currency, resulting in deflation: 'The pound had an average deflation rate of 0.38% per year since 1870, producing a cumulative price change of 7.37%' (Webster, 2024).

Tracking inflation and deflation requires the tracking of quantities of detailed information that was difficult before computers. Picking a plausible reference currency was the best option. People track the hyperinflation in Germany in the early 1920s using the US dollar exchange rate. Inflation stopped abruptly in 1923 when the German central bank (*Reichsbank*) issued a new currency which had no precious metal behind it, only the theoretical value of the economy. Without reliable information, inflation is hard to predict or to control.

Fact checking and plagiarism

Fact-checking sites have become part of the contemporary political landscape, especially during elections. Exaggerations and untruths have never been absent from political life. One example is the advertisement on buses in the UK about how leaving the European Union would save £350 million per week that would be available for the National Health Service (NHS). This was untrue for many reasons, among them the fact that (a) the UK did not pay that amount to the EU and (b) it received significant money back from the EU. The lie was nonetheless politically effective because of the financial problems of the NHS (Conversion Uplift, 2024). The Berkeley University Library has a guide to primarily American fact-checking sites, and lists six that it finds reliable. Some US candidates dispute their impartiality.

Plagiarism has become a political tool as well as a scholarly issue. *New York Times* reporter Alexandria Alter (2024) wrote about allegations against the author of the 2018 book *White Fragility*: 'The allegations against DiAngelo follow several other cases in which plagiarism and research misconduct accusations were leveled at academics and administrators who promote diversity, equity and inclusion initiatives, Bailey said. Similar complaints have been filed against diversity officers at Harvard, Columbia, the University of California, Los Angeles, and the University of Wisconsin-Madison.' Plagiarism concerns were also raised in Germany against the Defense Minister Karl-Theodor zu Guttenberg in 2011, who lost his doctoral title after large-scale plagiarism was exposed. The Education Minister Annette Schavan faced similar plagiarism accusations, which led to her losing her doctorate, though that case was less clear. More recently the first Black woman president of Harvard, Claudine Gay, was attacked for plagiarism:

> Investigations by the Washington Free Beacon and the New York Post, at least partially instigated by the conservative activist Christopher Rufo and his crusade to chase 'wokeism' and diversity initiatives from all corners of society, turned up nearly 50 instances of alleged plagiarism in Gay's academic writing. According to the Harvard board, a school subcommittee and independent panel charged with investigating the plagiarism allegations against Gay found 'a few instances of inadequate citation' but 'no violation of Harvard's standard for research misconduct …'
>
> (Lawrence, 2024)

Plagiarism is a dangerous political weapon because the definition is so imprecise.

Book banning

The American Library Association (ALA) is concerned about efforts to ban books in a number of US states: 'ALA's Office for Intellectual Freedom [OIF] documented 1,247 demands to censor library books and resources in 2023. The number of titles targeted for censorship surged 65% in 2023 compared to 2022, reaching the highest levels ever documented by OIF in more than 20 years of tracking …' (ALA, n.d.) Some publishers have also protested:

> The Florida law, enacted last year, requires school districts to allow parents and other residents to limit children's access to library materials. The lawsuit – filed by Penguin Random House, the nation's biggest publisher, and other companies – argues that the rule has caused a blanket purge of hundreds of books across the state, and created a 'regime of strict censorship in school libraries.'
>
> (Closson, 2024)

Florida is not the only state that wants to restrict books on socially controversial topics: 'More than 4,300 books were removed from schools across 23 states in a six-month period last year, according to PEN America, a free speech organization' (Closson, 2024).

Social media are harder to censor. Even so, information scientists are not committed to the same level of unrestricted free speech as Elon Musk. According to Arwa Mahdawi's *Guardian* article (2024), Elon Musk likes 'to refer to himself as a "free speech absolutist"'. Social media platforms like X (formerly Twitter) were implicated in the summer 2024 riots in Southport and elsewhere in England: 'Experts have said Musk's decision to allow figures such as the British far-right activist Tommy Robinson, whose real name is Stephen Yaxley-Lennon, back onto X has played a part in the spread of online disinformation' (Sinmaz, 2024). Information about the person who allegedly sparked the riot was also in the social media: 'Before the suspect's identity was confirmed, false claims proliferated online that he was a Muslim asylum seeker who had arrived in the UK by boat. In the wake of these messages, members of the far right – guided by social media – have gathered in towns and cities across the country with some shouting anti-immigration and Islamophobic slogans' (Sinmaz, 2024). Social media too often has no mechanism for restraining verbal violence.

Social media also provide a range of information that can put young people at risk. A study by University College London and the University of Kent entitled 'Safer Scrolling: How Algorithms Popularise and Gamify Online Hate and Misogyny for Young People' (Regehr et al., 2024) warns:

> With this report, we highlight how the affordances of social media platforms, exemplified in this research by the recommender systems of TikTok, actively amplify and direct harmful content to young people.... After only 5 days of TikTok usage, our research shows a fourfold increase in the level of misogynistic content being presented on the 'For You' page of an individual's TikTok account.

The social media sites have their own vocabulary which may appear standard, like 'Red Pill' and 'Black Pill', but have special meanings for 'incel' groups. '[I]ncel refers to a person, usually a man, who express resentment, rage, and hostility towards women for denying them relationships and sex' (Regehr, 2024). The relatively closed communities on social media tend to reinforce extreme behaviours. The roots of this could be seen in the early e-mail lists that had little or no moderation. E-mail lists that belong to particular academics or social communities tend today to be self-moderating.

Censorship

Censorship is an issue for many information scientists, but culture plays a strong role in what counts as censorship. The World Press Freedom Index ranks countries based on the following criteria: 'pluralism, media independence, media environment and self-censorship, legislative framework, transparency, and the quality of the infrastructure that supports the production of news and information' (World Press Freedom Index, 2024).

Information science needs to keep restrictions in cultural perspective. The World Press Freedom questionnaire expresses Western definitions of press freedom that are not universal, even in countries like the USA. Today 'pluralism' is especially under attack in some American states. The Reporters sans frontières's World Press Freedom Index ranks Germany at 10, the United Kingdom at 23, the United States at 55 and China at 172. In recent years many politically right-wing organisations have complained about what they consider censorship by more liberal academic communities. One example is what happened to New College of Florida:

> Mr. DeSantis and his allies vowed in January to transform the liberal arts institution, known as Florida's 'public honors college,' into a bastion of conservatism. More than a third of last year's faculty members – about three dozen – are gone. So are about 125 students who chose not to return.... The pronounced change in climate has led to a flurry of legal challenges. Alumni, faculty and students have sued, claiming free-speech violations that they say amount to academic censorship.
>
> (Mazzei, 2023)

Some American conservatives frame their arguments as an attack on their own freedom to speak. For example: 'Republican states spent years swooping in to bolster safe spaces for conservative voices at public universities in the name of fighting liberal censorship' (Perez, 2024).

Unlike in the 1960s, the right wing may be the demonstrators:

> 'You can't just have a blanket exclusion at a public university for speech activity, protests, marches, demonstrations and loud speeches,' Mark Rotenberg, the top lawyer for the Hillel International organization and a Reagan-era Justice Department official, said in an interview. 'That is completely clear from long-standing constitutional precedent. But by the same token, protesters do not have a right, including at public universities, to simply call their shots as they want.'
>
> (Perez, 2024)

From an information science perspective, understanding censorship requires a nuanced understanding of cultures and the local situations.

Medical information: COVID-19

Accurate medical information became an issue during the COVID-19 pandemic, especially in the USA. Then-president Trump made a number of verifiably false statements about the pandemic: he 'repeatedly expressed his surprise at the scale of the coronavirus as it spread around the world and raced across the US' (Milman, 2020). He also thought that it would disappear, and yet claimed to have taken it seriously early on. He promised vaccines and, when they did not reach people, accused some of hoarding, and at one point he seemed to think it was a form of flu (Milman, 2020). The number of untrue statements became a political issue during the 2022 US mid-term elections.

The claim that hydroxychloroquine could cure COVID was not only untrue, but increased deaths: those who tried it 'were 11% more likely to die from the virus, according to a new scientific study' (Vargas, 2024). Trump's claims 'about anti-malaria medication led to a surge in prescriptions for the drug'. Eventually the Food and Drug Administration 'was forced to warn that hydroxychloroquine could cause irregular heartbeats and other cardiac trouble' (Vargas, 2024). Such false claims are historically not all that unusual, but the timing in this case was bad. Rumours abounded that COVID originally came from a particular market in Wuhan, China, or that it was released from a Chinese lab. Even now it is not completely clear where the virus originated, but the possible Chinese connection made COVID more of a political issue than if the place of origin had been a neutral or Western location.

This repeats a pattern that has historical roots going back to medieval plagues, at a time when the existence of rodent-borne bacterial infections was completely unknown. People looked for someone to blame:

> Some people believed that the way to do this was to purge their communities of heretics and other troublemakers – so, for example, many thousands of Jews were massacred in 1348 and 1349.... Some upper-class men joined processions of flagellants that traveled from town to town and engaged in public displays of penance and punishment: They would beat themselves and one another with heavy leather straps studded with sharp pieces of metal while the townspeople looked on.
>
> (History.com, 2023)

This kind of behaviour did nothing to mitigate the effects of the plague or its spread, any more than the false information about hydroxychloroquine did to mitigate the COVID pandemic.

Medical information: HIV

COVID-19 was only one of many communicable diseases that became a political issue. Many people associated HIV with homosexual practices. The US National Institutes of Health (2024) describes it as follows:

> HIV stands for human immunodeficiency virus, which is the virus that causes HIV infection. The abbreviation 'HIV' can refer to the virus or to HIV infection. AIDS stands for acquired immunodeficiency syndrome. AIDS is the most advanced stage of HIV infection.... HIV can be transmitted from one person to another when certain bodily fluids are shared between people. Bodily fluids that can transmit HIV include blood, semen ('cum'), pre-seminal fluid ('pre-cum'), vaginal fluids, rectal fluids, and breastmilk. HIV can be transmitted during vaginal or anal sex, through sharing needles for injecting drugs or tattooing, by getting stuck with a needle that has the blood of someone with HIV on it, through pregnancy, and through breastfeeding.

The initial political reaction was 'to treat the epidemic as a joke' (Lopez, 2015), and misinformation about HIV was widespread. 'The exchanges are hugely revealing. For one, they show just how little was known about the disease when the epidemic first broke – people thought it was exclusive to gay people, and thought that it could be transmitted through saliva, even though HIV can only be transmitted through blood, semen, pre-cum, rectal fluids, vaginal fluids, and breast milk…' (Lopez, 2015).

The scale of the HIV epidemic is often underestimated. The statistics from UNAIDS (2024) are: '39.9 million [36.1 million–44.6 million] people globally were living with HIV in 2023. 1.3 million [1 million–1.7 million] people became newly infected with HIV in 2023. 630,000 [500,000–820,000] people died from AIDS-related illnesses in 2023.' The news media began to pay attention when well-known figures like Rock Hudson acquired the disease.

Climate information

Climate misinformation has grown over time: 'Republican leaders have staked out different positions on climate and energy issues. Some, including President Donald Trump, have called climate change a "hoax" and downplayed the link between human activity and a warming planet' (Tyson and Kennedy, 2024). A part of the problem involves industries whose profits have benefited from the consumption of fossil fuels. Cultural habits also play a role. Americans tend to live in houses or in the countryside where it is almost impossible to escape a dependence on cars. Despite evidence about the role of fossil fuels, '[a]mong Republicans, large shares back increasing the production of fossil fuel sources: 73% favor more offshore oil and gas drilling and 68% favor more hydraulic fracturing' (Tyson and Kennedy, 2024).

Age plays a role in attitudes towards climate issues:

> Younger Republicans stand out from their older GOP counterparts on some climate and energy issues. For instance, a large majority of Republicans ages 18 to 29 (79%) say human activity, such as the burning of fossil fuels, contributes at least some to climate change – including 35% who think human activity contributes a great deal. A much smaller share of Republicans ages 50 and older (47%) say human activity contributes a great deal or some to climate change.
>
> (Tyson and Kennedy, 2024)

Legal frameworks to achieve climate goals can help in theory. Most countries have signed the Paris Agreement: 'The Paris Agreement is a legally binding international treaty on climate change. It was adopted by 196 Parties at the UN Climate Change Conference (COP21) in Paris, France, on 12 December 2015. It entered into force on 4 November 2016' (UNFCCC, 2024). However, internal political pressure has kept many countries from reaching their 'legally binding' goals, something that has often been true for international treaties over the centuries. The problem with the Paris Agreement and most other international agreements is the lack of enforcement internally and externally. Short-term political gains tend to win in the end.

The problem is a measure of distrust in the news media. In 2023 the American Pew Research Center did a survey about the public's attitudes towards climate change. 'Interviewees widely rejected the national news media as a credible source for climate information. They see these outlets as presenting information that suits their own agendas. Interviewees generally expressed greater openness toward hearing from scientists on climate change because of their subject matter expertise' (Pasquini et al., 2023). Yet, survey participants supported local measures to improve air and water quality, and 'stressed the importance of respecting individual freedoms – and individual choice – in any energy transition. This theme was underscored by criticism of policies like ending the production of new gas-powered vehicles' (Pasquini et al., 2023).

The dependence of Americans on cars is an important factor here that is not universal. *Tagesspiegel* reported a survey in Germany that found a significant 12% decline in car use in Berlin between the beginning of the pandemic in 2019 and December 2023. Berlin's extensive public transit system is one reason, but Hamburg saw a reduction of 7% and car-friendly Munich saw a 5% reduction (Böldt, 2024). New car registrations have grown in the UK, but fuelled mainly by fleet registration rather than purchase of private cars: 'Private buyer uptake fell by 17.7% to 50,458 units, while business registrations declined by 16.1%, to 2,609' (SMMT, 2024).

Conclusion

Politics and information are so intertwined that many find it difficult to separate them, which is one of the problems with issues like the COVID-19 or global warming. Misinformation is historically common, because getting accurate information requires a level of trust in scientific sources. Scientific training at universities has helped to provide better information, and there is broad hope that better international communication also helps. In the end, however, for political purposes, it is not the reliability of facts that matters for some, but their use for winning office. This is the centuries-long reality of politics, where information just serves as a tool to achieve goals.

Little has changed since the time of Thucydides and Cicero. Power is what matters in politics, and power determines the value and meaning of information, even if later generations recognise that the information was wrong. Information scientists can hope that Shakespeare's famous line in the *Merchant of Venice* that 'the truth will out' will work in the long run. For most people, it is the short term that matters, which may explain why the truth failed to come out during the debates over Brexit and the discussion about COVID-19.

Summary and Conclusion

Context matters: 'Man ist eben so gut Zeitbürger, als man Staatsbürger ist' (Schiller, 1795). Or, in English, 'people are citizens of their time as well as their state'. This is one reason why information science needs a historical perspective.

The goal of this book has been to introduce readers to the history, philosophy and applications of the academic field that we currently call 'information science'. The book has looked beyond contemporary research projects in order to consider the full scope of the science of information. The ideas came out of discussions with scholars over multiple decades and in multiple countries. The main emphasis has been on European and American experiences, where the author is most at home, but has also included China, India and the Islamic world. A book like this must always be a work in progress because information science changes constantly and topics that seem urgent now, like information falsification, may seem less urgent to future generations.

In some sense this book is an ethnography of the field, based on the personal experiences of the author, who has a long history of using ethnographic methods. The emphasis on history has grown in part out of the fact that information science is a young field, and most practitioners have only a vague sense of its intellectual origins beyond its connection to library science, which is itself a comparatively modern field. Computing technology is an essential part of how we view information science today, and it helps that the author has decades of hands-on professional computing experience.

Philosophers understand that all scholarly fields have their own ways of thinking. With a few exceptions, information science scholars have no formal training as philosophers, but that does not mean that they lack philosophical approaches to information. Today many information scientists focus on the economic value of information and on how to repurpose information for commercial enterprises. Historically, people have regarded information more generally as a way to think about solving problems. Today's focus on the commercial value of information is almost the antithesis of the medieval use of information to understand God's will, but philosophies change over time. The desire to use information for human purposes remains constant.

Information-based applications are almost inescapable today, and have always played a role in human society. Today people talk more explicitly about information and how to acquire it and to use it efficiently. The official institutions of modern society, such as schools, universities and training programmes, are examples of how pervasive the demand for information has become. Every professional field today has a clear information aspect, which is sometimes bound up with specific training programmes. The library degree requirement in many countries is a simple and obvious example. Programming and other technical fields have escaped some of the training requirements insofar as they represent careers open to talent where capable people can learn to do the work on their own. In that sense there is a resemblance to art and music.

One of the contemporary information tasks is addressing false information, which comes up in an astonishing array of forms. Sometimes it is political, which is typical especially for an election cycle, but misinformation is not limited to that. Climate issues are an example, as seen in Marjorie Taylor Greene's suggestion that the US National Oceanic and Atmospheric Administration might cause hurricanes (Horvath, 2024). In fact, misinformation is far from new and has appeared in different forms on different topics using different media. At one time much misinformation came in the form of gossip that neighbours whispered from one person to another. Today the misinformation is often found on social media for everyone to see. It will take time to understand the full implication of this shift to digital gossip and what its consequences may be.

Scholarly information today suffers from articles with a range of reliability problems that range from data falsification to plagiarism. Some of this scholarly misinformation appears to come from the pressure to get more articles out without adequate checking. Mechanisms exist to deal with such problems, but the traditional safety net, peer review, is under heavy pressure because journals have trouble getting reliable people who can spend enough time to produce careful reviews. Shoddy reviewing only exacerbates the problem of creating quality information.

Several external factors exacerbate the problem. Some universities count how many articles a scholar publishes in certain journals with a certain ranking over a limited time. Historically we know that some of the most important scholars wrote relatively few works. The philosopher Ludwig Wittgenstein is a famous example: he produced only one unpublished work during his years at Cambridge, which was published after his death, but it is work that remains significant. The push for quantity appears to come in part from overburdened administrators who lack the skills (or time) to read the academic output of the scholars they must evaluate. This has led to a reliance on numerical rankings that measure short-term impact. The problem is historically new and comes largely as a consequence of the need to justify costs at universities. More publications is not the same as creating more scholarly knowledge or more information. As in most manufacturing operations, quality matters, and poor quality damages reputations.

Those who want to transform information science into a commercially viable profession whose graduates earn high salaries and produce easily definable goods will probably fail, not because the field lacks value but because money making is not the goal of information science. What makes information science useful is the way in which its practitioners transform the world into something comprehensible in terms that others can digest and apply to their own experience. Of course, not everyone wants reliable information. It is often easier to live in a fantasy world where facts do not matter for decision making. Nonetheless, information science is unlikely to go away, because rational people will always need information to do their work and live their lives.

References

Abalkina, A. (2014) Journal Hijackers Still Infiltrate Scopus Despite its Efforts, *Retraction Watch* (blog), 18 June, https://retractionwatch.com/author/anna-abalkina.

Abbott, A. (2001) *Chaos of Disciplines*, University of Chicago Press.

Abbott, D. (2008) What Is Digital Curation? *Digital Curation Centre*, www.dcc.ac.uk/sites/default/files/documents/resource/briefing-papers/what-is-digital-curation.pdf.

ALA (American Library Association) (n.d.) Censorship by the Numbers: Banned Books, www.ala.org/bbooks/censorship-numbers.

ALA (American Library Association) (2024) www.ala.org.

Alekna, J. N. (2020) Reunified through Radio: Media, Technology, and Politics in Modern China 1923–1958, https://dataspace.princeton.edu/handle/88435/dsp01rx913s82t.

'Alex' (2024) How Does AI Image Generation Work? *Hypotenuse AI*, www.hypotenuse.ai/blog/how-do-ai-image-generators-work.

ALISE (n.d.) History, https://alise.org/page/About.

ALISE (2024a) Council of Deans, Directors, and Chairs, https://alise.org/page/CDDC.

ALISE (2024b) Journal of Education for Library and Information Science (JELIS), www.alise.org/page/JELIS.

ALISE (2024c) ALISE Book Series, https://alise.org/page/Book-Series.

Alter, A. (2024) Author of 'White Fragility' Faces Accusations of Plagiarism, *New York Times*, 29 August, www.nytimes.com/2024/08/29/books/robin-diangelo-white-fragility-accusation-plagiarism.html.

Amos, J., Morelle, R. and Francis, A. (2024) Pompeii: Breathtaking New Paintings Found at Ancient City, *BBC News*, 11 April, www.bbc.com/news/science-environment-68777741.

Archaeology Magazine (2024) The World's Oldest Writing, www.archaeology.org/issues/213–1605/features/4326-cuneiform-the-world-s-oldest-writing.

Arles Tourism Board (2024) Arles Amphitheater, https://provence-alpes-cotedazur.com/en/things-to-do/culture-and-heritage/monuments/arles-amphitheater.

Arnold, J. H. and Goodson, C. (2012) Resounding Community: The History and Meaning of Medieval Church Bells, *Viator*, **43** (1), 99–130, www.academia.edu/1431766/with_John_Arnold_Resounding_Community_The_History_and_Meaning_of_Medieval_Church_Bells_Viator_43_1_January_2012_99_130.

ASIS&T (n.d.) Bibliography of the History of ASIS&T, www.asist.org/about/history-of-asist.

ASIS&T (2025) ASIS&T Partners with GMP, www.asist.org/2025/01/23/ed-january-2025-copy.

Atkins, D. (2003) Revolutionizing Science and Engineering through Cyberinfrastructure: Report of the National Science Foundation Blue-Ribbon Advisory Panel on Cyberinfrastructure, *National Science Foundation*, www.nsf.gov/cise/sci/reports/atkins.pdf.

Augustyn, A. (2024) Papyrus: Definition, History and Facts, *Encyclopedia Britannica*, www.britannica.com/topic/papyrus-writing-material.

Balter, M. (2015) Human Language May Have Evolved to Help Our Ancestors Make Tools, *Science*, www.science.org/content/article/human-language-may-have-evolved-help-our-ancestors-make-tools.

Barker, V. (2015) U.K. Tabloid 'The Sun' Ends Topless Tradition, *NPR*, 20 January, www.npr.org/2015/01/20/378660076/u-k-tabloid-the-sun-ends-topless-tradition.

Bates, M. J. (2010) Information Behavior, *Encyclopedia of Library and Information Sciences*, https://pages.gseis.ucla.edu/faculty/bates/articles/information-behavior.html.

Bayerische Staatsbibliothek (2023) Die Bayerische Staatsbibliothek in Zahlen – 2023, www.bsb-muenchen.de/ueber-uns/portraet/in-zahlen.

Bayerische Staatsbibloithek (2024) Chronik, www.bsb-muenchen.de/ueber-uns/portraet/chronik.

Becker, S. O., Hornung, E. and Woessmann, L. (2011) Education and Catch-up in the Industrial Revolution, *American Economic Journal: Macroeconomics*, **3** (3), 92–126, www.aeaweb.org/articles.php?doi=10.1257/mac.3.3.92.

Berkeley School of Information (2024) Online Master's in Data Science from UC Berkeley: Master of Information and Data Science, www.ischool.berkeley.edu/programs/mids.

Berlitz (2024) 214 Chinese Radicals: What Do They All Mean? A Handy Guide, www.berlitz.com/blog/chinese-radicals-list.

Berners-Lee, T. (2024) The WorldWideWeb Browser, www.w3.org/People/Berners-Lee/WorldWideWeb.html.

Bero, L. (2019) When Big Companies Fund Academic Research, the Truth Often Comes Last, *The Conversation*, 3 October, www.sydney.edu.au/news-opinion/news/2019/10/03/when-big-companies-fund-academic-research-the-truth-often-comes.html.

Bhattacharjee, Y. (2013) The Mind of a Con Man, *New York Times Magazine*, 26 April, www.nytimes.com/2013/04/28/magazine/diederik-stapels-audacious-academic-fraud.html.

Bibliothèque nationale de France (2023) La BnF en chiffres, www.bnf.fr/fr/la-bnf-en-chiffres.

Bibliothèque nationale de France (2024) Histoire de La Bibliothèque Nationale de France, www.bnf.fr/fr/histoire-de-la-bibliotheque-nationale-de-france.

Bild Zeitung (1984) 19. Juli 1984 zum 40. Geburtstag: 80 nackte Frauen eingesperrt, www.ebay.de/itm/296446690821 [2024].

Bloch, M. (1953) *The Historian's Craft*, Vintage.

Böldt, D. (2024) Trotz Bevölkerungswachstum in Berlin: Anzahl privater Autos geht seit zwei Jahren zurück, *Der Tagesspiegel Online*, www.tagesspiegel.de/berlin/trotz-bevolkerungswachstum-in-berlin-anzahl-privater-autos-geht-seit-zwei-jahren-zuruck-12301916.html.

Borth, D. (2024) Telephone: History, Definition, Invention, Uses, and Facts, *Encyclopedia Britannica*, www.britannica.com/technology/telephone.

Bortolotti, G. (2023) A Homage to Tomatoes, the King of Italian Cooking, *Issimo* (blog), 28 April, https://issimoissimo.com/buonissimo/a-homage-to-tomatoes-the-king-of-italian-cooking.

Bowden, H. (2005) *Classical Athens and the Delphic Oracle*, Cambridge University Press, https://assets.cambridge.org/052182/3730/excerpt/0521823730_excerpt.htm.

Breugel, P. (1566) *The Wedding Dance*, Detroit Institute of Arts, https://dia.org/collection/wedding-dance-35573.

Britannica (2025a) Alessandro Volta, www.britannica.com/biography/Alessandro-Volta.

Britannica (2025b) Information Science, www.britannica.com/science/information-science.

Britannica (2025c) Skype, www.britannica.com/technology/Skype.

Britannica (2025d) Black Death, www.britannica.com/event/Black-Death.

Britannica (2025e) Newspaper, www.britannica.com/topic/newspaper.

Britannica (2025f) Bombing of Dresden, www.britannica.com/event/bombing-of-Dresden.

Britannica (2025g) Strategic Bombing, www.britannica.com/topic/strategic-bombing.

Britannica (2025h) Scopes Trial, www.britannica.com/event/Scopes-Trial.

Brook, T. (2023) *The Price of Collapse: The Little Ice Age and the Fall of Ming China*, Princeton University Press.

Buck, S. (2023) When Does Science Self-correct? Lessons from a Replication Crisis in Early 20th Century Chemistry, *Substack, The Good Science Project* (blog), https://goodscience.substack.com/p/when-does-science-self-correct-lessons.

Butler, J. (2024) Deepfakes of Australian Politicians Including Penny Wong and Katy Gallagher Used in Investment Scams, *Guardian*, 7 June, www.theguardian.com/australia-news/article/2024/jun/08/deepfakes-of-australian-politicians-including-penny-wong-and-katy-gallagher-used-in-investment-scams.

ByteScout Team (2021) Cobol vs Fortran Ultimate Comparison, *ByteScout* (blog), https://bytescout.com/blog/cobol-vs-fortran.html.

Cambridge Dictionary (2024) Technology, https://dictionary.cambridge.org/dictionary/english/technology.

Campbell, W. J. (2014) No, Politico: Hearst Did Not Cause the Spanish-American War, *Media Myth Alert* (blog), https://mediamythalert.com/2014/06/20/no-politico-hearst-did-not-cause-the-spanish-american-war.

Canadian Association for Information Science (CAIS) (2023) https://cais-acsi.ca.

Canadian Federation of Library Associations (2016) Foreign Credentials Position Statement, https://cfla-fcab.ca/en/guidelines-and-position-papers/foreign-credentials-position-statement.

Carr, N. (2008) How Many Computers Does the World Need? Fewer than You Think, *Guardian*, 21 February, www.theguardian.com/technology/2008/feb/21/computing.supercomputers.

Chairman's BAO (2024) Top 10 Rude Gestures in China: Chinese Middle Finger, www.thechairmansbao.com/blog/gestures-to-avoid-in-china.

Charles University (2024) History of Charles University, https://cuni.cz/UKEN-106.html.

The Chartered Institute of Library and Information Professionals (CILIP) (2024) www.cilip.org.uk.

Clegg, N. (2021) In Response to Oversight Board, Trump Suspended for Two Years; Will Only Be Reinstated If Conditions Permit, *Meta* (blog), 4 June, https://about.fb.com/news/2021/06/facebook-response-to-oversight-board-recommendations-trump.

CLOCKSS (2024) Why CLOCKSS? https://clockss.org/about/why-clockss.

Closson, T. (2024) Major Publishers Sue Florida over Banned School Library Books, *New York Times*, 29 August, www.nytimes.com/2024/08/29/us/florida-book-ban-lawsuit.html.

Cohn, N. (2024) The Shaky Foundation of Trump's Lead: Disengaged Voters, *New York Times*, 24 April, www.nytimes.com/2024/05/24/upshot/trump-biden-polls-voters.html.

Columbia Law School (2024) COVID-19 Data Misrepresented by Florida Governor, *Sabin Center for Climate Change Law*, https://climate.law.columbia.edu/content/covid-19-data-misrepresented-florida-governor.

Conversion Uplift (2024) The Boris Johnson Brexit Bus Lie of £350m, https://conversion-uplift.co.uk/brexit/the-boris-johnson-brexit-bus-lie-of-350m.

Copeland, B. (2018) Artificial Intelligence Programming Language, *Encyclopedia Britannica*, www.britannica.com/technology/artificial-intelligence-programming-language.

Crease, R. P. (2014) Feynman's Failings, *Physics World*, **27** (3), 25, https://doi.org/10.1088/2058–7058/27/03/34.

Cummings, M. (2023) What Self-driving Cars Tell Us about AI Risks, *IEEE Spectrum*, 30 July, https://spectrum.ieee.org/self-driving-cars-2662494269.

Cunningham, C. (2016) The Dawning Moon of the Mind by Susan Brind Morrow, *Journal of Astronomical History and Heritage*, **19** (2), 233.

Cunningham, J. M. (2023) Why Do Some People Call Football 'Soccer'? *Encyclopedia Britannica*, www.britannica.com/story/why-do-some-people-call-football-soccer.

Curchin, L. A. (1995) Literacy in the Roman Provinces: Qualitative and Quantitative Data from Central Spain, *The American Journal of Philology*, **116** (3), 461–76, https://doi.org/10.2307/295333.

Davey, M., Kirchgaessner, S. and Boseley, S. (2020) Surgisphere: Governments and WHO Changed Covid-19 Policy Based on Suspect Data from Tiny US Company, *Guardian*, 3 June, www.theguardian.com/world/2020/jun/03/covid-19-surgisphere-who-world-health-organization-hydroxychloroquine.

DeNoon, D. J. (2005) Why 7 Deadly Diseases Strike Blacks Most, www.webmd.com/hypertension-high-blood-pressure/features/why-7-deadly-diseases-strike-blacks-most.

Department of Homeland Security (2021) Increasing Threats of Deepfake Identities, www.dhs.gov/sites/default/files/publications/increasing_threats_of_deepfake_identities_0.pdf.

Department of Islamic Art (2001) Figural Representation in Islamic Art, www.metmuseum.org/toah/hd/figs/hd_figs.htm.

Deutsche Biographie (n.d.) Dziatzko, Karl Franz Otto, www.deutsche-biographie.de/pnd116263601.html.

Deutsche Digitale Bibliothek (n.d.) www.deutsche-digitale-bibliothek.de/person/gnd/116185198.

Deutsche Nationalbibliothek (2024) Bücher, www.dnb.de/DE/Sammlungen/Buecher/buecher_node.

Deutsches Historisches Institut (2019) Leopold von Ranke: Auszüge aus seinen Schriften (1824–1881), ghdi.ghi-dc.org/sub_document.cfm?document_id=358&language=german.

Dilmegani, C. (2024) Large Language Model Training in 2024, https://research.aimultiple.com/large-language-model-training.

Domain Name Stat (2024) Country Domain Name Registrations, https://domainnamestat.com/statistics/country/others.

Dong, G., Wang, H., Sun, J. and Wang, X. (2024) Evaluating and Mitigating Linguistic Discrimination in Large Language Models, *arXiv*, 10 May, https://doi.org/10.48550/arXiv.2404.18534.

Dretske, F. (2007) The Metaphysics of Information. In *Wittgenstein and the Philosophy of Information: Proceedings of the 30th International Ludwig Wittgenstein-Symposium in Kirchberg*, De Gruyter, https://doi.org/10.1515/9783110328462.

Duits, K. (2022) Tokyo 1925: The Birth of Radio, *Old Photos of Japan*, www.oldphotosjapan.com/photos/890/japan-first-radio-broadcast-1925.

Dutwin, D. (2024) Understand the 2024 Election by Knowing How Polls Work, *Scientific American*, 5 March, www.scientificamerican.com/article/what-can-election-2024-polls-really-tell-us.

Egger, P. (2022) New Institute for the History of Knowledge in the Ancient World, www.fu-berlin.de/en/featured-stories/research/2022/zodiac/index.html.

Ellis-Petersen, H. (2024) India Elections: Exit Polls Show Narendra Modi Expected to Win Historic Third Term, *Guardian*, 3 June, www.theguardian.com/world/article/2024/jun/03/india-election-results-exit-polls-narendra-modi-victory.

El-Zalabany, H. M. H. (2024) Mobile Information Literacy among Higher Education Students, dissertation, https://doi.org/10.18452/29178.

Eser, A. (2024) Linux User Statistics Statistics: Market Data Report 2024, https://worldmetrics.org/linux-user-statistics.

Ethnologue (2024) Ethnologue Free, www.ethnologue.com/language/eng.

Etymonline (2021) Origin and History of College, www.etymonline.com/word/college.

Fellmann, J. (1978) The Earliest European Sanacritists, *Linguistics*, **16**, (205), 61–2, www.degruyter.com/document/doi/10.1515/ling.1978.16.205.61/html?lang=en.

Fischer, D. E. and Fink, D. (2024) Television, *Encyclopedia Britannica*, www.britannica.com/technology/television-technology.

Foote, K. D. (2023) A Brief History of Large Language Models, *DATAVERSITY* (blog), www.dataversity.net/a-brief-history-of-large-language-models.

Förderverein SenderKW e.V. (2024) 100 Jahre Rundfunk, https://100jahrerundfunk.de/english.

Frankfurter Allgemeine Zeitung (2017) Jeder zehnte deutsche Jugendliche kann programmieren, *FAZ.NET*, 19 October, www.faz.net/pro/d-economy/jeder-zehnte-deutsche-jugendliche-kann-programmieren-15253986.html.

Freiberger, P. A. and Swaine, M. R. (2023) Difference Engine, *Encyclopedia Britannica*, www.britannica.com/technology/Difference-Engine.

Freie Universität zu Berlin (2011) Information Technology and Media, www.fu-berlin.de/en/studium/studienangebot/abv/infomedien/index.html.

Friederici, A. and Anwander, A. (2020) The Roots of Language, www.mpg.de/earlier-evolutionary-origin-of-the-human-language-pathway-discovered.

Fuchs, I. and Freeman, G. (2024) BITNET History, *LivingInternet* (blog), www.livinginternet.com/u/ui_bitnet.htm.

Funk, C., Tyson, A., Kennedy, B. and Pasquini, G. (2023) What Americans Think about COVID-19 Vaccines, *Pew Research Center*, www.pewresearch.org/science/2023/05/16/what-americans-think-about-covid-19-vaccines.

Gifford, A. (2023) Over 10,000 High Schools Don't Teach Compsci, *GovTech*, 1 November, www.govtech.com/education/k-12/code-org-over-10–000-high-schools-dont-teach-compsci.

Giles, J. (2005) Internet Encyclopaedias Go Head to Head, *Nature*, **438** (7070), 900–1, https://doi.org/10.1038/438900a.

Goodman, R. S., Patrinely, J. R., Stone, C. A. and Zimmerman, E. (2023) Accuracy and Reliability of Chatbot Responses to Physician Questions, *JAMA Network Open*, **6** (10), https://doi.org/10.1001/jamanetworkopen.2023.36483.

Goodwin, A., Joseff, K., Riedl, M. J., Lukito, J. and Woolley, S. (2023) Political Relational Influencers: The Mobilization of Social Media Influencers in the Political Arena, *International Journal of Communication*, **17**, https://ijoc.org/index.php/ijoc/article/view/18987/4070.

Grainger College of Engineering (2024) Illiac I, https://physics.illinois.edu/people/history/ILLIAC-I.

Gregersen, E. (2024) Technology: Definition, Examples, Types and Facts, *Encyclopedia Britannica*, www.britannica.com/technology/technology.

Greifeneder, E. and Schlebbe, K. (2022) How Things Fit Together: A General Model of the Information Behaviour Field, *edoc-Server*, https://edoc.hu-berlin.de/handle/18452/25947.

Gross, T. (2022) From Slavery to Socialism, New Legislation Restricts What Teachers Can Discuss, *NPR*, 3 February, www.npr.org/2022/02/03/1077878538/legislation-restricts-what-teachers-can-discuss.

Grout, J. (2024) The Death of Cicero, *Encyclopedia Romana*, https://penelope.uchicago.edu/~grout/encyclopaedia_romana/calendar/cicero.htm.

Grundberg, A. and Gernsheim, H. E. R. (2025) Camera Obscura Photography, *Encyclopedia Brittanica*, www.britannica.com/technology/camera-obscura-photography.

Gruppetta, S. (2022) Coding in the Curriculum for Key Stages 2, 3 and 4, *codetoday*, 5 July, www.codetoday.co.uk/post/coding-in-the-curriculum-for-key-stages-2-3-and-4.

Gusenbauer, M. (2019) Google Scholar to Overshadow Them All? Comparing the Sizes of 12 Academic Search Engines and Bibliographic Databases, *Scientometrics*, **118** (1), 177–214, https://doi.org/10.1007/s11192-018-2958-5.

Hacker News (2014) It Seems This Claim Has Been Made Forever: COBOL Was Supposed to Make Programmers Unnecessary, 30 July, https://news.ycombinator.com/item?id=8109327.

Hall, M. (2024) Facebook, *Encyclopedia Britannica*, www.britannica.com/money/Facebook.

Hansen, N. and Becker, H. (2013) Featured Publication: Photography and the American Civil War, *Metropolitan Museum of Art*, www.metmuseum.org/articles/photography-and-the-american-civil-war.

Hanson, M. A., Barreiro, P. G., Crosetto, P. and Brockington, D. (2023) The Strain on Scientific Publishing, *arXiv.org*, https://arxiv.org/abs/2309.15884v1.

Harvard College Writing Program (2024) What's Wrong with Wikipedia? https://usingsources.fas.harvard.edu/what%E2%80%99s-wrong-wikipedia.

Hashimoto, U. (1963) An Historical Synopsis of Education and Science in Japan from the Meiji Restoration to the Present Day, *Impact of Science on Society*, **XIII** (1), 3–23.

Haskins, C. H. (1957) *The Rise of Universities*, Cornell University Press, www.gutenberg.org/files/63574/63574-h/63574-h.htm.

Heidelberg University (2024) History – Heidelberg University, www.uni-heidelberg.de/en/university/history.

Hillebrand, V. (2024) Is Helping Them All that Technologies Can Do? The Challenges of Digital Ageism in User Studies Involving Older Adults, PhD dissertation, Humboldt University of Berlin, https://doi.org/10.18452/30017.

Hinderer, W. (2009) Das Theater als politische Anstalt: Friedrich Schillers Kritik am System totalitärer Herrschaft und sein Plädoyer für eine humane Gesellschaft, https://literaturkritik.de/id/13627.

Historic England (2024) Coventry Cathedral, https://historicengland.org.uk/whats-new/features/blitz-stories/coventry-cathedral.

History.com (2023) Black Death – Causes, Symptoms and Impact, www.history.com/topics/middle-ages/black-death.

Hoh, A. H. (2021) The History of Printing in Asia According to Library of Congress Asian Collections – Part 1: 4 Corners of the World, *Library of Congress Blogs*, http://blogs.loc.gov/international-collections/2021/06/the-history-of-printing-in-asia-according-to-library-of-congress-asian-collections-part-1.

Horvath, B. (2024) False Conspiracy Theories about Hurricane Milton Continue to Swirl Despite Outcry from Officials, *NBC News*, 10 October, www.nbcnews.com/tech/internet/hurricane-milton-conspiracy-theory-government-storm-biden-rcna174558.

Huang, A. (2017) The Origins of Computing: The Sumerians, the Abacus and Binary Code, *Medium* (blog), https://medium.com/@Ashley_Huang/the-origins-of-computing-the-sumerians-the-abacus-binary-code-15289c3ced16.

Hudon, E. G. (1964) Literary Piracy, Charles Dickens and the American Copyright Law, *American Bar Association Journal*, **50** (12), 1157–60, www.jstor.org/stable/25723046.

Huld, A. (2023) China Data Protection Regulations in 2023 and 2024 Outlook, *China Briefing News*, 22 November, www.china-briefing.com/news/china-data-protection-regulations-2023–2024.

Humboldt-Universität zu Berlin (2016) Short History, Humboldt-Universität zu Berlin, www.hu-berlin.de/en/about/history/huben_html.

IBM (2023) AI Code-Generation Software: What It Is and How It Works, *IBM Think*, 19 September, www.ibm.com/blog/ai-code-generation/www.ibm.com/blog/ai-code-generation.

IBM Corp. (2021) What Is Data Science? *IBM Think*, 21 September www.ibm.com/topics/data-science.

IBM Corp. (2022) What Are Foundation Models? *IBM Blog*, 9 May, https://research.ibm.com/blog/what-are-foundation-models.

IBM Corp. (2023) What Are Large Language Models (LLMs)? *IBM Think*, 2 November, www.ibm.com/topics/large-language-models.

IFLA (2014) Guidelines for Library Services to Persons with Dyslexia – Revised and Extended, www.ifla.org/wp-content/uploads/2019/05/assets/lsn/publications/guidelines-for-library-services-to-persons-with-dyslexia_2014.pdf.

IFLA (2024) Our History, www.ifla.org/history.

Ingram, D. (2024) Fewer People Are Using Elon Musk's X as the Platform Struggles to Attract and Keep Users, According to Analysts, *NBC News*, 22 March, www.nbcnews.com/tech/tech-news/fewer-people-using-elon-musks-x-struggles-keep-users-rcna144115.

Iowa State University (2016) Trains: A History, https://intrans.iastate.edu/news/trains-a-history.

Jena University (2024) History of the University, www.uni-jena.de/en/28485/history-of-the-university.

JenaKultur (2017) Der Gott der Romantiker – Goethe in Jena, www.romantikerhaus-jena.de/de/714952.

Johns Hopkins University (2022) The Hidden Risks of Hearing Loss, www.hopkinsmedicine.org/health/wellness-and-prevention/the-hidden-risks-of-hearing-loss.

Jones, M. (2015) History of Social Media: The Invention of Online Networking, https://historycooperative.org/the-history-of-social-media.

Jordan, T. (2024) *Information Politics: Liberation and Exploitation in the Digital Society*, Pluto Press.

JSTOR (2024) JSTOR: Mission and History, https://about.jstor.org/mission-history.

Juhaňák, L., Zounek, J., Záleská, K. Bárta, O. and Vlčková, K. (2019) The Relationship between the Age at First Computer Use and Students' Perceived Competence and Autonomy in ICT Usage: A Mediation Analysis, *Computers & Education*, **141** (1 November), 103614, https://doi.org/10.1016/j.compedu.2019.103614.

Kamali, O. (2023) Tokens, the Secret Language of AI, https://omarkama.li/blog/tokens-the-secret-language-of-ai.

Kamisar, B. (2024) Poll: Biden and Trump Supporters Sharply Divided by the Media They Consume, *NBC News*, 29 April, www.nbcnews.com/politics/2024-election/poll-biden-trump-supporters-sharply-divided-media-consume-rcna149497.

Kaplan, L. (2003) Inuit Snow Terms: How Many and What Does It Mean? www.uaf.edu/anlc/research-and-resources/resources/archives/inuit_snow_terms.php.

Kashyap, K. (2021) Data Protection Commission Fines WhatsApp €225 Million for Breaching GDPR Laws, *Spiceworks Inc* (blog), www.spiceworks.com/it-security/data-security/news/data-protection-commission-fines-whatsapp-e225-million-for-breaching-gdpr-laws.

Kashyap, K. (2022) 94% of U.S. Companies Are Ill-Prepared to Comply with GDPR Requirements in Spiceworks, www.spiceworks.com/it-security/data-security/articles/us-companies-ill-prepared-to-comply-with-gdpr.

Kaube, J. (2020) *Hegels Welt*, Rowohlt.

Kellaway, L. (2013) The Arrival of Women in the Office, *BBC News Magazine*25 July, www.bbc.com/news/magazine-23432653.

Kerr, D. (2023) California Orders Cruise Driverless Cars off the Roads because of Safety Concerns, *NPR*, 24 October, www.npr.org/2023/10/24/1208287502/california-orders-cruise-driverless-cars-off-the-roads-because-of-safety-concern.

Khan Academy (2024) Transmission Control Protocol (TCP), www.khanacademy.org/computing/computers-and-internet/xcae6f4a7ff015e7d:the-internet/xcae6f4a7ff015e7d:transporting-packets/a/transmission-control-protocol—tcp.

King and Allen Limited (2016) A Brief History of Trousers, https://kingandallen.co.uk/journal/article/a-brief-history-of-trousers.

King's College London (2016) Student Guidance on Academic Honesty and Integrity, https://docs.google.com/viewer?url=https%3A%2F%2Fwww.kcl.ac.uk%2Fcampuslife%2Facservices%2Fconduct%2Fstudent-guidance-on-plagiarism.pdf.

Knox, T. M. (2024) Georg Wilhelm Friedrich Hegel, *Encyclopedia Britannica*, www.britannica.com/biography/Georg-Wilhelm-Friedrich-Hegel.

Kobayashi, C., Glover, G. H. and Temple, E. (2008) Switching Language Switches Mind: Linguistic Effects on Developmental Neural Bases of 'Theory of Mind', *Social Cognitive and Affective Neuroscience*, **3** (1), 62–70, https://doi.org/10.1093/scan/nsm039.

Krishnamurti, B. (2024) Dravidian Languages, *Encyclopedia Britannica*, www.britannica.com/topic/Dravidian-languages.

Krishnan, N. (2023) Justice for Neanderthals! What the Debate about Our Long-dead Cousins Reveals about Us, *Guardian*, 19 September, www.theguardian.com/science/2023/sep/19/justice-for-neanderthals-what-the-debate-about-our-long-dead-cousins-reveals-about-us.

Kynaston, D. (2015) The Old Boys Review – Fascinating but Flawed History of Public Schools, *Observer*, 30 March, www.theguardian.com/books/2015/mar/30/the-old-boys-by-david-turner-the-decline-and-rise-of-public-schools.

Laliberté, A. (2019) Religious Traditions in Politics: Buddhism, *Oxford Research Encyclopedia of Politics*, https://doi.org/10.1093/acrefore/9780190228637.013.691.

Larsen, R. (2009) History of the iSchools, *iSchools.org*, https://ischools.org/resources/Documents/History-of-the-iSchools-2009.pdf.

Lavington, S. (2010) A Brief History of British Computers: The First 25 Years (1948–1973), *BCS*, www.bcs.org/articles-opinion-and-research/a-brief-history-of-british-computers-the-first-25-years-1948-1973.

Lawrence, A. (2024) Harvard's Claudine Gay Was Ousted for 'Plagiarism'. How Serious Was It Really? *Guardian*, 6 January, www.theguardian.com/education/2024/jan/06/harvard-claudine-gay-plagiarism.

Lechêne, R. (2025) Koenig's Mechanical Press (early 19th Century), *Encyclopedia Britannica*, www.britannica.com/topic/printing-publishing/Koenigs-mechanical-press-early-19th-century.

Lennon, L. (2023) The 'Morris Worm': A Notorious Chapter of the Internet's Infancy, *Cornellians: Cornell University* (blog), https://alumni.cornell.edu/cornellians/morris-worm.

Lévy, M-F. (1998) Television, Family and Society in France 1949–1968, *Historical Journal of Film, Radio and Television*, 1 June, https://doi.org/10.1080/01439689800260131.

Liebman, M. (2019) Sir Isaac Newton and the Sextant, https://marcliebman.com/sir-isaac-newton-and-the-sextant.

Lietzow, R. (2020) Do China's Imperial Examinations Predict Modern Regional GDP Distribution? *China Focus* (blog), https://chinafocus.ucsd.edu/2020/12/29/do-chinas-imperial-examinations-predict-modern-regional-gdp-distribution.

Linto, E. (2024) How to Use an AI Image Generator to Create Visuals (Detailed Guide), *Photoroom*, www.photoroom.com/blog/how-to-use-ai-image-generator.

LMU Munich (2024) Data Science (Master/Hauptfach), www.lmu.de/de/studium/studienangebot/alle-studienfaecher-und-studiengaenge/data-science-master-hauptfach-4483.html.

Lopez, G. (2015) The Reagan Administration's Unbelievable Response to the HIV/AIDS Epidemic, *Vox*, 1 December, www.vox.com/2015/12/1/9828348/ronald-reagan-hiv-aids.

Lumas Photo Art (2024) The History of Photography, www.lumas.de/en/history-photography.

Luscombe, R. (2024) Florida Is Swamped by Disease Outbreaks as Quackery Replaces Science, *Guardian*, 3 March, www.theguardian.com/us-news/2024/mar/03/florida-measles-outbreak-preventable.

Mahdawi, A. (2024) What a Surprise! Free Speech Absolutist Elon Musk Doesn't Really Love Free Speech, *Guardian*, 6 April, www.theguardian.com/commentisfree/2024/apr/06/elon-musk-free-speech-lawsuits.

Mailland, J. (2017) Minitel, the Open Network before the Internet, *The Atlantic* (blog), 16 June, www.theatlantic.com/technology/archive/2017/06/minitel/530646.

Maliks, R. (2022) Kant and the French Revolution. In *Elements in the Philosophy of Immanuel Kant*, Cambridge University Press, https://dokumen.pub/kant-and-the-french-revolution-1108438733-9781108438735.html.

Malone, J. A. (2014) 2014 Office of Research Integrity, https://ori.hhs.gov/ori-policy-plagiarism.

Manning, C. (2020) Artificial Intelligence Definitions. https://hai.stanford.edu/sites/default/files/2020-09/AI-Definitions-HAI.pdf.

Marx, L. (1963) *The 18th Brumaire of Louis Bonaparte*, International Publishers.

Matthias, M. (2024) WeChat: Overview, History, and Facts, *Encyclopedia Britannica*, www.britannica.com/topic/WeChat.

Mayernik, M. S. (2023) Data Science as an Interdiscipline: Historical Parallels from Information Science, *Data Science Journal*, **22**, 16.

Mayo Clinic (2024) Dyslexia – Symptoms and Causes, www.mayoclinic.org/diseases-conditions/dyslexia/symptoms-causes/syc-20353552.

Mazzei, P. (2023) Sports Are In, Gender Studies Are Out at College Targeted by DeSantis, *New York Times*, 22 September, www.nytimes.com/2023/09/22/us/new-college-florida-desantis.html.

McCallum, S. (2023) 40 Years of Technology in Libraries: A Brief History of the IFLA Section on Information Technology, 1963/64–2003, *IFLA*.

McCarthy, J. (1979) History of LISP, http://jmc.stanford.edu/articles/lisp/lisp.pdf.

McGillem, C. D. (2024) Telegraph, *Encyclopedia Britannica*, www.britannica.com/technology/telegraph.

McGraw, M. and Stein. S. (2021) It's Been Exactly One Year since Trump Suggested Injecting Bleach. We've Never Been the Same, *Politico*, 23 April, www.politico.com/news/2021/04/23/trump-bleach-one-year-484399.

McHugh, J. (2021) The World's First Anti-Vaccination Movement Spread Fears of Half-Cow Babies, *Washington Post*, 14 November, www.washingtonpost.com/history/2021/11/14/smallpox-anti-vaccine-england-jenner.

McNeill, W. H. (1976) *Plagues and Peoples*, Anchor Books.

Mehra, A. (2023) Things to Consider for Data Collection and Preprocessing for LLMs, *Labellerr*, 2 June, www.labellerr.com/blog/data-collection-and-preprocessing-for-large-language-models.

Melton, J. V. H. (1988) *Absolutism and the Eighteenth-century Origins of Compulsory Schooling in Prussia and Austria*, Cambridge University Press.

Metz, C. (2023) Chatbots May 'Hallucinate' More Often than Many Realize, *New York Times*, 6 November, www.nytimes.com/2023/11/06/technology/chatbots-hallucination-rates.html.

Milman, O. (2020) Seven of Donald Trump's Most Misleading Coronavirus Claims, *Guardian*, 28 March, www.theguardian.com/us-news/2020/mar/28/trump-coronavirus-misleading-claims.

Mitch, D. (1999) The Role of Education and Skill in the British Industrial Revolution. In *The British Industrial Revolution: An Economic Perspective*, 2nd edn, ed. J. Mokyr, Westview Press.

Morales, C. (2021) Pennsylvania Woman Accused of Using Deepfake Technology to Harass Cheerleaders, *New York Times*, 14 March, www.nytimes.com/2021/03/14/us/raffaela-spone-victory-vipers-deepfake.html.

Morris, G. E. (2024) Who Is Favored to Win the 2024 Presidential Election? *FiveThirtyEight*, https://projects.fivethirtyeight.com/2024-election-forecast.

Mozilla (n.d.) Browser History: Epic Power Struggles that Brought Us Modern Browsers, www.mozilla.org/en-US/firefox/browsers/browser-history.

Nasution, M. K. M., Syah, E. R. and Elveny, M. (2023) What Is Data Science? In *Data Science with Semantic Technologies*, CRC Press.

National Institutes of Health (2024) HIV and AIDS: The Basics, https://hivinfo.nih.gov/understanding-hiv/fact-sheets/hiv-and-aids-basics.

National Science and Media Museum (2020) A Short History of the Internet, www.scienceandmediamuseum.org.uk/objects-and-stories/short-history-internet.

Naylor, T. (2013) TripAdvisor Restaurant Reviews: How Much Can You Trust Them? *Guardian*, 30 July, www.theguardian.com/lifeandstyle/wordofmouth/2013/jul/30/tripadvisor-restaurant-reviews-trust-travel.

NeuroNation (2017) Multilingualism – Harm or Benefit for Our Brains? www.neuronation.com/science/en/multilingualism-harm-or-benefit-for-our-brains.

News CNE (2021) The Battle for Angkor 1970–1975, https://cne.wtf/2021/02/06/the-battle-for-angkor-1970-1975.

Nicholas, M. (2018) Storing and Accessing Books in Ancient Libraries, *Brewminate: A Bold Blend of News and Ideas* (blog), https://brewminate.com/storing-and-accessing-books-in-ancient-libraries.

Norman, J. (2004) The Suanpan, a Chinese Version of the Abacus, *History of Information*, www.historyofinformation.com/detail.php?id=233.

Oktaviana, A. A., Joannes-Boyau, R., Hakim, B. et al. (2024) Narrative Cave Art in Indonesia by 51,200 Years Ago, *Nature*, **631**, 814–18, https://doi.org/10.1038/s41586-024-07541-7.

Oliver, G. and Harvey, R. (2016) *Digital Curation*, Facet Publishing.

Oppy, G. and Dowe, D. (2021) The Turing Test. In *The Stanford Encyclopedia of Philosophy*, ed. E. N. Zalta, https://plato.stanford.edu/archives/win2021/entriesuring-test.

Oransky, I. (2024) Up to One in Seven Submissions to Hundreds of Wiley Journals Flagged by New Paper Mill Too, *Retraction Watch* (blog), 14 March, https://retractionwatch.com/2024/03/14/up-to-one-in-seven-of-submissions-to-hundreds-of-wiley-journals-show-signs-of-paper-mill-activity.

Orduna-Malea, E., Ayllón, J. M., Martín-Martín, A. et al. (2015) Methods for Estimating the Size of Google Scholar, *Scientometrics*, https://doi.org/10.1007/s11192-015-1614-6.

ORI (The Office of Research Integrity) (1994) ORI Policy on Plagiarism, https://ori.hhs.gov/ori-policy-plagiarism.

Oxford University (2014) Introduction and History, https://web.archive.org/web/20141020082611/http://www.ox.ac.uk/about/organisation/history.

Oxford University Faculty of English (2018) 18th Century, www.english.ox.ac.uk/18th-century.

Paddison, L. (2023) With 200 Lasers and a Peppercorn-Sized Fuel Capsule, Scientists Inch Closer to Mastering Fusion Energy, *CNN*, 20 December, www.cnn.com/2023/12/20/climate/nuclear-fusion-energy-breakthrough-replicate-climate/index.html.

Pallant, J. (2007) *SPSS Survival Manual*, 3rd edn, McGraw Hill.

Pasquini, G., Spencer, A., Tyson, A. and Funk, C. (2023) Why Some Americans Do Not See Urgency on Climate Change, *Pew Research Center* (blog), 9 August, www.pewresearch.org/science/2023/08/09/why-some-americans-do-not-see-urgency-on-climate-change.

PBS (2024) The Greeks: The Origins of Theatre: The First Plays (Continued), www.pbs.org/empires/thegreeks/background/24b_p1.html.

Perez, J. Jr (2024) Campus Free Speech Is Getting Murky for Republican Governors, *Politico*, 27 April, www.politico.com/news/2024/04/27/republican-states-colleges-free-speech-israel-gaza-complicated-00154702.

Petras, V. (2023) The Identity of Information Science, *Journal of Documentation*, **80** (3), 579–96, https://doi.org/10.1108/JD-04-2023-0074.

Pew Research Center (2005) Technology Experts and Scholars Foresee a Bigger Role for the Internet in People's Personal and Work Lives in the Next Decade, www.pewresearch.org/internet/2005/01/09/technology-experts-and-scholars-foresee-a-bigger-role-for-the-internet-in-peoples-personal-and-work-lives-in-the-next-decade.

Pew Research Center (2023) Social Media and News Fact Sheet, www.pewresearch.org/journalism/fact-sheet/social-media-and-news-fact-sheet.

Pidd, H. (2011) German Defence Minister Stripped of Doctorate for Plagiarism, *Guardian*, 24 February, www.theguardian.com/world/2011/feb/24/german-defence-minister-guttenberg-plagiarism.

Pimentel, T. et al. (2023) On the Effect of Anticipation on Reading Times, *Transactions of the Association for Computational Linguistics*, **11**, 1624–42, https://doi.org/10.1162/tacl_a_00603.

Plant, I. (2004) Women Writers of Ancient Greece and Rome: An Anthology, www.equinoxpub.com/home/women-writers-ancient-greece-rome-anthology-ian-plant.

Portico (2024) www.portico.org.

Protect (2024) Breach of Personal Data and Whistleblowing, https://protect-advice.org.uk/breach-of-personal-data-whistleblowing.

Public Broadcasting Service (2025) Development of Radio, www.pbs.org/wgbh/americanexperience/features/rescue-development-radio.

Pytlowany, A. (2018) *Ketelaar Rediscovered: The First Dutch Grammar of Persian and Hindustani*, LOT Publications.

Ramírez, M. (2024) Optimism Isn't Very 'European': But in 2024, Let's Celebrate These Reasons for Hope, *Guardian*, 2 January, www.theguardian.com/commentisfree/2024/jan/02/europe-optimism-2024-hope-train-olympics-charger.

Ranasinghe, N., Karunanayaka, K., Cheok, A. D., Fernando, O. N. N., Nii, H. and Gopalakrishnakone, P. (2011) Digital Taste and Smell Communication. In *Proceedings of the 6th International Conference on Body Area Networks*, Institute for Computer Sciences, Social-Informatics and Telecommunications Engineering, https://dl.acm.org/doi/10.5555/2318776.2318795.

Rankin, J. L. (2023) Learning to Code Isn't Enough, *MIT Technology Review*, April, www.technologyreview.com/2023/04/20/1071291/learn-to-code-legacy-new-projects-education.

Ravado, R. (2022) A Brief History of Typing, Typists, Sex and the Typewriter, *HubPages*, https://discover.hubpages.com/business/A-Brief-History-of-Typing.

Ray, M. (2023) WikiLeaks, *Encyclopedia Britannica*, www.britannica.com/topic/WikiLeaks.

Regehr, K., Shaughnessy, C. N., Turner, A., Zhao, M. and Cambazoglu, I. (2024) *Safer Scrolling: How Algorithms Popularise and Gamify Online Hate and Misogyny for Young People*, www.ascl.org.uk/ASCL/media/ASCL/Help%20and%20advice/Inclusion/Safer-scrolling.pdf.

Reich, V. and Kiefer, R. (2012) Digital Preservation Matters: Research Information, www.researchinformation.info/interview/digital-preservation-matters.

Rohde, R. (n.d.) 'Zur Geschichte der bibliothekswissenschaftlichen Ausbildung in Berlin', *Seite*, Institut für Bibliotheks- und Informationswissenschaft, www.ibi.hu-berlin.de/de/institut/gebaeude/gesch-ausbildung.

Romanino, A. (2009) The Standard Model of Particle Physics, *Inspire*, https://inspirehep.net/literature/850372.

Sadhu, S. (2024) Top 60 Social Media Influencers in 2024: Who's Leading the Chart, *SocialPilot* (blog), www.socialpilot.co/blog/top-social-media-influencers.

Samelson, Y. I. (2024) 11 Best Deepfake Nude Makers, *Morning Dough* (blog), www.morningdough.com/ai-tools/best-deepfake-nude-maker.

Sample, I. (2010) Language and Toolmaking Evolved Together, Say Researchers, *Guardian*, 3 November, www.theguardian.com/science/2010/nov/03/language-hand-toolmaking-evolution.

Schemmel, M. (2012) The Transmission of Scientific Knowledge from Europe to China in the Early Modern Period. In *The Globalization of Knowledge in History*, Max-Planck-Gesellschaft zur Förderung der Wissenschaften.

Schiller, F. (1795) Ueber Die Ästhetische Erziehung Des Menschen, www.projekt-gutenberg.org/schiller/aesterz/aesterz.html.

Schlebbe, K. (2023) The Role of Mobile Devices in Young Children's Information Behavior, PhD thesis, Humboldt University of Berlin, Faculty of Philosophy, http://dx.doi.org/10.18452/25942.

Science Museum (2024) 2LO Calling: The Birth of British Public Radio, www.sciencemuseum.org.uk/objects-and-stories/2lo-calling-birth-british-public-radio.

Seadle, M. (1991) *Automating Mainframe Management Using Examples from MV and MVS*, McGraw Hill.

Seadle, M. (2017) *Quantifying Research Integrity*, Morgan Claypool.

Seadle, M. (2021) Transfer and Transformation: Leadership in a Time of Change, *Bibliothek Forschung und Praxis*, **45** (2), 249–54, https://doi.org/10.1515/bfp-2021-0014.

Seadle, M. (2022) *The Measurement of Information Integrity*, Routledge.

Seadle, M. and Havelka, S. (2023) Information Science: Why It Is Not Data Science, *Data and Information Management*, Special Issue on Data Science and Information Science, **7** (1), 100027, https://doi.org/10.1016/j.dim.2023.100027.

Seadle, M., Chu, C., Stöckel, U. and Crumpton, B. (2016) *Educating the Profession: 40 Years of the IFLA Section on Education and Training*, De Gruyter Saur.

Sefton, C. (2013) What Exactly Is the 'Five (Consecutive) Word' Plagiarism Rule? *StackExchange*, https://writing.stackexchange.com/questions/7546/what-exactly-is-the-five-consecutive-word-plagiarism-rule.

Seltzer, R. (2022) Restrictions Threaten 'Integrity of Our System of Higher Education', Groups Say, in *Higher Ed Dive*, 8 June, www.highereddive.com/news/restrictions-threaten-integrity-of-our-system-of-higher-education-groups/625159.

Senders, S. (2008) Academic Plagiarism and the Limits of Theft. In *Originality, Imitation, and Plagiarism*, ed. by C. Eisner and M. Vicinus, University of Michigan Press.

Shallit, J. (1995) Brief History of Computer Science, https://cs.uwaterloo.ca/~shallit/Courses/134/history.html.

Shapin, S. (2024) Story of Eau, *London Review of Books*, **46** (13), www.lrb.co.uk/the-paper/v46/n13/steven-shapin/story-of-eau.

Sheffield University (2024) Data Science, www.sheffield.ac.uk/postgraduate/taught/courses/2024/data-science-msc.

Sinmaz, E. (2024) Why Are People Rioting across England and How Many Are Involved? *Guardian*, 6 August, www.theguardian.com/politics/article/2024/aug/05/why-people-rioting-across-england-how-many-involved.

Sintetos, T. (2015) LISTSERV: The Original Social Media, *LISTSERV at Work*, www.lsoft.com/news/social-issue2-2015.asp.

Sivin, N. (1973) Copernicus in China. In *Études sur l'audience de la théorie héliocentrique: Conférences du symposium de l'UIHPS, Toruń*, ed. International Union of the History and Philosophy of Science, Zakład Narodowy Imienia Ossolińskich.

Smith, D. (2022) 'Trump Is Not My God': How the Former President's Only Vaccine Victory Turned Sour, *Observer*, 5 February, www.theguardian.com/us-news/2022/feb/05/donald-trump-vaccine-republicans-operation-warp-speed.

Smith, G. N. (2024) How (Not) to Deal with Missing Data: An Economist's Take on a Controversial Study, *Retraction Watch* (blog), 21 February, https://retractionwatch.com/2024/02/21/how-not-to-deal-with-missing-data-an-economists-take-on-a-controversial-study.

Smith, R. (1997) *The Norton History of the Human Sciences*, W. W. Norton.

SMMT (2024) New Car Market Growth Continues despite Declining Private Demand, www.smmt.co.uk/2024/05/new-car-market-growth-continues-despite-declining-private-demand.

Sneader, W. (2000) The Discovery of Aspirin: A Reappraisal, *BMJ: British Medical Journal*, **321** (7276), 1591–4.

Southern, R. W. (1970) *Western Society and the Church in the Middle Ages*, Penguin Books.

Specht, J. (2017) The NOTIS History Webpage, https://notis-history.northwestern.edu.

Staatliche Museen zu Berlin (2016) Rembrandt Research Project Completed: Berlin Paintings in the Rembrandt Database, www.smb.museum/en/whats-new/detail/rembrandt-research-project-completed-berlin-paintings-in-the-rembrandt-database.

Staatsbibliothek zu Berlin (2025a) History: Staatsbibliothek zu Berlin, https://staatsbibliothek-berlin.de/en/about-the-library/history.

Staatsbibliothek zu Berlin (2025b) Für Forschung und Kultur, https://staatsbibliothek-berlin.de/die-staatsbibliothek/portraet.

Steiner, G. (1987) *Martin Heidegger*, University of Chicago Press, https://press.uchicago.edu/ucp/books/book/chicago/M/bo3644853.html.

Stephens, M. (1999) History of Television, https://stephens.hosting.nyu.edu/History%20of%20Television%20page.html.

Stephenson, J. (2024) Alabama Public Library Service Board Will Not Renew ALA Membership, *Alabama Reflector* (blog), 30 January, https://alabamareflector.com/2024/01/30/alabama-public-library-service-board-will-not-renew-ala-membership.

Strunk, W. Jr and White, E. B. (1959) *Elements of Style*, https://faculty.washington.edu/heagerty/Courses/b572/public/StrunkWhite.pdf.

Study.com (2024) History of Radio: Timeline and Invention: Lesson, https://study.com/academy/lesson/history-of-the-radio.html.

Surowski, D. B. (2000) History of the Educational System of China: Projects for International Education Research, www.math.ksu.edu/~dbski/writings/history.html.

Syvertsen, T. and Enli, G. (2020) Digital Detox: Media Resistance and the Promise of Authenticity, *Convergence*, **26** (5–6), 1269–83, https://doi.org/10.1177/1354856519847325.

Szalai, J. (2024) How Robots Learned to Write So Well, *New York Times*, 7 February, www.nytimes.com/2024/02/07/books/review/literary-theory-for-robots-dennis-yi-tenen.html.

Tampa Bay Times (2022) Why Are so Many Floridians Still Dying from COVID? Editorial, 9 September, www.tampabay.com/opinion/2022/09/09/floridas-tough-covid-summer-now-what-editorial.

Thompson, L. (2024) The University of Sheffield: Data Protection Policy, www.sheffield.ac.uk/media/17203/download?attachment.

Thucydides (2019) *The Melian Dialogue*, translated by R. Crawley, Book 5, Chapter 17, http://academics.wellesley.edu/ClassicalStudies/CLCV102/Thucydides—MelianDialogue.htm.

Timm, T. (2024) Elon Musk Has Become the World's Biggest Hypocrite on Free Speech, *Guardian*, 15 January, www.theguardian.com/commentisfree/2024/jan/15/elon-musk-hypocrite-free-speech.

Toynbee, A. (1934–61) *A Study of History*, Volumes I–X, Oxford University Press.

Tyson, A. and Kennedy, B. (2024) How Republicans View Climate Change and Energy Issues, *Pew Research Center* (blog), 1 March, www.pewresearch.org/short-reads/2024/03/01/how-republicans-view-climate-change-and-energy-issues.

Tysver, D. A. (2022) When Should a Patent Application Be Filed? *Bitlaw Guidance*, www.bitlaw.com/guidance/patent/when-to-file-a-patent-application.html.

UNAIDS (2024) Global HIV and& AIDS Statistics – Fact Sheet, www.unaids.org/en/resources/fact-sheet.

UNFCCC (2024) The Paris Agreement, https://unfccc.int/process-and-meetings/the-paris-agreement.

University of Chicago Library (2024) The Berlin Collection: The Collection, www.lib.uchicago.edu/collex/exhibits/extbc/history/the-collection.

University of Michigan (2004) Ahead of Its Time: U-M Computing Center Celebrates 45 Years, *Michigan News*, 7 September, https://news.umich.edu/ahead-of-its-time-u-m-computing-center-celebrates-45-years.

University of Michigan (2019) Claude Shannon: Father of the Information Age, *Alumni News*, 18 March, https://ece.engin.umich.edu/stories/claude-shannon-father-of-the-information-age.

Unterberg, S. (2024) Jäger und Gejagte; Die Enthüllungen des VroniPlag Wiki und ihre Auswirkungen auf Prominente, *Spiegel Panorama*, 1 May, www.spiegel.de/panorama/bildung/plagiatsjaeger-die-enthuellungen-des-vroniplag-wiki-und-ihre-auswirkungen-auf-prominente-a-98520406-de24-42aa-9375-499edc389211.

US National Institute on Aging (2023) How to Find Reliable Health Information Online, www.nia.nih.gov/health/healthy-aging/how-find-reliable-health-information-online.

Utrecht University (2022) Notes on Hegel's Lectures Published, News, 10 January, www.uu.nl/en/news/notes-on-hegels-lectures-published.

Vargas, R. A. (2024) Malaria Drug Trump Touted as Covid Cure Increased Chance of Death – Study, *Guardian*, 12 January, www.theguardian.com/world/2024/jan/12/hydroxychloroquine-covid-increase-chance-death-trump.

Varian, M. (1991) VM and the VM Community: Past, Present, and Future, www.cs.tufts.edu/~nr/cs257/archive/melinda-varian/neuvm.pdf.

Vericat, F. L. (2015) Her Master's Voice: Dictation, the Typewriter, and Henry James's Trouble with the Speech of American Women, *South Atlantic Review*, **80** (1–2), 1–23, www.jstor.org/stable/soutatlarevi.80.1-2.1.

Voth, H-J., Caprettini, B. and Trew, A. (2022) *Fighting for Growth: Labor Scarcity and Technological Progress during the British Industrial Revolution*, Adam Smith Business School Working Paper Series, www.gla.ac.uk/media/Media_900972_smxx.pdf.

Walravens, H. (1997) Copper-Engraving in China: The First Chinese-European Co-operative Project in the Field of Art, *Art Libraries Journal*, **22** (1), 16–19, https://doi.org/10.1017/S0307472200010269.

Wang, D. (2024) WeChat conversation with Dr Di Wang.

Wang, M., van Leeuwen, B. and Li, J. (2020) Female Education. In *Education in China, ca. 1840–present*, Brill, https://doi.org/10.1163/9789004442252_005.

Webster, I. (2024) £100 in 1870–1890, CPI Inflation Calculator, www.in2013dollars.com/uk/inflation/1870.

Werner, E. K. (2015) The Dawning Moon of the Mind: Unlocking the Pyramid Texts, *Library Journal*, **140** (17), 91–3, https://search.ebscohost.com/login.aspx?direct=true&db=buh&AN=110530420&site=ehost-live.

West, C. (2022) Radio: A Brief History, *Oxford Open Learning* (blog), 9 February, www.ool.co.uk/blog/radio-a-brief-history.

White, W. (2024) DJT Stock Alert: Truth Social Keeps Losing Users, *InvestorPlace* (blog), 10 May, https://investorplace.com/2024/05/djt-stock-alert-truth-social-keeps-losing-users.

WHO (2024) Data Collection and Analysis Tools, www.who.int/data/data-collection-tools.

Wiik, L. (2024) How Modern Tokenization Works, *Medium* (blog), 21 April, https://medium.com/@lars.chr.wiik/how-modern-tokenization-works-d56013a78f1e.

Wikipedia (2025a) James Burrill Angell, https://en.wikipedia.org/wiki/James_Burrill_Angell.

Wikipedia (2025b) Basic English, https://en.wikipedia.org/wiki/Basic_English.

Wikipedia (2025c) Truth Social, https://en.wikipedia.org/wiki/Truth_Social.

Wikipedia (2025d) Golden Age of Radio, https://en.wikipedia.org/w/index.php?title=Golden_Age_of_Radio&oldid=1217569952.

Wikipedia (2025e) History of Television, https://en.wikipedia.org/wiki/History_of_television.
Wikipedia (2025f) Lynx, https://en.wikipedia.org/wiki/Lynx.
Wikipedia (2025g) BITNET, https://en.wikipedia.org/wiki/BITNET.
Wikipedia (2025h) Minitel, https://en.wikipedia.org/wiki/Minitel.
Wikipedia (2025i) HTTPS, https://en.wikipedia.org/wiki/HTTPS.
Wikipedia (2025j) Lamarckism, https://en.wikipedia.org/wiki/Lamarckism.
Wikipedia (2025k) Abacus, https://en.wikipedia.org/wiki/Abacus.
Wikipedia (2025l) Sextant, https://en.wikipedia.org/wiki/Sextant.
Wikipedia (2025m) International Federation of Robotics, https://en.wikipedia.org/wiki/International_Federation_of_Robotics.
Wikipedia (2025n) Deep Blue (Chess Computer), https://en.wikipedia.org/wiki/Deep_Blue_(chess_computer).
Wikipedia (2025o) Large Language Model, https://en.wikipedia.org/wiki/Large_language_model.
Wikipedia (2025p) Isaac Asimov, https://en.wikipedia.org/wiki/Isaac_Asimov.
Wikipedia (2025q) Swastika, https://simple.wikipedia.org/wiki/Swastika.
Wikipedia (2025r) Potato, https://en.wikipedia.org/wiki/Potato.
Wikipedia (2025s) Chinese Painting, https://en.wikipedia.org/w/index.php?title=Chinese_painting&oldid=1231056290.
Wikipedia (2025t) Theatre, https://en.wikipedia.org/wiki/Theatre.
Wikipedia (2025u) Islamic Culture, https://en.wikipedia.org/wiki/Islamic_culture.
Wikipedia (2025v) Angkor Wat, https://en.wikipedia.org/wiki/Angkor_Wat.
Wikipedia (2025w) The Feynman Lectures on Physics, https://en.wikipedia.org/wiki/The_Feynman_Lectures_on_Physics.
Wikipedia (2025x) Literacy, https://en.wikipedia.org/wiki/Literacy.
Wikipedia (2025y) Pharmaceutical Industry, https://en.wikipedia.org/wiki/Pharmaceutical_industry.
Wikipedia (2025z) Etching, https://en.wikipedia.org/wiki/Etching.
Williamson, E. (2024) Cast as Criminals, America's Librarians Rally to Their Own Defense, *New York Times*, 3 February, www.nytimes.com/2024/02/03/us/book-bans-librarians.html.
Williamson, L. (2024) The Slowly Evolving Truth about Heart Disease and Women, *American Heart Association News*, 9 February, www.heart.org/en/news/2024/02/09/the-slowly-evolving-truth-about-heart-disease-and-women.
Wilson, T. D. (2000) Human Information Behavior, *Informing Science*, **3** (2), 49–55, https://doi.org/10.28945/576.
Wolf, Z. (2024) Analysis: The Deepfake Era of US Politics Is upon Us, *CNN Politics*, 24 January, www.cnn.com/2024/01/24/politics/deepfake-politician-biden-what-matters/index.html.

World Press Freedom Index (2024) World Trends in Freedom of Expression and Media Development, www.unesco.org/en/world-media-trends/world-press-freedom-index.

Wu, J., Yang, S., Zhan, R., Yuan, Y., Wong, D. F. and Chao, L. S. (2024) A Survey on LLM-Generated Text Detection: Necessity, Methods, and Future Directions, *arXiv.org*, https://arxiv.org/html/2310.14724v3.

Wulf, A. (2022) *Magnificent Rebels: The First Romantics and the Invention of the Self*, John Murray.

Xiaoping, L. (2001) *Significant Changes in the Chinese Television Industry*, The Brookings Institution, www.brookings.edu/wp-content/uploads/2016/06/li_01.pdf.

Yasin, S. and Hina, G. (2023) Women's Education in Ancient India in the Light of the Hindu Scriptures and Scholars, *Pakistan Journal of Social Research*, **5** (2), 718–25.

Yi, Z. (2013) *History of Library Developments in China*, IFLA, https://library.ifla.org/143/1/164-yi-en.pdf.

Yurcaba, J. (2023) Montana State Library Withdraws from National Library Group over President's 'Marxist Lesbian' Comment, *NBC News*, 13 July, www.nbcnews.com/nbc-out/out-news/montana-state-library-withdraws-national-library-group-presidents-marx-rcna94130.

Zhang, T. (2005) Literacy Education in China, *UNESCO Digital Library*, https://unesdoc.unesco.org/ark:/48223/pf0000146208.

Zinkina, J., Korotayev, A. and Andreev, A. I. (2013) Mass Primary Education in the Nineteenth Century, *Social Studies*, www.sociostudies.org/almanac/articles/mass_primary_education_in_the_nineteenth_century.

Index